Naming Adult Autism

Naming Adult Autism

Culture, Science, Identity

James McGrath

ROWMAN & LITTLEFIELD
INTERNATIONAL

London • New York

Published by Rowman & Littlefield International Ltd
Unit A, Whitacre Mews, 26-34 Stannary Street, London SE11 4AB
www.rowmaninternational.com

Rowman & Littlefield International Ltd. is an affiliate of Rowman & Littlefield
4501 Forbes Boulevard, Suite 200, Lanham, Maryland 20706, USA
With additional offices in Boulder, New York, Toronto (Canada), and Plymouth (UK)
www.rowman.com

British Library Cataloguing in Publication Data
A catalogue record for this book is available from the British Library

ISBN: HB 978-1-78348-040-1

Library of Congress Cataloging-in-Publication Data Is Available

978-1-78348-040-1 (cloth)
978-1-78348-041-8 (paper)
978-1-78348-042-5 (electronic)

Printed in the United States of America

This book is dedicated with love and thanks to the National Health Service of the UK. The workers of the NHS help us into and out of the world; they are also there for us along the way, and ask for nothing in return.

Contents

Acknowledgements

To complete this book over three busy academic years, it was necessary to start writing by two o'clock most mornings. Against the solitude and occasional stresses involved with this routine, my daytime work as a senior lecturer at Leeds Beckett University provided grounding, stimulation and invaluable encouragement from friends and colleagues. I am deeply grateful to these people for their academic and personal support: Penny Andrews. Sue Chaplin. Nick Cox. Laura Ettenfield. Max Farrar. Caroline Herbert. Nasser Hussain ('Finished is better than perfect'). Lady Colette McGill. Emily Zobel Marshall. Fern Pullan. Jayne Raisborough. Rachel Rich. Ruth Robbins. Katy Shaw. William Sparling. Annisa Suliman. Beverley Swinbourne. 'T'. Zoë Tew-Thompson. Lindsay Trelford. Susan Watkins. Alison Wilde. Never forgetting Matthew Caygill (1955–2016).

The guidance and encouragement of editors and other staff at Rowman & Littlefield International has been crucial throughout this project. Thank you especially to: Catherine DeMello. Elaine McGarraugh. Sinead Murphy. Martina O'Sullivan. Holly Tyler. Michael Watson. Peer reviewers provided indispensable guidance at various stages, from proposal to publication. Thanks and great respect here to: Helen Davies. John Duffy. Kate Fox. Rachel Rich. Zoë Tew-Thompson. Mitzi Waltz. Susan Watkins. Paul Wheeler. (And Anonymous). Although our critical interpretations of (and esteem for) certain texts may still differ, your intellectual input has been pivotal. Hannah Spruce provided a wise and perceptive commentary on the penultimate draft of this book, as well as discussing many of the related texts along the way. Joanne Limburg kindly shared the manuscript of *The Autistic Alice* with me ahead of its publication.

I am deeply grateful to the staff of Leeds Autism Diagnostic Service – particularly Frances Needham and Alison Stansfield – for their insights and encouragement. Although at times we may have slightly different views on certain medical models of autism, you have listened to me without judging. I have benefited personally and intellectually from your expertise.

A number of students from Leeds Beckett University deserve distinguished thanks here for the support they have given to this book and to a series of talks I gave on some of the themes addressed. Thank you in particular to: Lizzie Anstiss. Saba Bettul. Symrun Chatha. Mel Dawson. Laura Duncan. Gemma Hickey. Lucybelle Holmes. Rose Korner. Daniel Mcloughlin. Madison Stephens. Andrew Ward (1978–2016).

The realization of this project also owes importantly to the presence or inspiration of the following individuals: Linda Chase Broda. Sarah Calderwood. Chris Davies. Matt Edwards. Janet Edwards. Laurence Grant. Christian Hogsbjerg. Nicholas Jones. Claire Luck. Eileen McGrath. Jenny McGrath. Paul Mills. Jane Morrow. Andrew Mucha. Julia Oakes. Emma Persand-Carter. Marv Scott. Roger Smith. Peter Street. Tara Stubbs. William Underhill. Melissa Watson. Tim Watson. Callum Westbrook. Most of all: thank you to my father, Tom McGrath.

Introduction

Culture and diagnosis

In this book, 'naming' is the accumulative shorthand for the following processes surrounding adult autism:

Calling. Characterizing. Chastising. Classifying. Confining. Constructing. Deconstructing. Debating. Defining. Dehumanizing. Demeaning. Demonizing. Demonstrating. Diagnosing. Disabling. Disclosing. Dismissing. Disturbing. Embodying. Empathizing. Enabling. Engineering. Essentializing. Evolving. Exemplifying. Exhibiting. Existentializing. Expanding. Experimenting. Exploiting. Feeling. Fictionalizing. Finding. Functionalizing. Gendering. Generalizing. Historicizing. Humanizing. Idealizing. Identifying. Infantilizing. Interpellating. Labelling. Liberating. Limiting. Locating. Magnifying. Mainstreaming. Marginalizing. Meta-labelling. Misrepresenting. Narrating. Narrowing. Neoliberalizing. Normalizing. Othering. Paratexting. Performing. Personifying. Philosophizing. Playing. Poeticizing. Portraying. Priding. Queering. Radicalizing. Reaching. Reading. Realizing. Redeeming. Redefining. Renaming. Repeating. Replaying. Replying. Screaming. Screening. Seeming. Sensing. Sexing. Silencing. Showing. Surveying. Voicing. Writing.

* * *

One term which this study of autism largely rejects is 'representation': a term integral to two early cultural studies, Stuart Murray's *Representing Autism: Culture, Narrative, Fascination* (2008) and Mark Osteen's edited collection *Autism and Representation* (2008). Those two pioneering books remain indispensable. Yet, as each in different ways illuminates, many so-called representations of autism – most of which are authored by and primarily aimed at neurotypicals (non-autistics) – rely on, and reinforce, misleading assumptions, stereotypes and expectations regarding autistic people.

Primarily, this book addresses *adult* autism. The past three decades have witnessed a shift in which a condition first conceptualized as an impairment in children has necessarily been redefined as a lifelong identity. Autistic adults feature frequently and prominently in culture and fiction. However, as the following chapters confront, our agency is not just excluded from but effectively *denied* in the many of the most influential narratives by non-autistics. My concern is that in the decade since Murray and Osteen's books appeared, the numbers of fictional and non-fictional narratives purporting to depict adult autism have continued to increase, but the meanings of autism (and adulthood) as conveyed in the culturally presiding texts – including scientific narratives – have become more narrow, more shallow and more oppressive.

Autistic people continue to be a source of (in Murray's phrase) *fascination* to audiences, as evidenced by the number of films, television series, documentaries and media articles featuring autistic people – or ideas about autistic people – which continue to appear. Yet, many of the most popular examples of this arguably bear a greater resemblance to *each other* than to actual autistic lives and identities. Tropes such as spectacular ability in mathematics, for instance, have become standard in fictions of autism since Barry Levinson's sensationally successful film *Rain Man* (1988) and Mark Haddon's noticeably similar construction of an autistic male in his comparably popular young adult novel *The Curious Incident of the Dog in the Night-Time* (2003). One of the most eminent and passionate commentators on autism, Canadian philosopher Ian Hacking has promoted the following wisdom: 'You've met one person with autism – you've met one person with autism'.[1] Sadly, this aphorism is less applicable to the most influential literary and screen fictions of autism. Of those, it remains true to say: *You've encountered one fictional character with autism. It's most likely a white male with savant-like ability in mathematics or science.* As will be critiqued through the book, this hegemonic pattern in fiction is powerfully – though often very questionably – endorsed by some of the world's most influential autism scientists.

It is symbolic of the emphasis throughout *Naming Adult Autism* that the most scientific tool available to scientists for diagnosing autism is not a piece of laboratory technology: it is a book – and a contentious one at that. It is the American Psychiatric Association's *Diagnostic and Statistical Manual of Mental Disorders 5* (*DSM-5*, 2013). At present, there are no biological tests available to reliably inform autism diagnostic procedures. Allen Frances, a subsequently disillusioned advisor on the diagnostic criteria for 'Asperger's Disorder' as included in *DSM-IV* (1994), reflects:

> The powerful new tools of molecular biology, genetics, and imaging have not yet led to laboratory tests for dementia or depression or schizophrenia or bipolar or obsessive-compulsive disorder or any other mental disorders. . . . We still do not have a single laboratory test in psychiatry.[2]

Narrative is thus essential to not just to the definition but the *detection* of autism. In exploring (and sometimes experimenting with) the effects of such a reality, this book is fundamentally concerned with promoting deeper, greater dialogue between the humanities and the sciences regarding the meanings of autism. This is an angry book about autism, but also an optimistic one.

The separation of 'science' and 'the arts' into what the novelist and physicist C. P. Snow called *The Two Cultures* is a relatively recent development – or stalling – in Western civilization. In the Renaissance era, the practices now known as science were considered part of the same sphere as the arts.[3] English definitions of 'science' in the current sense date back only to the 1830s.[4] More burdensome though, for attempts to promote interaction between the sciences and humanities, is the spectre of what were somewhat immaturely called 'the science wars' (at their height in the 1990s). In those debates, some literary and cultural theorists sought to deconstruct science by stressing its *narrative* components, and thus its subjectivity and limitations.[5] In turn, some scientists argued that such critics had no idea what they were actually talking about, because the values of the humanities and the sciences are essentially incompatible.[6] The leading interventions from both corners of that quarrel read more like competing monologues than sincere attempts at promoting or achieving greater mutual understanding or respect. But that was a generation ago. And though this book questions certain scientific hypotheses concerning autism, the point is to promote *discussion* between the humanities, the sciences and autistic people. So I do not suggest that science is 'wrong' about how autism should be defined or understood, but that the picture the sciences provide is incomplete. Two of the harshest scientific critics of the humanities, Alan Sokal and Jean Brincmont, cautioned in 1997 against philosophical and literary approaches to scientific texts because 'factual and theoretical arguments' are the basis of science, 'not the words used'.[7] Yet, in the assessment, diagnosis and cultural portrayal of autism, language is central to what is tested, what is concluded, what is narrated. To return to the words of Allen Frances earlier, 'We still do not have a single laboratory test in psychiatry' – and, as the present book will detail, several of the most widely used narrative-based tests in autism assessment are both medically and socially problematic. I write as a senior lecturer in literary studies, but also as an adult diagnosed autistic. I am no trained scientist. It is therefore unsettling that even *I* can identify major limitations (if not discrepancies) in the methodologies and conclusions of the UK's most medically influential autism research centres – and that is before we even get to 'the words used' (which we nonetheless will).

In focusing on 'naming', this book primarily addresses cultural and medical narratives of autism – that is, how autism is surrounded by texts, and how these shape both diagnostic and public understandings of the term. However, this book does not endorse a *merely* social model of understanding this

condition. My stance on what constitutes any 'essence' of autism follows
the emphasis of Ian Hacking (1999): autism presents an *interactive* self, in
which the social and biological are continually converging.[8] To quote Tom
Shakespeare:

> It is valid and indeed very important to be sceptical about labelling and scepti-
> cal about categories. But it is very dangerous indeed to consider that this means
> impairments do not exist or do not matter.[9]

So if autism is, as most experts and autistic people concur, a biological
reality – however incompletely understood it might remain – then why give
so much attention to how it is named and narrated? My answer is that narrative quite literally defines how we regard autism itself, and thus, how this
identity is perceived, as well as experienced. This book therefore is not just
about naming autism itself, but naming (and questioning) certain narrative
conventions (or cultural disorders) evident in how this subjectivity and identity is portrayed from outside, and how notions of adult autism are socially
reinforced via scientific, diagnostic and cultural texts.

Naming Adult Autism focuses on narratives, not least fictions, for two core
reasons. First, as chapter 1 addresses, autistic people are often the subjects
of novels, and yet are widely assumed to be unlikely to *read* fiction: a supposition often transparently evident in the vacuous stereotypes that populate
many of the best-known novels, films and television series that claim to feature autistic characters. But my focus on narrative, including scientific (and
pseudo-scientific) texts, has a deeper agenda. Autism is, however mysterious,
an embodied reality for countless adults.[10] There is no known 'cure'; there
probably never will be; and I do not endorse the search for one. But what
can be altered are the ways in which society responds to and often oppresses
autistic adults. And this is why it is imperative to focus on how autism is
portrayed and narrated. The political and thus humanitarian urgency of doing
so is likely to increase in the coming decades.

If 'prevention' of autism via prenatal screening becomes available, it will
not just be science impacting on the future of autism – including its possible obliteration – but culture, too. If autism is demonized, as it has often
been by the controversial charity 'Autism Speaks', then such narratives will
almost inevitably shape some decisions around abortion. This is a key reason
why, as biogenetic research develops, the critical study of autism's cultural
depictions will become increasingly vital. Yet while there are various causes
for both fear and anger in how adult autism is named and conjectured from
outside, this book – both as a whole and through most of its chapters – seeks
to offer what is broadly an arc-shaped narrative, in which the focus advances
from oppression towards liberation. In other words, the stereotype-laden texts

addressed and occasionally attacked are mainly confined to the early discussions: the more progressive and empowering narratives are given the greater space, towards the chapters' endings.

* * *

AN INTRODUCTION TO FIVE CHAPTERS

A core concern of this book is the relationship of fiction to autism. Characters named by authors, publishers and producers as being autistic or having Asperger syndrome regularly feature in a range of fictional narratives, both in literature and on screen. At the same time, many psychiatric studies – and several highly influential diagnosticians – assert that autistic people, by definition, do not 'get' fiction. This highly problematic assumption and generalization is challenged in chapter 1, 'Outsider Science and Literary Exclusion: A Reply to Denials of Autistic Imagination'. The chapter traces the emergence of associations between autism and STEM subjects (science, technology, engineering, mathematics), and of assumptions that the autistic mind is incompatible with the values of the arts and humanities. Via Percy Bysshe Shelley, I reflect on the historical celebration of *imagination* as a vital organ in the functioning of human society. I then outline how medical discourse in the late 1970s formalized assumptions that autistic children lack imagination. The discussion of 'autism and the machine' traces how, since the 1960s, the skills of autistic people have been likened to the functions of computers, and how this association has since become a reductive cliché. I then contemplate the vulnerable future of autism itself amid emerging clinical policies, which seek to exclude genes that are possibly associated with the condition from sperm banks and IVF treatment.

Chapter 1 also addresses the portrayal of autism in relation to STEM subjects in two works by major Canadian novelists: Douglas Coupland's *Microserfs* (1995) and Margaret Atwood's *Oryx and Crake* (2003). Coupland's novel carried the since widely quoted (though as we shall see, decontextualized) words: '*All* tech people are slightly autistic'.[11] Atwood's novel imagines a future in which Crake, an autistic scientist, destroys the human race to create an 'improved' humanoid species which lacks humanity's supposedly faulty interest in the arts, and is unable to read or write.

As well as being a persistent motif in literary novels, the idea that autistic people are unable to enjoy or understand fiction is embedded in diagnostic screening tools used by clinicians to help decide whether or not an adult should be formally assessed for autism. The main proponent of this assumption remains Simon Baron-Cohen, Director of the University of Cambridge's Autism Research Centre. Professor Baron-Cohen was the principal designer of the 'Adult Autism-Spectrum Quotient Test' (2001), a screening or gatekeeping tool still widely used. Chapter 1 uncovers a series of methodologically unsound biases in the scoring of this questionnaire's statements. Baron-Cohen's 'test' was in fact designed for two separate purposes. One was to create a new means for clinicians to screen adults for autism diagnostic referral – but the other was to test, if not prove, Baron-Cohen's headline-friendly theory that scientists and mathematicians show a higher number of autistic traits than the general population. It seems that the two aims of the questionnaire conflicted, then conflated. The 2001 journal article launching the questionnaire was titled 'The Autism-Spectrum Quotient (AQ): Evidence from Asperger Syndrome/High-Functioning Autism, Males and Females, Scientists and Mathematicians'. The last three words, although pivotal, have remained oddly overlooked. The questionnaire's statements regarding a predilection for numeracy are counted as autistic traits in their own right, meaning that numeracy and autism have become directly – but implicitly – equated. A possible result is that some mathematicians may have higher AQ scores simply because they are mathematicians – but not necessarily because they are autistic. Meanwhile, statements on the questionnaire involving the enjoyment of fiction are scored negatively – again, reinforcing the notion that literature is exclusively the realm of neurotypicals. For these and other reasons, I express doubts about the questionnaire's relevance to ongoing national surveys of autistic traits in the adult population, and concerns about its usefulness as a diagnostic screening tool.

The chapter revisits the research of Hans Asperger from the 1930s to the 1970s to reveal how Baron-Cohen's usages of the (posthumously introduced) term 'Asperger syndrome' problematically ignore the Austrian paediatrician's various emphases that an appreciation of fiction and the arts was strikingly expressed by many of his patients. The chapter concludes by reconsidering the relationship between science and narrative in autism research, contemplating the wider cultural ramifications posed by what amounts to the literary exclusion of autistic agency. I conclude that there needs to be greater dialogue between the sciences and the humanities – including autistic perspectives from both sides – if knowledge about autism is to meaningfully advance.

'Metaphors and Mirrors: The Otherness of Adult Autism' is the title of chapter 2, which highlights both the cultural and the medical unease regarding what it means, or could mean, to be an autistic adult. The chapter visits some of the many ways in which mirrors have served as metaphors and, sometimes, diagnostic tools in autism psychiatry. I point to asymmetries between how autistic mirror-gazing has been viewed from scientific perspectives, and how it has been diversely narrated in autistic autobiographies.

I look at how the otherized figure of the adult autist becomes a focus of projection. Normalcy cannot be sure of its own existence unless it has corresponding notions of otherness, and the set of traits, or ways, known as 'autistic' sometimes serve this need. With chapter 2, I attempt to metaphorically take up the mirror and hold it back up to some of the values questionably projected onto autism.

Adapting and expanding on key contentions from Foucault's *Madness and Civilization*, I look at how the figure of the autistic adult has been part segregated from and part exhibited in early 21st-century culture. The social otherizing of behaviours (or *expressions*) associated with autism is illustrated with reference to writings by Simon Armitage and to the UK television series *The Office*. Chapter 2 contemplates how the figure of the child continues to haunt the very meanings of adult autism. Nowhere is this more basely evident than in a certain procedure integral to the internationally recognized *Autism Diagnostic Observation Schedule™*, in which adults being assessed – and observed – by psychiatric panels are asked to 'respond to' a set of toys designed for pre-school children. I critically reflect on the methodological bizarreness of this procedure and ask why possible alternative procedures are not used.

One continual indicator of the scientific uncertainties surrounding autism is the prevalence of metaphor (another realm supposedly off-limits to autistic people). Expanding on previous critical studies, chapter 2 addresses how metaphor tends to surface in autism science discourse in the absence of factual explanations. Medical and cultural portrayals of parents to autistic children since the 1950s are considered. Sometimes, it seems as if what cannot be said about childhood autism becomes implied about *adult* autism. Chapter 2 confronts such implications when addressing how, though there is now greater sensitivity than previously towards the parents of autistic children, the parents of autistic adults remain caricatured in a manner that was otherwise largely discarded by the 1970s. After reviewing the now-discredited 'refrigerator parent' theory (and metaphor) prevalent in the 1960s, I criticize its re-enactment in 21st-century popular culture. In these fictions, the ageing mothers of autistic adults grotesquely embody the scientifically archaic notion that autism is a reflection of parental rejection. I critique how such depictions have resurfaced as metonyms for autism itself, and how such tropes indicate a cultural tendency in which few ideas are deemed too offensive to project onto autistic adults and their families. The chapter then considers how autism itself has become a metaphor, adapting Mitchell and Snyder's terms of 'narrative prosthesis'. In this, I explore one of the first cultural texts to extensively (and variously) invoke autism as a metaphor for the wider human condition: The Who's 1969 rock opera *Tommy*, written primarily by the band's guitarist and lead songwriter, Pete Townshend. *Tommy* remains an unusual autism narrative because – partly owing to its timing, in an era when Kanner's notion of 'severe' impairment was dominant, and Asperger syndrome had yet to be clinically recognized – it dares to centralize a *preverbally* autistic character. In spite of certain problematic aspects then – not least, the emphasis on 'cure' – this 1969 rock album remains unusually pertinent, for the realms of culture and literature have rarely since foregrounded preverbal autistic adulthood.

Themes of metaphor, otherness and agency culminate with chapter 2's focus on autism and poetry. First, I reflect on the Australian poet Les Murray's 'It Allows a Portrait in Line Scan at Fifteen' (1994), and the complexities it confronts between self, autism and other. I then look at a full sequence of poems on autism in British writer Joanne Limburg's *The Autistic Alice* (2017). Limburg's third full poetry collection, this opens with a thematically (and formally) daring 21-poem title sequence narrating an autistic life from infancy through to adulthood. A partial retelling of Lewis Carroll's *Through the Looking-Glass, and What Alice Found There* (1871), Limburg's collection empoweringly articulates not just the absurdity, but the *impossibility* of normalcy.

*   *   *

I use the name 'new classic' adult autism as shorthand for how the realities and thus the complexities of autistic experience have been marginalized. The term highlights how the dominant fictional and scientific narratives together popularize notions of adult autism constructed according to bourgeois, patriarchal and *neurotypical* ideas of success (or even recognition). Chapter 3 is thus titled 'Against the "New Classic" Adult Autism: Narratives of Gender, Intersectionality and Progression'. While the previous chapter addressed metaphor, this one begins by confronting an even more prevalent narrative feature surrounding autism: cliché. Science and culture often present us with *ideals* of adult autism – that is neurotypical notions of achievement. In this process, other hegemonic values are revealed: via tendencies to prioritize the white, middle-class, able-bodied male. 'New classic' is obviously an oxymoron, and I use it to address both the superficiality and (I hope) the transience of this cultural fixation and burden.

One of the most media-pleasing of all the Cambridge Autism Research Centre's projects has proven to be Baron-Cohen's theory of autism as the 'extreme male brain'. Chapter 3 considers the obstacles this creates to the cultural (and potentially the diagnostic) recognition of autistic girls and women. I examine the theory's debt to Hans Asperger's early research, and thus to ideas about gender and intelligence that were more prevalent in the 1940s than they are now. I draw from Simone de Beauvoir's *The Second Sex* (1949) as a partial counterpart to Professor Baron-Cohen's popular 2003 book *The Essential Difference*, which positions the 'male' and 'female' brains as binaries. Baron-Cohen's scientific research, which underpins the book and its arguments about autism, is then closely examined. Several methodological weaknesses are identified and discussed.

Chapter 3 then considers the convergence of Baron-Cohen's configuration of the adult autist as a high-achieving white male with the same idea in four of the most commercially successful fictions that use autism. A trajectory is traced from Levinson's *Rain Man* (1988), via Haddon's *Curious Incident of the Dog* (2003), through the American situation-comedy *Big Bang Theory* (2007–) to Graeme Simsion's best-selling romantic comedy novel *The Rosie Project* (2013). I look at how, within and between these four texts, cultural recognition of the impairments involved with autism has receded, almost to the point where an emphasis on white male high achievement (in STEM areas, of course) is virtually all that is left of the autistic profile. Applying several of Adorno and Horkheimer's sometimes-terrifying observations on the power of culture industries from *Dialectic of Enlightenment* (1944), I consider why and how the supposed 'representations' that most trivialize adult autism have become the most popular. However, with reference to autism fictions at least, the chapter does not fully concur with Adorno and Horkheimer's belief that dominant patterns in popular culture can never be meaningfully subverted. Here, the chapter turns toward a series of adult autism portrayals which, while neither as sensationalist nor as popular as the 'new classic' fictions, signal how authors, producers and audiences have always been open to more progressive considerations of autism – even if some dominant tropes still persist.

Bron/Broen (*The Bridge*) is a Scandinavian television drama (2011–2016) foregrounding an autistic detective, Saga Norén. As well as being one of few female autistic screen characters, Saga often appears less *oblivious* to social conventions than scornful of them. The UK television drama *The Syndicate* (2015), through the character of Godfrey Watson, positions adult autism at the intersection of both racial minority and working-class labour. In British novelist Clare Morrall's Bildüngsroman *The Language of Others* (2008), intersectionality is again crucial to a deeper engagement with what it can mean and entail to be autistic. Via the lead character and main narrator, Jessica Fontaine, Morrall intertwines the social and sensory pressures of autism with the shifting identities of childhood, adolescence, marriage, parenthood and work. Morrall's 2008 novel also remains subversive but unusual through the fact that it is the character herself who shows the agency to recognize and name her own autism (in contrast with *The Bridge* and *The Syndicate* – which, as I also discuss, shy away from the name).

American writer Meg Wolitzer's *The Interestings* (2013) is a novel of – among much else – autism in relation to family, friendship and relationships (all of which are often strained here, and not just by autism). Through this novel's empathic engagements with what can be deemed 'autistic' in a person, combined with how it allows readers to make up our own minds about its characters, Wolitzer's *The Interestings* is one of the most refreshing autism narratives discussed in this book. Chapter 3 thus begins by attacking cliché and ends by celebrating innovation in narratives of adult autism. However, a conspicuous gap across this spectrum of perspectives is addressed: the reasons and procedures of adult autism diagnosis have seldom been narrated in *any* autism fiction, and this creates certain problems.

'Title' is the name of the minimalist chapter 4. In partial harmony with the scientific nature of the psychiatric texts addressed in *Naming Adult Autism*, this chapter adopts an experimental approach and contemplates the medical model of autism within my own most literalist autistic terms.

This book primarily discusses the role of texts, both 'cultural' and 'scientific', in creating certain understandings of autism. In the final chapter of *Naming Adult Autism*, I begin to address the capacity of autistic people – as individuals and communities – to influence broader perceptions of what autism/s might actually mean. Thus, chapter 5, 'Performing the Names of Autism', addresses the agency of autistic people in defining the usage of this name. I begin by addressing the formal retraction of the (interchangeable) names 'Asperger syndrome' and 'Asperger's Disorder' in the US (and, it is likely by the time you read this, in the UK too). The American Psychiatric Association's divisive decision to remove the name 'Asperger's' from *DSM-5* (2013) – despite maintaining concurrence with Hans Asperger's own observations on autism – is contextualized as, in part, a reaction to what it failed to foresee as the phenomenon of self-diagnosis in response to *DSM-IV* (1994), as most subversively epitomized by the widespread adoption of the name 'Aspie'. The role of popular culture in prompting this move is also considered.

The frustrations of realizing one's own neurodivergence are juxtaposed with religious faith in Les Murray's Psalm-like 2006 poem 'The Tune on Your Mind'. Chapter 5 responds to tensions between form, content and allusion in Murray's variations on the naming of autism in the poem. I then move into comparable matters of constraint and subversion to explore the contestability of the name autism, using Judith Butler's terms of performativity as rigid social (and in this case, psychiatric) structure, and *performance* as individual (and collective) agency. The chapter, and thus the book, concludes by experimenting with some possibilities of autistic criticism as a textual practice and, in the Butlerian sense, performance. Here, having prioritized a range of narratives which, in various ways, overtly *name* adult autism, I engage with two quite different texts. E. M. Forster's 1910 novel *Howards End* is contemplated as an evocation of adult autism via the childlike, wise and unpredictable character of Mrs Wilcox. I consider how Forster's novel, written decades before autism as we know it was first named, presents a convincing and provocative depiction of autism in an era when now familiar stereotypes and tropes had yet to be formed. I also illustrate how, in *Howards End*, autistic sensibilities intersect with another marginalized subjectivity which has yet to be significantly addressed in autism fiction: same-sex love. Finally, chapter 5 turns to another genre, song. Roland Orzabal's 1982 composition 'Mad World' – now best known for the 2001 version recorded by Michael Andrews and Gary Jules – has been the focus of much discussion and deep empathy from autistic adults. But the composition also endures as a mainstream, if quirky, song of widespread appeal. In listening to 'Mad World', the chapter ends by considering how moments of art can resonate with both autistic and non-autistic people, and how this opens up further possibilities of autistic criticism.

AN INTRODUCTION TO AUTISM, INTERPELLATION AND IDENTITY

To respond to being called, or 'hailed', is to become a subject: to obey. 'Interpellation' is Louis Althusser's term for this process.[12] Using the dramatic and symbolic example of a police officer shouting 'Hey, you there!', Althusser delineates how the person who turns around in response to the call becomes caught up in somebody else's exercise of power – which, in turn, is part of a whole vaster network of authority.[13] One could pretend to ignore the police officer's shouting or even shout an impolite name back. But the point here regarding the term 'interpellation' is that to believe or even sense that one is being hailed is to become part of a process of subjection. Althusser outlines the example of the police officer's shout to illustrate his key contention: *'The existence of ideology and the hailing or interpellation of individuals are one and the same thing'* (my emphasis).[14] Ideology makes us subjects, and interpellation is the means by which it does so. To listen to the radio news is to be interpellated. We may of course disagree with how it is being narrated to us – but in order to do that, we have to listen.

To 'look at me when I'm talking', 'pay attention' or 'leave the flowers alone, dear' are all, in Althusser's sense, examples of being interpellated. Although in strict linguistic terminology, those examples are actually imperatives, Althusser's principal concern is not functional grammar, but *ideology*, and how it becomes manifest. Thus, the key point here is that (like the police officer's shout), the three speech examples at the start of this paragraph all position the recipient as a subject to processes of authority. For some autistic people, such commands can be mysterious, somewhat unnatural, even point-less orders to process and perform. Autism is, in Jim Sinclair's powerful phrase, 'a way of being'.[15] However, like any way of being, autism is also a social position. Sometimes, this position can accidentally – or naturally – disrupt the distribution of authority.[16] And so in turn, certain children, and the adults they become, find themselves frequently being made or *turned* into subjects in a more profound sense of being otherized, through the name of autism as a medical, social and cultural category. As chapter 4 reflects, to be diagnosed autistic during adulthood can be a most profound experience of interpellation.

Diagnostic assessment for autism involves not just the clinicians' own perceptions of you, but their readings of accounts of how others – primarily, others in positions of authority – have perceived you. Narratives of a per-son's childhood are vital to adult autism assessment, because these help qualified specialists to establish whether the client's autistic traits have been present since early infancy (as in the case of autism), or whether the person is presenting a different condition which developed later. But the extensive diagnostic focus on the childhood of the adult being assessed also implicates 'high' interpellation because it so largely invokes the narratives of authority figures. School reports, medical records and recollections from parents can shape the diagnostic outcome of adult autism assessment. The role of inter-pellation in adult autism assessment is also openly manifest in the Cambridge Autism-Spectrum Quotient questionnaire (2001) through statements begin-ning with phrases such as 'People often tell me that I'm. . .'.

But it is apt, perhaps unwittingly so, that Asperger syndrome (or for a time, in America, Asperger's Disorder) is named after the paediatrician who first observed and published on the condition: for the possessive 'Asperger's' emphasizes not the individual person but *the witness's (or diagnostician's) perception of the individual*. Asperger's syndrome – or Asperger syndrome – has, since its medical conception, involved (however well intentioned) processes of *othering*. However, a more radical implica-tion of this is that 'autism' may exist less in the 'autistic' individual than in the brain of the beholder. In other words, it takes *two* people to render autism present in one.

*   *   *

Culturally and medically, the naming of adult autism is a subjective process. This does not detract from the importance of *what* is being named, as well as how, when and by whom. Autism has never been *merely* a name.[17] It is an embodied experience of the sensory, the social, the cerebral and emotional, as well as of how these intersect. So before we go further, here is the place to briefly outline the history of how autism has been recognized, and how it is identified today.

The historical and political subjectivity of the American Psychiatric Association's *Diagnostic and Statistical Manual of Mental Disorders* (*DSM*) is critiqued in chapter 5. Nonetheless, the diagnostic criteria for 'Autism Spectrum Disorder' presented in the *DSM*'s most recent, fifth edition (2013) remain largely concurrent with those outlined by the two publications which first, separately, identified autism as a distinct medical category: Leo Kanner's 'Autistic Disturbances of Affective Contact' (1943) and Hans Asperger's '"Autistic Psychopathy" in Childhood' (1944). In 2015, the investigative research of Steve Silberman revealed that two of Kanner's colleagues, Georg Frankl and Anni Weiss, had previously worked in Europe with Hans Asperger; this may explain how Kanner (who published first) arrived at the name and concept of autism as similarly conceptualized by Asperger through the 1930s.[18] However, there were also significant distinctions in how the two paediatricians used the term. Kanner, working in Baltimore, described what has since been called 'classic' autism, in which speech was often significantly limited. Conversely, Asperger (researching in Vienna) profiled children whose language use, while idiosyncratic, was less limited than in classic autism. Furthermore, Asperger – unlike Kanner – emphasized the intellectual *abilities* of his patients, alongside their significant social impairments. As chapter 1 details, Asperger's work did not begin to receive widespread medical recognition until the 1980s, after Lorna Wing had formulated his 1944 observations into 'Asperger syndrome' as a distinct clinical category within autism. Yet in noticeable ways, Kanner's emphasis on apparent restrictions of language use still shapes many social expectations surrounding autism itself. Chapter 5 confronts how the very act of naming oneself autistic – and more subversively, that of critiquing the dominant meanings of this term – often elicits reactionary suppositions that those who can speak of and intellectualize this identity cannot, by definition, be 'genuinely' autistic. In assuming autism and self-expression to be somehow incompatible, such reactions threaten to severely undermine all possibilities of autistic agency.

In relation to the seminal articles by Kanner and Asperger, two points warrant emphasis here. First, Kanner and Asperger were paediatricians. Thus, both the focus and the contexts of their research primarily concerned child development. And, as chapter 2 explores, *adult* autism remains both culturally and clinically marginalized against the figure of the child. Yet second, the very fact that 'autism' was conceptualized almost simultaneously on two separate continents reflects how it was, in one crucial sense, the different groups of people *observed* by Kanner and Asperger who effectively 'defined' the name: the two researchers merely named a way of being already present in humanity.

*   *   *

To delineate the diagnostic criteria for autism, it is useful to begin with three stipulations regarding *how* the core traits are manifest. First, the 'symptoms' (discussed later) must be evident from early childhood. This is in order to distinguish autism – a biogenetic and lifelong condition – from other psychiatric conditions it may sometimes resemble, such as schizophrenia.[19] Second, autism is diagnosed when the 'disturbances' it presents do not come under broader categories of what *DSM-5* summarizes as 'intellectual disability'.[20] However, the most pivotal diagnostic mandate for autism is also the least recognized in mainstream cultural fictions. In *DSM-5*, this crucial mandate states that diagnosis should be given only when symptoms present clinically significant impairment in social, occupational, or other important areas.[21]

As chapter 3 addresses, a misleading, influential and unfortunate implication perpetuated by many of the most prominent literary and screen fictions of autism is that this condition is diagnosable merely by some kind of novelty tick-list of quirks. An effect of this misrepresentation is as follows: any 'significant impairment', disadvantage or suffering caused for adults by the combination of autistic traits and an ableist society tends to be culturally unrecognized or, worse, denied. Many fictions which proclaim to show a character 'on the spectrum' are ultimately representing autism not as impairment, disability or diversity, but autism as mere spectacle.

AUTISM DIAGNOSTIC CRITERIA: SOCIAL COMMUNICATION AND INTERACTION

Aspects and experiences of autism – and, in other words, the diagnostic criteria for the condition – are discussed at length across the following chapters. At this point, however, it is useful to introduce and begin reflecting on some of autism's defining traits. While chapters 1 and 2 critically compare numerous medical texts, I ground the focus here on the most recent and influential source, *DSM-5*.

The two main diagnostic criteria for 'Autism Spectrum Disorder' in *DSM-5* revolve around 'deficits' in interaction, and 'restricted' patterns of behaviour and activities.[22] Together, these criteria of apparent social withdrawal reinforce the etymology of 'autism' from the Greek *autos*, meaning 'self'.

Further properties and implications of the name 'autism' will be explored in chapters 2 and 5. Here however, it is instructive to closely consider the diagnostic criteria themselves, plus an implication rarely addressed in depth or at length in most scientific narratives of autism: that is, how some of the defining 'deficits' or tendencies may intersect.

DSM-5's core diagnostic criteria for Autism Spectrum Disorder begins by referring to ongoing 'deficits in social communication and social interaction', which can be present in 'multiple contexts'.[23] Obviously, 'communication' and 'interaction' both centre on verbal and non-verbal *language*. Yet this obviousness – which makes humanities and social science perspectives immediately pertinent to autism research – is oddly understated in *DSM-5*'s psychiatric narrative, much as it is in virtually all scientific texts on autism. Under the first criterion of deficits in social communication and interaction, *DSM-5* presents three subcategories.

The first subcategory, '[d]eficits in social-emotional reciprocity', invokes the 'spectrum' element of autism by listing examples from 'failure' of 'normal' interactive conversation to 'failure to *initiate* or *respond* to social interactions' (my emphasis).[24] As chapter 5 discusses via characters in Forster's *Howards End* (1910), autism can become socially discernible in tendencies to either give seemingly excessive detail in conversation or, as part of the same continuum, to be painfully uncertain of when to speak and what to say (thus saying very little), especially in group settings. Meanwhile, at further points along this spectrum are figures discussed in chapter 2. Les Murray's 'It Allows a Portrait in Linescan at Fifteen' (1994) describes a boy who began to speak as an infant before ceasing to talk for several years; the lyrics and music of The Who's *Tommy* (1969) contemplate the experiences and subjectivity of a boy (through to early adulthood) who withdraws from seemingly *all* communication and interaction. *DSM-5*'s ranging examples of social communication differences may encompass various levels of impairment, yet they indicate a struggle shared by the most socially able and the most socially disabled autistic people.

A subcategory of 'deficits' in communication detailed in *DSM-5* concerns nonverbal interaction. Primarily, this involves differences in using and interpreting body language, including tone of voice. It can be harder for autistic than non-autistic people to non-verbally intuit whether and when another person is hinting, irritated, joking, flirting and so on. Yet, as this book's various footnote narratives seek to articulate by illustration, 'failure' to *respond* in social interactions is a two-way process. The verbal and non-verbal communication and gestures of autistic people are themselves apt to be misinterpreted by others, perhaps especially neurotypicals. Apparent 'abnormalities' in eye contact – or in effect, *differences* in eye contact between two people when at least one is autistic – are often the site of such confusion. This can be disadvantageous in testing settings such as job interviews, especially if the person's autism is not known to (or is inadequately understood by) others present. Such instances point to deeper implications of the diagnostic criteria in *DSM-5*'s definition of autism: it is conceptualized according to a set of traits which are all deemed (with little critical flexibility) somehow undesirable.

Autistic traits can converge to create potentially misleading suppositions regarding autistic subjectivity from the outside. For instance, differences in eye contact might be viewed as a lack of interest in other people.[25] Again though, this notion of impairment may be read very differently by an autistic and a neurotypical person. For instance, if my eye contact with you is inconsistent during a conversation (whether formal or friendly), it is probably because I am thinking carefully and deeply about what we are verbally saying to each other; because I *am* interested in you, and am giving our words my full concentration. It remains true that some autistic people – like some non-autistic people – have little interest in the experiences or perspectives of other individuals, but at times, what may be taken as autistic indifference to others is actually more of a difference in *expression*.

DSM-5 presents three subcategories of 'deficits' that typically manifest in autism: these concern conversation; non-verbal communication; and the development of relationships. Together, these constitute the first diagnostic criterion for ongoing impairments in communication and interaction. The manual acknowledges how the 'severity' of these may vary widely between individuals diagnosed autistic, and how these traits might require different levels of support, though specific recommendations for this are not provided.[26]

A matter of increasing urgency now is the need for research into autism and old age. The American Psychiatric Association admits that consequences of autism for the elderly are largely 'unknown', although social isolation and difficulties in seeking support are posited as notable risks.[27] Greater medical and professional awareness of autism in old age is now being encouraged by the UK's National Autistic Society, but it is notable that ageing autistic people remain almost entirely unrepresented in literature and culture.[28] That said, an imminent work of note is the forthcoming sixth book by Wigan-based poet Peter Street. This as-yet-untitled volume reflects on Street's past and present in view of his being diagnosed autistic aged 68.[29]

AUTISM DIAGNOSTIC CRITERIA: RESTRICTED AND REPETITIVE PATTERNS

The second major diagnostic criterion for autism concerns '*Restricted, repetitive patterns of behaviour, interests or activities*' as evident in at least two of four subcategories. These are repetitive movements; a need for 'sameness'; intensely 'fixated interests'; and over- or under-reaction to sensory stimuli.[30]

In autism communities, the making of repetitive movements has its own recognized name: 'stimming' (short for 'self-stimulation'). Stimming may be performed consciously or unconsciously. Its expressions can range from being barely perceptible to others to becoming the focus of much unwanted attention. The sustained tensing or stretching of a muscle might be pleasurable; it might also create discomfort for the autistic person. But either way, it can help to physically and mentally 'conduct' autistic consciousness away from an unwanted sensory stimuli which *cannot* be controlled, such as the echoing din of a shopping mall, or the glare of an intense office strip light which for others goes unnoticed.

Needs for 'sameness' and repetitive routines can lead to extreme distress when seemingly (to others) minor changes occur.[31] Yet there can also be extreme delight in small changes. All of the routines and fascinations beloved of autistic people were new to us once. Perspective is key. I might visit the same café daily for months and have the same drink at the same early opening time at the same quiet table. If ever someone else is at my table, I cannot stay. I just walk off to work too early, feeling distractingly unright. That is distress at small change. But what I also need to emphasize here is that every single visit to that café is distinct for me. The daylight is different. The moods are unique. Some mornings, combinations of light and shade might remind me of a previous visit, and there is a pleasing feeling not of repetition, but continuity. But no two of my morning visits are ever entirely the same. Some routines can make the everyday feel new, every day. To an outsider, all this can still seem 'restricted'. Yet normative values can shadow such views. My preference for sameness is such that I have rarely been able to share daily life with 'a partner'. It also means that as yet, I have never truly wanted to do so. Every day has been somehow enough in itself.

The capacity for 'fixated interests' has its own name in autism communities: monotropism, a term explored in chapter 2. Nevertheless, in diagnostic rhetoric – whose function is to define not human diversity, but merely human disorder – the 'restricted' interest of autistic people continue to be outlined in restrictively pejorative terms of 'abnormality'.[32]* But it is in this subcategory

---

* **Elsewhere**

Sometimes, such preoccupations can seem, to others, morbid. Yet, perspective is crucial. Some Autism psychiatrists would probably be interested to note that, between the ages of four and six, I chronically pestered my parents – and any family we visited – to take me to a local graveyard. What I actually meant was *churchyard*. Admittedly, the names and dates on every grave were fascinating to me, having just learnt to read, then to read 'without pointing', then to read 'in my head' (that is, silently). Yet I never much considered what was underneath the soil. The most profound reason for my utter love of churchyards was their peacefulness. In a semi-rural area, they were the stillest, quietest places. I was fascinated, too, by the architecture of churches: they were unlike any other buildings I could see elsewhere.

of autism diagnostic criteria more than any other that social position (and privilege) becomes significant. For autistic academics, researching and lecturing on favourite topics, monotropism is not just acceptable; it is essential. Yet there are many more autistic people with comparably intense, critical knowledge on different subjects who might not have the chance to become academics. This is a loss not just to these individuals but to academic communities and the knowledge economy at large.

The fourth subcategory of restricted, repetitive behaviour patterns presented in *DSM-5* concerns unusual or extreme responses to sensory stimulation. The sensory dimension of autism is also of great importance when debating the boundaries between impairment and mere difference. The problem here is that autism can be a neurological 'difference' which *becomes* an impairment when environments – and societies – still too rarely consider or accommodate it.

Intense responses to sensory stimuli can bear a vital though underrecognized correspondence with seemingly unusual or repetitive motor movements. For instance, an 'abnormal' habit related to autism in *DSM-5* is walking on tiptoes.[33] This remains entirely natural to me whenever not wearing shoes. It has to do with avoiding contact of my heel-bones with the floor, which (even on carpets or rugs) issues a throb right through my nervous system, culminating in my lower jaw. 'Abnormal' physical gestures can sometimes be the body's logical response to forms of hypersensitivity.

*   *   *

Above and elsewhere, I have presented certain personal examples to reinforce that autism can be lived on the inside of the body and mind in more complex, nuanced ways than tend to be speculated in psychiatric narratives. But to autistic readers, it could already be apparent that my tendencies and experiences are drastically different from your own. It remains imperative to reinforce that autism presents a deeply diverse set of circumstances within one life, or even one day – let alone in all autistic lives. My citations of personal experience in footnotes thus appear on occasion in this book for two reasons. First they are there because I have yet to see such perspectives and details acknowledged (or *adequately* acknowledged) in the psychiatric, scientific or literary narratives by non-autistics that surround, and potentially enclose, autism itself. Second, I offer these footnotes not to imply that all nor even many autistic people share similar experiences, but indeed to demonstrate that autistic sensibilities are more varied and nuanced than the dominant ideas confronted may suggest. Autism itself, plus its critical significance, has become one of my own 'fixated interests'. And, as various citations across the chapters will show, I am not alone in this.

This book focuses on autistic *ability* almost as often as impairment: therefore, a political and ethical question must be voiced. What about each one of the autistic people who do *not* read, nor indeed, express themselves in verbal language, let alone through the privilege of academic study? They all deserve much more here than an attempt from me to theorize my own stance towards some kind of easy resolution. They all deserve much more than I know how to offer. Just like anybody else, I cannot claim to speak 'for' any other person's subjectivity or experience (autistic or non-autistic). However, I stress here that what many autistic people can and should do is speak of what we know and how it feels, and to name oppression and exclusion when we sense them. Doing so is politically vital in an era when neurotypically dominated psychiatric and cultural discourses *do* uncritically assume to speak for autistic individuals. This book is a reply to such narratives from an autistic and literary critical perspective; *one* such reply, from *one* such perspective.

NOTES

1 Ian Hacking, 'Making Up Autism', Inaugural C. L. Oakley Lecture in Medicine and the Arts, University of Leeds, 13 May 2013.

2 Frances, *Saving Normal*, 10.

3 See Kuhn, *The Structure of Scientific Revolutions*, 161.

4 See Snow, *Two Cultures*, xi–xii.

5 See for instance Locke, *Science as Writing* and Ross, *The Science Wars*.

6 See for example Gross and Levitt, *Higher Superstition*; Sokal and Brincmont, *Intellectual Impostures*.

7 Sokal and Brincmont, *Intellectual Impostures*, 185.

8 Hacking, *The Social Construction of What?*, 116.

9 Shakespeare, *Disability Rights and Wrongs*, 69–70, Kindle Location 1446.

10 For a sustained consideration of embodiment as a physical reality amid social constructs, see Shakespeare and Watson, 'The Social Model of Disability', 27–29.

11 Coupland, *Microserfs*, 159.

12 Althusser, 'Ideology and Ideological State Apparatuses', 117–18.

13 Althusser, 'Ideology and Ideological State Apparatuses', 118.

14 Althusser, 'Ideology and Ideological State Apparatuses', 118.

15 Sinclair, 'Don't Mourn for Us'.

16 For a variant on this suggestion of neurodivergence as a natural or even evolutionary disruption to social order, see Milton, 'Nature's Answer to Over-Conformity'.

17 For an opposing perspective, see Timimi, Gardner and McCabe, *The Myth of Autism*.

18 Silberman, *Neurotribes*, 167–68.

19 American Psychiatric Association, *DSM-5*, 50, 58.
20 American Psychiatric Association, *DSM-5*, 51.
21 American Psychiatric Association, *DSM-5*, 50.
22 American Psychiatric Association, *DSM-5*, 50.
23 American Psychiatric Association, *DSM-5*, 50.
24 American Psychiatric Association, *DSM-5*, 50.
25 American Psychiatric Association, *DSM-5*, 50.
26 American Psychiatric Association, *DSM-5*, 52.
27 American Psychiatric Association, *DSM-5*, 57.
28 See National Autistic Society, *Ageing with Autism*.
29 My thanks to Peter Street for his correspondence regarding his current work.
30 American Psychiatric Association, *DSM-5*, 50.
31 American Psychiatric Association, *DSM-5*, 50.
32 American Psychiatric Association, *DSM-5*, 50.
33 American Psychiatric Association, *DSM-5*, 55.

Chapter 1

'Outsider Science' and literary exclusion: A reply to denials of autistic imagination

Scientific narratives often assert that autistic people – supposedly predisposed to 'systemizing' and lacking empathy – are, by definition, indifferent to or confused by fiction. In a process exacerbated since the late 1990s, autistic ability has come to be associated somewhat exclusively with STEM (science, technology, engineering, mathematics) areas. The standard implication is that the arts and humanities, and particularly literary studies, are the province of neurotypicals only. Yet the rarely questioned assumption that autistic people are automatically unlikely to enjoy, critically engage with or express themselves through literature has become problematic for a spectrum of reasons. Medically, the implications are considerable. Assumptions about STEM and autistic talent are encoded in certain questionnaires used to screen for autism, potentially making some autistic adults less likely to receive a diagnosis or indeed recognition – simply because they happen to read novels. Culturally, too, the dismissal of autistic literary sensibilities is troubling. It both signifies and reinforces deeper, dehumanizing suppositions that autistic people are devoid of imagination. Moreover, as widely disseminated scientific beliefs that autistic adults struggle to comprehend fiction have become steadfast, the past two decades have also yielded countless novels that depend on standard but often simplistic notions of autism for character construction. Tellingly, few 'autistic' characters in novels are ever portrayed reading fiction. In Margaret Atwood's *Oryx and Crake* (2003), an autistic adult is even depicted as ideologically (and destructively) opposed to the existence of art and literature in the world. In effect, the autism narratives in both science and fiction critiqued in this chapter collusively perpetuate what is becoming a barbarically clichéd assumption: that autistic people are good at either STEM subjects or nothing. I argue that this notion both underestimates and undermines autistic diversity, and address possible consequences of this. The chapter thus details where and why it is both scientifically and culturally necessary to rethink certain dominant theories which have hitherto excluded literary engagement – and by extension, imagination itself – from the namings, and the meanings, of adult autism.

The main scientific narratives of autistic ability critiqued in this chapter come from the University of Cambridge's Autism Research Centre (UCARC) and are led by the centre's director Simon Baron-Cohen (Professor of Developmental Psychopathology). The name and notion that most extensively characterizes Baron-Cohen's interpretation of autistic subjectivity is *systemizing*. Summarizing the UCARC's ongoing research into systemizing and autism, the centre's website defines the former: '*Systemizing is the drive to analyse or construct a system. A system is anything that follows rules*' (my italics).[1] The examples of systemizing listed on the website are noticeably geared towards the practical and the scientific. Systemizing can be 'mechanical', 'abstract' (e.g., 'number patterns'), 'natural' or 'collectible' (e.g., 'classifying objects').[2] Thus, the key feature of the autistic mind as defined by UCARC excludes any interest in *people*. Although UCARC is a cross-disciplinary unit, its principal investigators' work includes neuroscience, biochemistry, psychiatry and psychology: none of the centre's affiliates or collaborators represent the humanities.

I title the processes and perspectives of the present chapter 'Outsider Science'. The term was introduced by science historian Margaret Wertheim (2011) as an equivalent to 'Outsider Art' or *Art Brüt*. Wertheim surveys the work of independent scholars who had little formal scientific training and yet, through experiment, made pioneering contributions to physics, biology and chemistry. I name this chapter 'Outsider Science' for much less grand but more specific reasons. First, I am not a trained scientist: my critique of scientific autism research is essentially *literary* in its questions regarding narrative and representation, but also in its focus on a particular aspect of autistic subjectivities and identities – namely the relationship of autism to literature itself. But, second, the scientific research addressed in the chapter also constitutes Outsider Science. The authors whose influential constructions of autism I critique are not, to my knowledge, autistic. Their scientific research, although invaluable, remains 'outside' the condition it narrates. Third, the chapter concerns Outsider Science in a more hypothetical manner: I am arguing for greater recognition of autistic sensibilities and identities which have so far been marginalized from dominant narratives. Thus, while I cite hitherto neglected evidence that autism and literary engagement have coexisted, can coexist and do coexist in many adults, my emphasis is also intended to point towards a wider reality: the fact that dominant autism portrayals in both science and culture are problematically reductive; propagating notions of uniformity at the expense of diversity or, indeed, equality.

The emphasis on autism and STEM talents since the 1990s is part of a cultural shift that gives increased attention to autism as a condition that – contrasting with dominant associations in the preceding half-century – does not necessarily mean a drastically limited lifestyle for all individuals so diagnosed. Essentially, the most culturally prominent narratives have switched from sensationalizing 'classic' autism, as conceptualized by Leo Kanner (1943), towards sensationalizing what has crudely (and ominously) been termed 'high-functioning' autism, based primarily on Hans Asperger's research (1944). This intensified focus on autism as a condition that can sometimes coexist with spectacular talent – even if, for most of us, it does not – ostensibly celebrates autism and autistic potential. However, it incurs expectations that could actually reinforce the disablement of many autistic people.

I write as an academic whose qualifications and profession are based in literary studies, but also from the seemingly inescapable perspective of an adult diagnosed autistic. In critically reviewing the most influential narratives of a link between autistic talents and STEM subjects, I do not suggest that such associations are inaccurate but that they present a misleadingly *incomplete* profile of what it means to be, and be diagnosed, autistic. Autistic literary authors and scholars (not unlike autistic adults in STEM areas) most likely constitute a minority when the fuller autistic spectrum is considered. Yet, as later citations will show, there are innumerable autistic individuals emerging in literary areas, and in this chapter, I begin to outline why their wider recognition is beneficial to both autistic and neurotypical communities.

Suggestions that autistic people don't 'get' fiction presuppose that we are excluded from the audience of a form which simultaneously exploits neurotypical curiosity about our condition and influences how others may think of us. But there is also a deeper reason to interrogate both scientific and cultural notions that autistic people are unable to identify with or express themselves via fiction. In recent scientific discourse and diagnostic texts, such assumptions reinforce a still more oppressive preconception: that autistic people, by definition, lack imagination.

*   *   *

CHILDHOOD AUTISM AND THE PSYCHIATRIC IMAGINATION

Reviewing Baron-Cohen's neuroscience monograph *Zero Degrees of Empathy* (2011), Terry Eagleton cautions against culturally engrained notions that imagination is an exclusively positive attribute.[3] The tendency criticized by Eagleton also marks the potentially dehumanizing implications of suggesting – or, indeed, imagining – that autistic people do not express, nor even *have*, imaginations of their own.

To briefly illustrate the literary and social reverence for imagination as a human property, radical poet and pamphleteer Percy Bysshe Shelley's essay 'A Defence of Poetry' (1821) is instructive:

> A man, to be greatly good, must imagine intensely and comprehensively; he must put himself in the place of another and many others; the pains and pleasures of his species must become his own. The great instrument of moral good is the imagination.[4]

Shelley clearly refers to the process which, almost a century later in 1909, would be named by psychologist Edward Titchener as *empathy*.[5] But even now, another century on, it is possible to see how, in autism discourse since the late 1970s, the naming of empathy drags behind it the conceptual baggage of 'imagination' at large. In effect, differences in *social* imagination as seen in autism remain conflated with suppositions of autistic impairment in all aspects and uses of imagination, including 'pretend play' in childhood as well as creativity, reading comprehension and intellectual originality *throughout* autistic life.

In 1979, Lorna Wing and Judith Gould – two most dedicated, progressive researchers on autism – recommended 'Abnormalities of Symbolic, Imaginative Activities' as a new diagnostic criterion for autism in children.[6] Two types of 'abnormalities' were identified: the absence of pretend play and demonstration of 'repetitive, stereotyped symbolic activities'.[7] Wing and Gould thus proposed what became known as the 'triad of impairments', naming autism in terms of apparent deficiencies in social skill, communication and imagination. In 1981, another influential article by Wing – elucidating and modifying Asperger's research to enable its clinical recognition as a 'syndrome' – further emphasized pretend play as the main signifier of imagination (or its lack).[8] However, a decade later, a study profiling individuals with Asperger syndrome from childhood to adulthood by psychologist Digby Tantam (1991) presented enough evidence of pretend play – and making up stories – to conclude that people with the syndrome 'are not always deficient in imagination', contrary to Wing (1981).[9] Interviewed about her work by autism historian Adam Feinstein in 2010, Wing confirmed:

> We now emphasize that it is *social* skills, communication and imagination which are impaired. Autistic children *do* have imagination, but it is not social (Wing's emphasis).[10]

Thus, 'play' is only equated with 'pretending' if it involves interaction with others. Yet despite Wing's honourable acknowledgement that her earlier usage of the term 'imagination' could have been more specific, the legacy of the 1979 terminology persists.

The most prominent research on autism and empathy itself has been authored by Baron-Cohen – who, from outside, defines autistic thought as a predisposition to systemizing, the effective cost of which is impairment in empathizing.[11] But despite presenting a more specific focus on empathy, UCARC's narratives tend less to nuance than to reinforce in bulk the older suppositions that autistic people are devoid of imagination itself. In UCARC's adult autism AQ test, 10 of the 50 statements were designed to assess imagination. These include questions relating to visualizing processes imagination, pretend play (but only with others), empathizing and the enjoyment and comprehension of fiction. The answers are scored in such a way that imagination itself is exclusively equated with neurotypicality.[12] Thus, in one of the most widely used diagnostic tools, created by some of the world's most prominent specialists, the assumption is implicit: autism means a lifelong lack of imagination. However, a more complex process is at work and one which the dominant scientific discourse around autism seldom acknowledges. To recognize this process, an 'inside' perspective is crucial.

Sociologist Dr Damian Milton – who himself has Asperger syndrome – has written extensively on what he terms the 'double empathy problem' between autistics and neurotypicals. In a 2012 article drawing on both sociology and philosophy to elucidate the double empathy problem, Milton justifiably argues that the

> 'empathy' so lauded in normative psychological models of human interaction refers to the ability a 'non-autism spectrum' (non-AS) individual has to assume understandings of the mental states and motives of other people. When such 'empathy' is applied toward an 'autistic person', however, it is often wildly inaccurate in its measure.[13]

Milton (2012) concludes:

> It is true that autistic people often lack insight about non-AS perceptions and culture, yet it is equally the case that non-AS people lack insight into the minds and culture of 'autistic people'.[14]

Although Milton refers here to narratives of empathy specifically, his emphasis on the uneven reciprocity between autistic and non-autistic perspectives is pertinent to 'outsider' narratives of autism and imagination itself. In short, autistic people are assumed to lack imagination because their expressions of it may not conform to neurotypical expectations. Yet, as with the double empathy problem, this also signifies a limitation or impairment of imagination on the part of neurotypicals – including, as Milton suggests, the authors of 'normative psychological models'. However, some prominent neuro-typical voices in autism discourse are beginning to advocate more empathic viewpoints.

One of the more innovative commentaries on autism from outside is Jonathan Alderson *Challenging the Myths of Autism* (2011). The author is a Toronto-based childhood autism consultant. I remain cautious of Alderson's optimism that a mid-way stance on 'cure' between scientists and autistics is possible.[15] However, I admire his separate implorations that something approaching a meeting point between autistics and non-autistics can be reached if the latter apply their own imaginations in more questioning ways. Alderson emphasizes that orthodox psychiatry has dismissed the presence of autistic imagination simply because it shows itself differently from neurotypical imagination. Alderson critiques another psychiatrist's narrative of a boy with Asperger syndrome, who was reported to show no evidence of 'imaginative play', preferring to manipulate toy trains in a 'routinized way'. Yet the same boy was observed to enjoy walking backwards, apparently imitating the sensation of riding in a train. As Alderson points out, the latter detail could actually be *proof* of the boy's 'capacity for make believe and imagination'.[16] And it's possible to go further: I would also suggest that playing with the *toy* trains in a routinized way can be read as an act of imagination.*

AUTISM AND THE MACHINE

Dr Sonya Freeman Loftis – a literary scholar who states her own autistic identity in *Imagining Autism* (2015) – points out that the common comparison of the autistic mind with a machine or computer suggests 'a less-than-human quality to those with cognitive differences'.[17] But why has autism, of all cognitive identities, been so conducive – or vulnerable – to associations with

---

* *Gateway*
    In my brief, distressing stint at nursery school (while Lorna Wing, miles away in London, was probably finalizing her 1981 manuscript), I was chastised for repeatedly wandering away from my seated peers during 'story-time' to try and enjoy the school's collection of toy cars and lorries alone. Like many a good little exemplar of autistic 'play', I was determined to position these toys into a neat line. I did so because that was how I often *saw* cars and lorries: in processions, on roads. Perhaps this literalism indicated lack of imagination. Yet to me, this ritual was a gateway into imagination itself. Kneeling above these toys, I was not merely imagining but *seeing* and *hearing* them as if they were actual vehicles, the size of reality. I imagined them forming a glorious procession down a particular lane, near my grandmother's house. I imagined I was somehow above this scene, and seeing the hedges, the church and the bench, as this whole convoy rolled along. Then my entire upper body flinched, as my flapping hands were grabbed by those of the nursery teacher, Ms Atwood (not her real name). My whole imagined scene disappeared as I was led back to the seated area to pretend to listen to a story.

machinery? As we shall see, science has proven itself more interested in how autistic adults systemize than how we empathize. Nonetheless, since computer technologies are created according to systems, often for the function of creating further systems, it makes logical sense that a computer scientist with Asperger syndrome is presented as a case study alongside a mathematician and a physicist in an early journal article on autism and systemizing skills by Baron-Cohen et al. (1999).[18] And, by the time the 1999 article appeared, associations of autism with both mathematics and computers were already long-standing in popular culture. Therefore, I will first discuss how the figure of the adult autist as the computer-esque computer programmer emerged in broadcasting, journalism and cinema.

Morten Tyldum's 2014 film *The Imitation Game* utilizes and projects the autism and computer association backwards to the Second World War period, portraying the life of polymath Alan Turing with accentuated autistic traits, based on post-Asperger 21st-century readings of biographical sources. However, the earliest cultural associations of autistic minds with computers occurred in the mid-1960s, following various media profiles of savant twin brothers George and Michael Flinn.[19] Born in 1940, the Flinn brothers had been variously diagnosed as autistic, psychotic and 'severely retarded'.[20] They also showed superlative talents in calculating days of the week on given dates centuries into the past and (with effect that quietly underlined the apparent otherness of these twins) thousands of years into the future. In retrospect, the Flinn brothers' media appearances together seem to have established two related antecedents for autism associations: first, with mathematics; second, with contemporary technology. For in the 1960s, a new labour-saving computer device was appearing in workplaces internationally: the desktop calculator, introduced in 1961. Popular associations of the autistic mind with machinery have since developed in loose accordance with technological progress and its social and cultural impact.

In Barry Levinson's film *Rain Man* (1988), Raymond Babbitt's autistic 'savant' abilities are formatively juxtaposed with the efficiency (and function) of a pocket calculator. As Raymond's autism is explained to his brother, a psychiatrist asks the autistic adult to mentally answer spectacular sums, to each of which Raymond responds swiftly and correctly, as is shown when the camera cuts to show the same digits on the calculator's display. The same handy trope of autistic intelligence persists into the 21st century. A 2007 documentary on the German autistic mathematician Rüdiger Gamm was titled 'The Human Calculator'; the phrase also headed a 2010 UK newspaper article on the eccentricities and possible autism of mathematician Paul Dirac.[21] But the deeper significance of such associations demands analysis. Numbers constitute an infinite system that transcends regional language boundaries. Numbers are mysterious because they have no known limits.

When combined with another mystery – autism – mathematical expertise can almost seem an infinite form of mental ability to those who do not share the combination. But this is a burdensome expectation to place onto autistic people – including brilliant autistic mathematicians.

Morgan Matthews's film *X+Y* (2014) is based on the real lives of British teenagers who competed in the 2006 International Mathematical Olympiad. The most devastating moment occurs after Luke – one of the film's several autistic characters – has been eliminated from the competition. When another contestant later discovers him slashing his arm with a razor, Luke begins to describe how his parents explained autism to him. 'It's alright being weird. As long as you're gifted'. But: 'If you're not gifted then – that just leaves weird. Doesn't it'.[22] What this fictionalized scene says about the character's parents is irrelevant here: for the deeper, twisted roots of what Luke is facing are ultimately cultural.

In his landmark study *Representing Autism: Culture, Narrative, Fascination* (2008), Stuart Murray observes how the autist-as-mathematical-genius trope, used to sensational acclaim in *Rain Man*, resurfaces in Mark Haddon's (comparably lauded) young adult novel *The Curious Incident of the Dog in the Night-Time* (2003).[23] In this context, Murray (2008) critiques the then recent television profiles of Daniel Tammet, a British adult with Asperger syndrome who demonstrates outstanding abilities in rapidly learning foreign languages and – of most interest to the media – in mathematics. In 2004, Tammet performed a record-breaking recital of *pi*, from memory, to 22,514 accurate digits. While recognizing Tammet's achievements, including a fine memoir (2006), Murray highlights how 'the backdrop of fiction, and the expectations produced by such fiction' after *Rain Man* and Haddon's novel created an eager cultural audience for Tammet as a real-life autistic person.[24] Amid all this, we see a paradox that will be addressed more fully in chapter 3: autistic people – including *exceptional* autistic people – are usually given cultural approval if they appear to closely resemble each other. Murray's commentary on the 'idiot savant' expectations of autism notes that a 2006 British documentary on the extraordinary memory of Kim Peek (on whom *Rain Man*'s Raymond Babbitt was partially based) referred to Peek as a 'living Google'.[25] Through this equation, Murray surmises an 'increasingly common idea that autism can be understood through comparisons with technology, and particularly computing'.[26] But surely, all this othering of autism, implicit in cultural notions like the 'human calculator' and 'living Google' motifs, is back to front. Computers imitate certain functions of human minds: not vice versa.

Ultimately, skills for numeracy and memory in autistic people, however spectacular, have more in common with neurotypical minds than with computers. However, this obviousness remains largely dormant in cultural narratives – including books concerning, as well as for, autistic children. A section in Adelle Jameson Tilton's *The Everything Parent's Guide to Children with Autism* (2010) is headed 'A Mind Like a Computer'.[27] *Our Brains Are Like Computers!* is the title of a guidebook on social skills for autistic children by Joel Shaul (2016).[28] But is the autistic-brain-as-computer analogy healthy for understandings of autism in a neurotypically dominated world? Computers have no rights. The nearest thing to human feeling embodied by a computer is exhaustion. Computers are here to *serve* – until a more efficient model arrives, or the present one expires.

* * *

So far, I have discussed cultural equations of the autistic mind and machinery. It is also important to consider the vulnerability of autism itself as a way of being at the present time of technological development. One of the gravest implications of a future that may involve science preventing or curing autism as funded by 'Autism Speaks' is that such human engineering could also acquire the potential to modify – or manipulate – the development of individual autistic minds. Yet even right now, scientific constructions of autism appear to be unconsciously exercising what could become a narrative arm of eugenics.

The Cambridge UCARC's 2015 report on autistic traits in UK adults is titled 'Sex and STEM Occupation Predict Autism-Spectrum Quotient (AQ) Scores in Half a Million People'. But what happens if we rearrange the nominal focal points of this scientific research? What if one day, sex and AQ scores 'predict' STEM occupations? What if prenatal testing – or engineering – eventually enables science to predict and influence the social and economic function of autistic adults?

Alongside its surveys of adult autistic traits and STEM talent, UCARC is leading longitudinal research into autism and fetal hormones. One of the centre's main findings is that 'fetal testosterone is positively associated with systemizing, attention to detail, and a number of autistic traits'.[29] Another recent publication involving UCARC (led by Baron-Cohen in collaboration with scientists across Europe) was a 2015 article in *Molecular Psychiatry*, declaring 'the first direct evidence of elevated fetal steroidogenic activity in autism' (steroidogenic activity is an organism's natural production of steroids).[30] The authors admit that the findings do not indicate 'the potential for such data as a prospective prenatal test of autism risk' but suggest how the reported discovery could be involved in such future research.[31] Now, I fully recognize that the UCARC has neither an agenda nor an allegiance with any interests concerning autism and genetic engineering.[32] However, what needs to be remembered is the fact that science and technology can often be brought into service of wider ideological forces.

The actual cause or causes of autism are still deeply unclear to even the world's leading scientists. But worryingly, eugenic agendas are now being implicated with the condition. In December 2015, Ari Ne'eman – founder of the Autistic Self Advocacy Network – wrote in *The Guardian* newspaper of how clinical policies have already begun to exclude autistic people from contributing to the gene pools involved in reproductive technology.[33] The London Sperm Bank now rejects donors who have autism, attention deficit hyperactivity disorder, dyslexia or obsessive compulsive disorder. Ne'eman also reported that the Western Australia Reproductive Technology Council has authorized an in vitro fertilization clinic to screen the gender of embryos before implantation. The same council has approved the rejection of male embryos from families in which autism is present (because autism is more often diagnosed in males).

Under the current coalescence of cultural and scientific narratives of autism, Aldous Huxley's *Brave New World* (1932) bears particular relevance. Huxley's novel envisions a future in which science – but more to the point, society's ruling powers – can 'predestine and condition' human beings to become, at one extreme, sewage workers, and, at another, 'future World Controllers'.[34] What would become of autism, in a post-eugenic future? We cannot know. However, increasingly urgent questions remain. How is autism being named and narrated in science and culture? And what might be the impact of such narratives on how autism is perceived by those wishing to cure or somehow change the essence of the condition – whether in one individual person or, indeed, within the whole of humanity?

COMPUTER CODING AND/AS LITERATURE: THE NAMING OF AUTISM IN DOUGLAS COUPLAND'S *MICROSERFS*

Having critiqued how autistic minds have been likened to machines, and considered certain wider technological forces in relation to autism, I now focus on the cultural figure of the adult autist as active *user* of the computer. Although many such cultural configurations of the Aspergic ICT (information and computer technology) specialist remain repressive, the association marks an evolving recognition of the presence and power of autism, even (and perhaps especially) when belying *hostility* towards autistic people. The present discussion thus overturns the focus of the section 'Autism and the machine' and emphasizes the computer as a signifier and indeed means of autistic agency. Although computer technology is usually synonymous with 'information', not imagination, these two cerebral realms have never been binaries. In Canadian author Douglas Coupland's novel *Microserfs* (1995), 'information' as stored and activated on computers is continually shown as the product and *expression* of human imagination – including autistic imagination. However, before looking at *Microserfs* more closely, the cultural context that spawned this innovative novel requires brief consideration.

As mass access to information technology progressed from pocket calculators to personal computers, popular metonyms for autistic minds similarly evolved. Jordynn Jack (2014) traces how the rhetorical trope of the male computer 'geek' as borderline autistic emerged through the 1990s. Critiquing how those who succeed in a computerized knowledge economy are caricatured as geeks, Jack considers how, 'to protect the character of the traditional male (now diminished in his economic productivity), those geeks are repeatedly cast as disabled, autistic, and abnormal'.[35] Effectively, then, the increased economic prowess attached to ICT success (epitomized by Bill Gates) yielded a crisis for masculinity as an identity conventionally associated with physical strength. Indeed, the male computer geek is most popular in culture when his portrayal is stripped of both physical strength and adult emotion. In the following discussion, I address how associations of autism with ICT talent have been spread by seminal journalistic texts and, particularly, Coupland's novel. In different ways, the manufacturing and reproduction of stereotypes is at work in these narratives (or, at least, in their legacies). What must also be named here is the compellingly yet conspicuously *anecdotal* essence of these texts – and the inevitability that observations which are difficult to prove accurate are often similarly difficult to prove wrong. Thus, anecdotal evidence can be peculiarly harder to counter than organized science (not least because the former tends to reach a much vaster audience). Nonetheless, as the following discussion proceeds, we will also see that some key autistic voices not only support popular associations of ICT talent with autism but importantly stress the role of computers in the formation of autistic community.

* * *

A semi-facetious yet pivotal moment in popularizing ICT associations with adult autism was *Time* magazine's 1994 article 'Diagnosing Bill Gates', which scrutinized selected media profiles of Microsoft's CEO to suggest that Gates has Asperger syndrome.[36] In 2001, science journalist Steve Silberman's essay 'The Geek Syndrome' was published in U.S.-based computer technology and science magazine *Wired*. Silberman anecdotally stressed a high prevalence of autism diagnoses in California's Santa Clara Valley, known as 'Silicon Valley' for its concentration of multinational technological corporations and their workers. Since Silberman's article, the association of adult autism with computer programmers has become one of the most popular tropes of autism narratives.

Although the IT trope is problematically dominant in cultural imaginings of autism, it is crucial to acknowledge the depth and vitality in which many autistic people engage with – and through – computers. A very positive and seemingly representative viewpoint on this is quoted by Silberman (2015). Carolyn Baird, who in 2000 became manager of Autism List, one of the first major online autism resources, commented:

> Autistic people seem to have an affinity with computers and many of them were already working in computer-related fields prior to the advent of the Internet. The appeal of a computer is that there is only one right way to tell it to do something – it doesn't misinterpret what you tell it and do something else as people do.[37]

Not all computer enthusiasts are autistics and not all autistics are computer enthusiasts. Many autistic people have no access to computers. And for older autistic adults who were not taught IT at school, the prospect of learning to use a laptop may seem insurmountably complex or, indeed, simply unnecessary. Nevertheless, Baird's comments in particular, but also Silberman's outsider emphasis on the allure of computers to (many) autistic people, valuably stress how access to such technology can potentially be liberating to thousands of people on the spectrum.

Coupland's *Microserfs* (1995) provided one of the earliest literary juxtapositions of autism, information technology and the workplace. The novel is a satire of the Microsoft empire and a contemplation of the evolving relationship between humanity and technology. Like Silberman, Coupland is also a contributor to *Wired*, and *Microserfs*' opening chapter appeared as a short story in the magazine in 1994.[38] *Microserfs* offers the following thought via the character of Karla, a computer programmer: 'I think *all* tech people are slightly autistic'.[39] A less sensational possibility might be that *working in technology demands skills in which some autistic people excel*. However, Karla's line – often positioned as *Coupland*'s view – has since been quoted as shorthand for a prominent cliché (and, worse, a clichéd expectation) regarding autistic adults.[40]

Although Coupland's novel is often reduced to Karla's comment that '*all* tech people are slightly autistic', in context, the suggestion stays ambiguous. Karla ventures the remark when the narrator's mother comments that the talented but unpredictable Michael (absent from the conversation) seems autistic. With unexpected switches between topics that imply her own neurodiversity, Karla then summarizes dyspraxia before swiftly announcing that 'Michael is an elective mute', after which she returns to closer associations of autism by stating that his brain is 'wide open' to some things but 'nailed shut' to others, making him 'a true techie geek'.[41] Daniel, the novel's narrator, proceeds to give his own observations of Michael's talent and impulsiveness, but is ambivalent over whether Michael is autistic. Through this hectic exchange of views, *Microserfs* keeps autism's relationship to 'tech people' demonstrably *debatable*, and the characters' uncertainty regarding the condition itself reflects a diagnosis in a state of semantic transition.

In and for its time, *Microserfs* was genuinely progressive as an early portrayal of autism less as impairment than mere difference. As I discuss later, too much emphasis on this may be culturally disabling to autistic people if it trivializes the condition's realities and complexities. But, here, *Microserfs* is particularly relevant as a literary exploration of adult autism and STEM. It is also compelling as a novel promoted with reference to its informal but immersive research. Coupland has described how, while planning the book, he spent six months living among software programmers, observing them as they worked and socialized.[42] And, in *Microserfs*, most characters (nearly all software programmers) convey traits associated with autism. However, as in most subsequent autism fiction, one character (Michael) is singled out as much more overtly autistic. With similar prescience for fictional autistic characters, Michael has no formal diagnosis, yet his manner, routines and talent both distinguish and isolate him from others. Michael's primary connection is with computers, not people.

Microserfs explores how far the human brain – but particularly the autistic brain – resembles a computer. Michael muses that he models his personality on machines; they 'never have to worry about human things'.[43] Similarly, 'Bill', the novel's all-powerful software tycoon (based on Gates), 'doesn't have to express emotion or charisma, because emotion can't be converted into lines of code'.[44] As a technological illiterate, I find *Microserfs'* references to silicon developments and their share index values alienating, but this accentuates the novel's satire of technology and capitalism as a two-pronged hegemony dictating much of mental and physical life. However, amid the novel's tentative yet resonant naming of autism, the centrality of computers to the narrative gains other meanings.

Coupland's novel evokes how computers can be both useful and beautiful. If it's true that autism and computer expertise are related, *Microserfs* must be one of the most autism-friendly novels to date. Interspersed with pages of software coding, *Microserfs* reminds us how such texts *are* literature for Michael: full of elegance, precision and wonder, they create connections between the self, others and the wider world. In such ways, the novel points to how being autistic and preferring programming to reading fiction is not to show lack of imagination but simply to exercise it in another way. *Microserfs* also recognizes the power of the computer as a social and even emotional prosthetic: Michael falls in love over the World Wide Web.

An additional implication of Coupland's work deserves emphasis. *Microserfs* and its 2006 sequel *JPod* juxtapose autism with ICT careers, yet by cautiously suggesting in his 2011 biography of Marshall McLuhan that the English literature professor turned media theorist had Asperger syndrome, Coupland indirectly shows how autistic subjectivities can yield innovation in the humanities.[45] Furthermore, interviews have paraphrased Coupland as stating that he has 'mild' autism himself: an important gesture from any novelist, while culture, science and fiction itself so often imply that autism precludes literary engagement or expression.[46]

MARGARET ATWOOD'S *ORYX AND CRAKE*: AUTISM AND LITERARY EXCLUSION

The positioning of autistic and literary thinking as antithetical is given ambiguous prominence in Canadian author Margaret Atwood's futuristic novel *Oryx and Crake* (2003), the first instalment of her 'MaddAddam' trilogy (2003, 2009, 2013). The novel satirizes the academic and cultural marginalization of the humanities (renamed 'Problematics') against the hegemony of economically lucrative STEM subjects. In the future of *Oryx and Crake* humans are divided between 'word people' and 'numbers people', who broadly signify neurotypicals and autistics, respectively. In some of the more subtle invocations of autism, the central character of Jimmy (a word person, viewed by numbers people as neurotypical) displays certain social struggles associated with Asperger syndrome. For instance, Jimmy has difficulty understanding other people's humour; he also experiences unease at certain social events.[47] However, like *Microserfs* and many subsequent texts featuring multiple Aspergic characters, Atwood's 'MaddAddam' trilogy casts a singular figure in whom autism is much more pronounced and thus otherized. This is the eponymous Crake of the first novel: a numbers person and recklessly amoral scientist who almost totally obliterates the human race and replaces it with a laboratory-created species, the Crakers. Designed according to the physical and psychological ideals of their autistic maker, Crakers are also created to serve Crake's political ends. These ends include the removal of art and literature from the world.

In the third novel in Atwood's trilogy, *MaddAddam* (2013), a less drastic depiction of autism emerges, as stories are told of Crake as a child (when his name was Glenn). For instance, *MaddAddam* describes Glenn's mysterious (to others) dislike of physical contact.[48] But in *Oryx and Crake* (and briefly in the second novel, *The Year of the Flood*, 2009), this character's autism is reduced to two relentlessly emphasized features: a total lack of empathy, and savant-like talents in both computer coding and laboratory innovation.[49] In the 2003 novel, Atwood's vocabulary for and around Crake's character marks the acceleration of STEM associations with autism by the early 21st century. Crake's casual conversation revolves around being 'objective' and following 'hypotheses' to 'logical conclusions'.[50] Contrasting with Jimmy, Crake is unmoved by a passage from *Macbeth* and dismisses art at large as serving the purely biological purpose of giving the artist sexual appeal.[51] Throughout *Oryx and Crake*, the main autistic character's distaste for art is conflated with his utter indifference to the suffering of others. Crake's autistic appearance is thus largely mechanical: not just in the sense that he so lacks human feeling, but in his narrative function of personifying political opposition to literature, art and imagination itself.

In *Oryx and Crake*, Harvard University has been replaced by the Watson-Crick Institute, a STEM-driven organization.[52] Watson-Crick, which Crake attends, is nicknamed 'Asperger's U.' in a chapter of that title. This interpellation of 'Asperger's' from local youngsters refers to the institute's resident 'brilliant weirdos', described thus:

Demi-autistic, genetically speaking; single-track tunnel-vision minds, a marked degree of social ineptitude – these were not your sharp dressers – and luckily for everyone there, a tolerance for mildly deviant public behaviour.[53]

This quotation carries *Oryx and Crake*'s pivotal reference to autism. 'Demi-autistic', technically meaning *semi*-autistic while phonetically reeking of 'demigod', encapsulates the novel's conjecture of autism as supreme talent combined with comic social impairment. Not unlike in *Microserfs*, there is considerable ambiguity as to whether autistic people are being satirized by Atwood's novel itself, or merely by its characters. It is the people outside Watson-Crick who nickname it 'Asperger's' university. One of those effectively excluded is Jimmy, whose perspective dominates *Oryx and Crake* (including the above quotation). The character of Crake and his checklist-like embodiment of millennial autistic features is thus viewed primarily according to Jimmy – whose feelings towards Crake are motivated by intellectual (and later, sexual) jealousy. In the novel's two sequels, Jimmy's perspective on many events in *Oryx and Crake* is revealed to have been limited. However, there are two narrative elements that do not change across Atwood's MaddAddam trilogy. The first is the continued prominence of autistic traits in Crake. For example, in *The Year of the Flood*, when he is depicted as a teenager and still known as Glenn, autism is not named but is metonymically re-established through the combination of his science-bound speech and the ostracizing terms in which different characters describe him: 'brainiac', 'cyborg' and 'geek'.[54] The second strand that remains even beyond the hostile Jimmy's perspective is Crake's STEM-happy determination to rid the world of the arts and humanities plus his vision that those made in his image must be incapable of 'symbolic thinking'.[55]

Semi-progressively, Atwood's 2003 novel employs the autistic community's own language by having Crake refer to Jimmy as 'neurotypical'.[56] The rareness of this term in fiction of the period was such that in 2008 *The Oxford English Dictionary* recorded its appearance in *Oryx and Crake* as an early usage of the noun.[57] However, the novel's actual invocation of the phrase uneasily serves to incur a familiarly clichéd assumption regarding autism. Crake tells Jimmy that 'neurotypicals' lack 'the genius gene', prompting Jimmy to fear that being neurotypical is 'now bad, in the gestalt of Crake'.[58] For in the gestalt of Crake and his kind at 'Asperger's' university, demi-autistics are beginning to reorder the world.

Despite Atwood's defence of the humanities in *Oryx and Crake*, Asperger syndrome has a primarily utilitarian function in the narrative, serving as a synonym for philistinism. In this sense, *Oryx and Crake* exemplifies what David Mitchell and Sharon Snyder (2000) had recently critiqued as the centuries-old literary usage of disability for 'narrative prosthesis'. To apply Mitchell and Snyder's phrase, autism is a prosthetic as 'a device of characterization' in Atwood's novel.[59] Notwithstanding the complexities of Jimmy's own character and perspective, narrative prosthesis is also at work in the sense that *Oryx and Crake depends* on autism – or certain, culturally familiar notions of autism – for characterization.

When comparing Atwood's 2003 novel with Coupland's 1995 *Microserfs*, the growing cultural fixation on the autistic adult as STEM genius becomes apparent. An intervening development was the increased attention to Asperger syndrome. Although the condition was added to *Diagnostic and Statistical Manual of Mental Disorders-IV* in 1994, its cultural recognition was gradual, and *Microserfs* names only 'autism'. Nonetheless, Coupland's infusion of clear yet ultimately minor autistic traits into Michael and other successfully employed adult characters indicates a shift in which Asperger's emphasis on autism and ability began attracting greater cultural attention than Kanner's on autism and impairment. While Coupland (1995) names autism but not Asperger syndrome, Atwood (2003) does almost the opposite. *Oryx and Crake* exemplifies how, following Silberman's 2001 'Geek Syndrome' article, cultural familiarity with Asperger syndrome was such that it could be invoked to google-ready readers without direct explanation of its being a form of autism or of what its symptoms involved. *Oryx and Crake* marks the association of autism with STEM becoming culturally naturalized: that is, taken as read. And, by the time of its publication, such beliefs were encoded in widely used screening tests for autism.

'Symbolic thinking of any kind' would signal 'downfall' for ruling powers, insists the autistic, civilization-dominating Crake.[60] Hence, Crakers, the
post-human species he creates, are designed to be unable to read.[61] The last
detail magnifies what, by 2003, was a scientifically endorsed supposition:
that autistic people, by definition, are somehow unable to be reached – or to
reach *out* – through fiction. Before comparing responses to Atwood's novel
from within the autism community it is important to identify and critique how
scientific narratives have rendered such assumptions about autism and fiction
both commonplace and misleading.

LIMITATIONS AND INACCURACIES
IN SIMON BARON-COHEN'S 'MINDS
WIRED FOR SCIENCE' NARRATIVE

Researchers are not unanimous in linking autistic talent predominantly with
STEM. Noteworthy here is psychiatrist Michael Fitzgerald, author of an academic monograph (2004) and two popular science books (2005, 2006) which
posthumously 'diagnose' writers, artists and musicians including W. B. Yeats,
Samuel Beckett, Vincent van Gogh, Andy Warhol, Ludwig van Beethoven
and Erik Satie with Asperger syndrome. Such case studies, Fitzgerald asserts,
'will surprise those that equate Asperger's syndrome with engineering and
mathematics'.[62] Fitzgerald is expansively cited in Ioan James's book on the
diversities of autistic talent (2006) and in literary scholar Julie Brown's study
of writers and autism (2010). However, Fitzgerald's challenge to the exclusive
association of autistic ability with STEM areas remains largely unacknowledged in subsequent publications by the most prominent – and, in terms of
both diagnostic texts and cultural dissemination, most influential – agency of
autism research.

One of the world's most prestigiously positioned, generously funded and
readily quoted autism-related organizations is the University of Cambridge's
Autism Research Centre, led by Simon Baron-Cohen. With the following
discussion, I argue that the UCARC's repeated assertions of a link between
autism and STEM talent are misrepresentative: not because the association
is invalid but because it has hitherto so rigidly excluded recognition of other
ways in which autistic talent can express itself.

*   *   *

To illustrate the main thrust of Baron-Cohen's narrative of autistic talent –
ongoing since the 1990s – his *Wired 2012* conference presentation, 'Autism
and Minds Wired for Science', is instructive.[63] Here, as through much of
his work, Baron-Cohen emphasizes how science and mathematics involve

related skills in systemizing. He states that autism is more prevalent in maths students than humanities students (a suggestion to which I will return). He stresses that his findings do not mean that all scientists have autism – nor that all autistic people are scientifically talented. Yet Baron-Cohen's *Wired* presentation asserts that autism

> may be linked to minds that are wired for science. Back in 2001, *Wired* magazine suggested that there might be a link between autism and scientific talent. If it's true, this may force us to rethink the nature of both. The idea actually goes back to Hans Asperger. . . . He wrote that '*For success in science, a dash of autism is essential*' [my emphasis]. . . . Well, this was just one man's observation, but the idea was picked up by Ioan James who published an article suggesting that . . . two early physicists and . . . four early Nobel Prize winners all had autism.[64]

Baron-Cohen names six deceased scientists and mathematicians as apparently autistic.[65] However, his three supporting citations in the quoted sequence – *Wired* (2001), Hans Asperger (1944) and James (2003) – are shadowed by epistemological shortcomings.

First, Baron-Cohen's citation of *Wired* (2001) in *Wired* (2012) is a somewhat insular point of evidence. Alongside Silberman's 'Geek Syndrome' article on Asperger syndrome and information technologists, the magazine's 1 December 2001 issue suggested a link between autism and STEM talents via an interview with Baron-Cohen himself.[66] Second, James (2003) consulted Baron-Cohen to arrive at his diagnoses of Newton and Einstein as cited by the latter (2012).[67] Yet though James (2003) focused on scientists, his article also asserted the compatibility of autistic talent with music, art and philosophy.[68] Himself a mathematician, James profiled the lives of historic writers, artists, musicians, social reformers and philosophers (alongside scientists and mathematicians) in his movingly empathic book *Asperger's Syndrome and High Achievement* (2006). Saliently advocating how autistic ability may express itself *across* the sciences, arts and humanities, James's research supports only partially Baron-Cohen's construction of autism as a condition mainly linked to scientific talent.

The third supporting source in Baron-Cohen's 2012 talk is most complex. Crediting Hans Asperger, the quote invokes vintage yet resounding authority. In Baron-Cohen's words, Asperger 'wrote that "*For success in science, a dash of autism is essential*"' (my italics).[69] As Baron-Cohen said this, the statement appeared on a slide, referencing 'Hans Asperger (1944)'. The source of this sound bite as presented remains mysterious. It does not appear in Frith's English translation (1991) of Asperger's 1944 paper ' "Autistic Psychopathy" in Childhood'. Asperger later made a similar statement – but with a paradigmatic difference unmentioned by Baron-Cohen (2012). Discussing the adult lives of some of his former child patients, Asperger's 1979 paper 'Problems of Infantile Autism' asserts:

> Indeed, it seems that for success in science *or art* a dash of autism is essential (emphasis added).[70]

That is not a rare quotation. It was reproduced accurately by James (2003) in one of Baron-Cohen's other cited sources.[71] Perhaps I am frustrated by the fact that Baron-Cohen missed Asperger's specification of science *or art* because, like many individuals observed by Asperger himself, I have 'pedantic tendencies veering towards the obsessional'.[72]

To be pedantic is to risk entirely missing larger meanings. A similar tendency in autism is tested in Baron-Cohen and Sally Wheelwright's *Adult Autism-Spectrum Quotient* (AQ) questionnaire (2001). One statement asks if you concentrate more on 'the whole picture' or 'small details': the latter preference being associated with autism.[73] I have two qualms about that, pedantically or not. First, if 'small details' are missing, we cannot have the 'whole' picture. Second, close readings of UCARC's publications linking autism with STEM talent indicate that perhaps the authors have themselves placed their focus too inflexibly, to the detriment of both diagnostic and cultural recognition of autistic diversity.

Baron-Cohen's research leadership on autism and Asperger syndrome at UCARC has involved (among much else) laboratory studies of genetics and hormones, designing psychometric tests and developing learning aids for autistic children. But in terms of impact through academic and popular science publications, two strands of Baron-Cohen's research have tended to dominate his contributions to wider public assumptions regarding autism. First, there is his conceptualizing of autism as a predisposition to systemizing rather than empathizing. Second, and in relation to the first proposition, Baron-Cohen contends that systemizing – and by extension, autism – can be equated with 'maleness' as a biological essence. Baron-Cohen's gendered construction of autism demands considerable critical space and is addressed in chapter 3. Here, I focus on his premise of systemizing as a prerequisite for STEM subjects and, more critically, on his tendency to dismiss the possibility that autism can in many people – even if they remain a minority – coexist with literary sensibilities and, indeed, with forms of empathy.

UCARC established its pursuit of a link between autism and STEM talents in a 1997 journal article, asserting a connection between engineering and autism. Yet the link found was indirect: based on survey responses from families of autistic children, the article reported 'an excess of engineers among the fathers and grandfathers'.[74] This 'excess' (possibly not the ideal word) was later explained thus: '1 in 8 of the fathers of children with autism is an engineer', but 'only 1 in 20 fathers of non-autistic children is an engineer' – or, at least, according to the study's own sample, concerning the families of 919 autistic children.[75] Replying in *Autism* journal, Wolff (1998) advised that UCARC's focus on engineering was too narrow and that perhaps 'more general intellectual ability' in autism families should be considered, as should the possible influence of social class on results.[76] However, Wolff's note of caution regarding social class was not heeded by UCARC.

Much of the centre's subsequent research on autism in relation to academic skill prioritizes Cambridge students and staff for its samples – thus, possible factors concerning class and prior education remain considerable, yet under-recognized in the centre's publications. In 1998, UCARC extended its focus with a further experiment: a survey asking about the number of people diagnosed autistic in the families of mathematics, physics and engineering students compared with literature students. In families of 641 maths, engineering or physics students, 6 autism cases were reported. In families of 652 literature students, only 1 autism diagnosis was recorded.[77] Therefore, a possible link between STEM students and autistic relatives – although still vague – was bearing repeated investigation. UCARC's 1997 and 1998 articles remain important because they appear to have shaped – and possibly biased – some of the content and thus the results of the centre's most ambitious tool for measuring autistic traits in adults.

BIAS IN THE ADULT AUTISM-SPECTRUM QUOTIENT TEST (2001): HISTORY AND LEGACY

Obviously, two decades is a very long time in scientific research – even in the study of autism, a still mysterious condition on which the first publications emerged in the 1940s. Underlying this chapter's present concern is thus the following question. Is it appropriate that a questionnaire designed nearly 20 years ago continues to be used – with no amendments since 2001 – as both a preliminary screening tool and the basis of a national study of autistic traits?

Scientifically, diagnostically and culturally, UCARC's most influential text is the *Adult Autism-Spectrum Quotient* (AQ) questionnaire (2001), devised by Baron-Cohen and Sally Wheelwright. Piloted in 1998, it was introduced as a means to assess 'the degree to which an adult with normal intelligence has the traits associated with the autistic spectrum'.[78] The AQ questionnaire contains 50 statements, with forced choices of 'definitely agree', 'agree', 'disagree' or 'definitely disagree'. Strength of agreement or disagreement does not affect scores.[79] Each statement adds one point to the respondent's Autism-Spectrum Quotient if answered a certain way. Approximately half each of the 'agree' and 'disagree' answers contribute as positive autism indicators.[80] The questionnaire was first published in 2001 in a journal article on its initial findings, co-authored by Baron-Cohen, Wheelwright and three experimental psychology undergraduates (Baron-Cohen at al., 2001). The list of statements has since remained unaltered and is still used for both research and diagnostic purposes.

In October 2015, open-access science journal *PLOS ONE* published a UCARC-led article reporting the results of the largest survey of AQ scores in UK adults yet undertaken (Ruzich et al., 2015).[81] The survey was launched on national television network Channel 4 in April 2014 with an appeal for viewers to complete the AQ test online, and 450,394 individuals obliged. Reinforcing UCARC's hypotheses as first disseminated in the late 1990s, the 2015 article is titled 'Sex and STEM Occupation Predict Autism-Spectrum Quotient (AQ) Scores in Half a Million People'. It concludes that 'traits commonly associated with autism are strongly linked to traits associated with being male and with STEM occupations, regardless of other factors'.[82] The article's abstract promises:

> These results support previous findings relating to sex and STEM careers in the largest set of individuals for which AQ scores have been reported and suggest the AQ is a useful self-report measure of autistic traits.[83]

Thus, UCARC's most ambitious and publicized study to date makes three claims: AQ seems to be determined by sex; autistic traits appear to link with STEM careers; and the AQ test (2001) remains 'useful' and, implicitly, reliable. Chapter 3 discusses the claims regarding autism and sex (UCARC doesn't 'do' gender). The purpose of the present commentary is to highlight how and where there are evident yet under-recognized discrepancies afoot between UCARC's use of its questionnaire to assess autism in STEM-occupied adults and its simultaneous insistence that the same questionnaire is a valid means of assessing autistic traits in the adult population at large. I will then discuss in this chapter's final section, 'The sySTEMizing focus and its implications for autistic diversity' why these and related discrepancies in UCARC's narratives are problematic not just for adults being tested for autism but for the currently marginalized place of autistic adults within the public sphere.

Statements used in the 2001 AQ test reflect the established 'triad' of autistic impairments – social skills, communication and social imagination – as conceptualized by Wing and Gould (1979) and the American Psychiatric Association (1994). However, UCARC's test also included statements relating to additional 'demonstrated areas of cognitive abnormality in autism'.[84]

Unfortunately, the 2001 article on the AQ test's design and trial does not clearly state *where* these additional tendencies were observed. But it is evident that the inclusion of 840 Cambridge students within the test's trial had an additional purpose, besides assessing autistic traits in adults at large. It allowed the authors

> to test if scientists differed from students in the humanities, given earlier reports (Baron-Cohen et al., 1998) suggesting that autism is more common in families of physicists, engineers, and mathematicians.[85]

The questionnaire's first major trial thus had two aims. But were these purposes (and results) entirely without conflict? UCARC's own hypotheses on links between autism and STEM (especially maths) seem to have influenced the inclusion of certain statements on the questionnaire – perhaps in premature if not misleading ways, as the following critique will address.

In December 2001, *Wired* published the AQ test online, making it accessible to audiences beyond academia. An introduction stated that the questionnaire provides 'a measure of the extent of autistic traits in adults' but 'is not a means for making a diagnosis'.[86] Yet *Wired* omitted to name the full title of the journal article which had, months earlier, launched the AQ test: 'The Autism-Spectrum Quotient (AQ): Evidence from Asperger Syndrome/High Functioning Autism, Males and Females, Scientists and Mathematicians'.[87] The last three words are paramount to this chapter's concern. UCARC's notion of 'Autism Quotient', and the questionnaire used to measure it, was trialled on four groups: 58 adults with Asperger syndrome or 'high-functioning' autism; 174 randomly selected controls; 840 Cambridge University students; and – complicating, if not compromising the article as the launch of a test for autistic adults in the general population – 16 winners of the UK Mathematics Olympiad.[88]

Despite or because of *Wired*'s preface that the test is not, by itself, a formal means of diagnosis, it has become an Internet novelty, and individuals are able to share their scores on social media for anyone (including researchers) to see. But while the questionnaire's cultural prominence as a diagnostic text is disproportionate to its role in final diagnostic stages (which usually depend on face-to-face consultations), UCARC's 2005 report on the validity of its own questionnaire concluded by advocating the test's usefulness to GPs (general practitioners): the gatekeepers of formal autism assessment for most people.[89] Helpfully, the National Autistic Society now provides its own adult autism checklist for GPs to use with patients, and this does not include survey-orientated questions about maths or literature.[90] Nonetheless, the AQ remains one of various questionnaires sent out by many autism clinics as preliminary screening tools, and its results can potentially influence whether an individual is referred for further assessment. This is troubling, given that the test was designed in part to assess mathematicians specifically.

Amid statements on preferences and skills relating to routine, conversation, friendship and socializing, four statements directly involve numeracy and four concern literacy. The numeracy statements ask whether the individual is 'fascinated' by numbers; 'fascinated' by dates; 'not very good' at remembering phone numbers (archaic, perhaps, in the age of speed dial); and 'not very good' at remembering dates of birth.[91] On literary-orientated thinking, questions involve whether the respondent can 'easily imagine' what characters look like when reading stories, whether they find 'making up stories' easy, whether it is 'difficult' to decipher characters' intentions in stories and this: 'I don't particularly enjoy reading fiction'.[92]

The negative suggestion of 'not particularly' enjoying fiction differs from the positive statements on being fascinated by numbers and dates in ways that encapsulate further implications of the AQ questionnaire. Here is the rarely stated detail which deserves more comment and greater, multidisciplinary debate: basically, numeracy itself has been conceptualized as an autistic 'trait' in its own right by one of the world's leading autism-related organizations, the UCARC. Literacy, meanwhile, has been categorized – or dismissed – as an indicator of neurotypicality.

Each response to the AQ statements indicating a proclivity for numeracy adds one point to a person's 'Autism Quotient', regardless of answers to the other questions. Responses suggesting comprehension and enjoyment of literature do *not* positively contribute to autism quotient. To convey a dislike of or disinclination to reading fiction *adds* to Autism Quotient. Thus, Atwood's positioning of autistic and neurotypicals as numbers people and word people, respectively, although crude, can be supported by scientific research. But how reliable is the evidence involved? The 840 Cambridge University students on whom the test was trialled included 454 working in sciences, 276 in humanities and 110 in social sciences.[93] Yet, given the difference in how the questions relating to numeracy and literacy are scored and ignored, respectively, this does not seem an unbiased group of controls. Baron-Cohen et al. reported:

> Scientists (including mathematicians) scored significantly higher than both humanities and social sciences students, confirming an earlier study that autistic conditions are associated with scientific skills. Within the sciences, mathematicians scored highest.[94]

But what this means is that mathematicians scored highly in a questionnaire including statements relating to numerical thinking. And what about the 'earlier study', reporting 'an association between science/maths skills, and autistic conditions' and apparently confirmed by the AQ trial?[95] This was the 1998 publication by Baron-Cohen et al. described earlier, assessing autistic traits not in student respondents themselves, but their families. The 1998 paper was not a full-scale article but featured as 'Research in Brief' in *Autism* journal. But can the AQ trial as reported in 2001 really be said to confirm the 1998 study when the subsequent questionnaire did not include any questions about family occupations? UCARC's assertions of a link between autism and STEM subjects remain intriguing, but more as an influential hypothesis than a stable conclusion.

With the summarized ambiguities of the AQ test in mind, some things remain to be asked (and answered). The test was designed for *two* purposes: to measure autistic traits in any adult with 'normal intelligence' and to measure autistic traits in STEM students.[96] It swiftly began to be used as a means of screening autism in *any* adult and continues to be distributed for such purposes. But if the test was simultaneously designed to support Baron-Cohen's existing hypothesis of a link between STEM and autism, then how reliable can it be for the rest of the population?

If one quotation indicates the epistemological limitations of how the UCARC links autism with STEM-thinking, it is this scientific definition of 'truth' from Baron-Cohen, the centre's director:

> Philosophers and theologians have long debated what we mean by truth. My definition of truth is neither mystical, nor divine, nor is it obscured by unnecessary philosophical complexity. Truth is (pure and simply) repeatable, verifiable patterns.[97]

Repeated patterns characterize Baron-Cohen's collaborative findings that link autistic tendencies to adults who study or work in science-based subjects. Yet a comparison of his quoted position with broader epistemological perspectives shows how UCARC's work prioritizes an orthodox scientific position – and, thus, how it remains (however authoritatively) only one of various possible standpoints. It is insightful here to note a more radical position on repeatable patterns from Paul Feyerabend (1975), philosopher of science and methodology:

> Hypotheses contradicting well-confirmed theories give us better evidence that cannot be obtained in any other way. Proliferation of theories is beneficial for science, while uniformity impairs its critical power. Uniformity also endangers the free development of the individual.[98]

Feyerabend has been criticized for goading excessive relativism.[99] However, his assertion is pertinent when applied to UCARC's constructions of autism. The trouble here is that one of the world's most influential autism research institutions has hitherto committed most of its work to repeating certain theories and findings to such an extent that their studies risk presenting autism in terms of sameness at the expense of diversity.

Attention to Baron-Cohen's previous publications on autism, STEM and maleness remains vital to any discussion of gender and occupation in autistic adults because these reports are the rather limited bases for (UCARC's) successive (and increasingly high-profile) research outputs on autism itself. As the earlier observations indicate, most of Baron-Cohen's evidence for the 'minds wired for science' theory comes from his centre's own experiments – and these contain various inconsistencies. Conspicuously, the 2001 AQ test continues to be used for research, for entertainment and even for diagnostic screenings. Yet this reputed 'scientific' tool for measuring autistic traits in any adult was actually created to establish a link between autistic tendencies and STEM subjects. And, as has been shown, the questions are scored in such a way that aptitude for mathematics is automatically counted as autistic in the questionnaire's design. Thus, Baron-Cohen's hypothesis (and aims to prove it) risks intruding on the scientific validity of 'Autism Quotient' as influentially conceptualized by UCARC.

Since UCARC's autumn 2015 report in *PLOS ONE* of its findings on sex and STEM occupations, the survey remains open to participants. UCARC is thus inviting a continually expanding 'big data' survey ostensibly showing autistic traits in the general population. At the time of writing (March 2017), the website of UK newspaper *The Daily Telegraph* is asking adults to 'take the original test' and 'help contribute to ongoing research'.[100] There is, however, a methodological flaw in how UCARC has either instructed or allowed the *Telegraph* to frame the test online. The appeal for responses to a survey aiming to show autistic traits as more prevalent in men features only on the website's 'men's' section. It is absent from this conservative newspaper's corresponding 'women's' section: a scientifically unusual oversight, perhaps, for a survey concerning sex differences.

Despite the earlier criticisms, I am at least glad to be able to answer the *Telegraph*'s online version of the questionnaire myself – and, in doing so, to demonstrate (however minutely) that there are some autistic males who work in non-STEM fields. However, I am frustrated – and, worse, unsurprised – to discover that UCARC's 'ongoing research' appears to marginalize any such data from the outset. On clicking to 'Start the test', four preliminary questions appear. These are not part of the AQ questionnaire itself: they ask about respondents' geographic location, gender, age and, most important here, 'occupation'. In UCARC's ongoing research on the likelihood of autistic traits according to employment, 20 occupations are listed in this multiple-'choice' question. STEM areas are represented four times ('civil engineering', 'engineering', 'computers and IT' and 'scientific and technical'). By contrast, *none* of the 20 categories listed mention the arts, culture or the humanities. Nor does the list offer a clear option of answering *unemployed* (and this at a time when it is estimated by the National Autistic Society that fewer than one in six autistic adults are in full-time employment).[101] Moreover, while two alternative answers are enabled after the 20 occupational categories – 'other' and more valuably, 'prefer not to say' – the former unsettlingly seems to indicate UCARC's lack of interest in recognizing autistic abilities outside of STEM.

RE-MEMBERING AUTISTIC IMAGINATION: ASPERGER, WING AND 'HARRO L.'

The section 'Childhood autism and the psychiatric imagination' illustrated how the scientific viewpoint emerged that autistic people lack imagination. In 'Autism and the machine', I considered how similar assumptions are reinforced by comparisons of autistic minds with computers. The discussion 'Computer coding and/as literature: the naming of autism in Douglas Coupland's *Microserfs*' ventured that computer programming, a process widely associated with autistic talent, can signify a form of creativity and even literature in its own right. However, as the sequence titled 'Margaret Atwood's *Oryx and Crake*: autism and literary exclusion' showed, literature in the more established sense has sometimes been complicit with science in reiterating that imagination is exclusively a neurotypical property. Then the previous two sections, on the work of Baron-Cohen and the UCARC, delineated how, in the past two decades, similar suppositions became encoded in scientific narratives and diagnostic tools concerning adult autism, most recently, in a report on the supposed national profile of autistic traits in the UK. Throughout the chapter so far, I have pointed towards oversights and contradictions in how such dismissals of autistic imagination have been constructed. In the following three sections, I present some of the actual, factual evidence that the name of autism can – and, originally, *did* – encompass the possession and expression of literary imagination in many individuals.

Re-membering: this term, first used in relation to disability by Helen Davies (2015), refers to an imaginative and critical process.[102] Basically, when we recall something we've experienced, we remember. But when we critically imagine a past we've never witnessed (say, by reading a novel from or set in the 19th century), we can *re-member* that period. To re-member is to consciously implicate history in present-day values: it is to reflect on how the past is speaking to us now.[103] Davies's study concerns the Victorian freak show and some of the individual 19th-century lives and bodies that were turned into a cultural spectacle on account of what we might now call disability. It is significant, as Davies notes, that the noun 'member' has been used to signify male or female genitalia.[104] Historical meanings of the verb 'dismember' include castration, as well as that of tearing off a person's limbs.[105] Crucially however, re-membering is not about imaginatively healing or normalizing disabled bodies of the past: it is instead about restoring something approaching the persons' (sometimes mutilated) agency, by letting their lives speak to the present. Davies is deeply attentive to the ethical complexities of this process: would these people have wanted to be made the subjects of published narratives after their death?[106] But to re-member is not to make any claim of 'rescuing' marginalized or forgotten people from history. To re-member is to demonstrate that the present *needs* awareness of these people's lives.

Later in the present sequence, as I critically assert the relevance of Hans Asperger's 1944 paper to the 21st century, I will consider some of the individuals whose lives inspired his definitions of autism. However, my terms and aims of re-membering differ from Davies's. The era on which I focus (ca. 1934–1944) is incompletely 'historical', in the sense that many of the people described in Asperger's publication may be alive today. But the main realm that separates the present from certain of the individuals portrayed by Asperger is not that of time but that of discourse in science and culture, and the capacity of narrative to select or ignore. The autistic imagination as 're-membered' in this discussion is most substantially evident in assertions by Asperger, which subsequent and possibly more influential autism researchers have disregarded. However, my focus is only partially on individual lives. The essential re-membering I hope to promote concerns autistic imagination and thus the meanings of autism itself. Nonetheless, individual lives remain integral to this process, for what I am ultimately emphasizing is the *diversity* of autistic subjectivity.

Despite the possible flaws in the AQ questionnaire and thus the *PLOS ONE* report, the results of the 2014–2015 survey reaffirm not just UCARC's own hypotheses on autism and STEM since the 1990s but also older clinical suppositions regarding autistic minds, which became prominent in the late 1970s. A dated yet influential narrative here is that of Lorna Wing, whose 1981 paper elucidated – then modified – Hans Asperger's own definitions of autism in order to advance 'Asperger syndrome' as a formally recognized medical diagnosis. As will be shown, Wing's own conceptions of Asperger syndrome later expanded considerably. However, in the decade prior to the first English translation of Asperger's 1944 article by Uta Frith in 1991, Wing's 1981 account remained a vital reference text on Asperger syndrome and may have limited subsequent recognition of autistic imagination and creativity.

Two of Asperger's contentions with which Wing (1981) disagreed concerned talent. First, Wing suggested that Asperger overestimated the imaginative flair that autistic people could show for verbal expression. Second, Wing was noticeably dismissive of Asperger's emphasis that autistic minds can be capable of original or creative thinking in adulthood. But before discussing these points of divergence, we need to appreciate the somewhat oppositional agendas of Asperger (1944) and Wing (1981). Asperger was working in Nazi-occupied Vienna when he published his article in the German journal *Archiv für Psychiatrie und Nervenkrankheiten* (*Archive of Psychiatry and Neuroscience*). It has been suggested that Asperger deliberately profiled the most intellectually able cases of autism to save autistic children at large from the very real threat of execution under the Nazi regime.[107] Wing was researching in London in 1981 – and stressing the need for recognition of Asperger syndrome as an impairing medical condition. Thus, while Asperger's paper periodically foregrounded autistic talent, Wing's was more concerned with emphasizing the cerebral and social *limitations* faced by people who warranted diagnosis with the syndrome. However, both clinicians were fundamentally concerned with the welfare of autistic people.

Dr Lorna Wing (1928–2014) was a psychiatrist whose daughter Susie (1956–2005) was diagnosed with autism aged three. Dr Wing co-founded what became the UK's National Autistic Society in 1962. Wing's 1981 introduction of Asperger syndrome to English-speaking audiences was transformative in enabling clinicians, parents, teachers and employers to recognize the genuine problems faced by certain individuals who might otherwise have been dismissed as simply 'odd' (a word used repeatedly in Wing's article).[108] Her 1981 narrative establishes how a medical diagnosis of Asperger syndrome as a distinct and clearly defined category of autism could help such people in a society which still equated autism 'with muteness and total social withdrawal' – in short, with Kanner's 1943 model of autism.[109]

In outlining Asperger syndrome as a clinical condition in its own right, it was necessary for Wing to stress that as a form of autism, it entailed significant limitations for children and adults so affected. In this context, Wing (1981) reinforces her 1979 assertion (in her article with Gould) of impaired imagination as a formal diagnostic criterion for autism.[110] However, while quietly reinforcing Asperger's observations that autistic people may often immerse themselves in mathematics, Wing in effect suggests the removal of imagination and creativity as observed by Asperger from the clinical profile of what autism and Asperger syndrome can entail.[111]

Wing (1981) stated that her experience as a psychiatrist did not support Asperger's summary that some autistic children show 'an especially intimate relationship with language'.[112] Instead, Wing countered, the language used by autistic children 'gives the impression of being learned by rote'.[113] Wing was also cynical about Asperger's suggestions that in adulthood, some autistics are capable of intellectual distinction in their chosen fields. Dismissing what she summarizes as Asperger's emphasis on 'originality and creativity' in autistic people, Wing posits:

> It would be more true to say that their thought processes are confined to a narrow, pedantic, literal, but logical, chain of reasoning. The unusual quality of their approach arises from . . . some aspect of a subject that would be unlikely to occur to a normal person who has absorbed the attitudes current in his culture.[114]

Wing (1981) thus presented a clinical assumption that autistic systemizing – whether seen in the infant lining up toy cars or in successful adult STEM specialists – somehow excludes the involvement of imagination. However, one of Wing's greatest gifts to autism science was her willingness to continually develop and, when necessary, openly contradict previous theories she had ventured. A 2001 interview in London's *Times* shows how, two decades after her first clinical account of Asperger syndrome, Wing had come to share Asperger's emphasis that autistic adults could indeed show great originality. Here, Wing named Albert Einstein as a candidate for retrospective diagnosis of Asperger syndrome.[115] Pertinently enough, an aphorism by Einstein published in 1931 declares:

> Imagination is more important than knowledge. For knowledge is limited, whereas imagination embraces the entire world, stimulating progress, giving birth to evolution. It is, strictly speaking, a real factor in scientific research.[116]

As such, it must become a more important factor in scientific conjectures of autistic minds.

It is possible that Asperger (1944) may have emphasized or even exaggerated the talents of certain autistic individuals in his care in order to protect them from the Nazis. But if that was the case (and we might never know), it would not diminish the world's evidence by now that autism, while an impairing and often distressing condition, can also yield invaluable and unique talent in many individuals. UCARC's evidence of this may be limited to STEM talents but is copious nonetheless.[117] Moreover, there are the various autistic scholars, writers and artists discussed in this book, including Damian Milton and Sonya Freeman Loftis as cited earlier. It should also be emphasized that despite the horrifying political context in which Asperger's 1944 research was published, his 1979 paper was no less emphatic that autism and talent frequently coexist. But what of Asperger's comments on autistic imagination and creativity?

Asperger (1979) suggested that 'for success in science or art a dash of autism is essential' after working with autistic people for almost five decades.[118] His inclusion of *art* in this assertion was no sudden expansion on his earlier publications. Asperger makes similar assertions in his seminal (and, regarding other observations, most frequently cited) 1944 paper. After summarizing defining traits of autism and, yes, the aptitude for science and maths in various children he observed, Asperger's 1944 commentary on 'Autistic Intelligence' adds that another 'distinctive' ability in some autistic children is their 'rare maturity' in responding to artworks. He continues:

> Autistic individuals can judge accurately the events represented in the picture, as well as what lies behind them, including the character of the people represented and the mood that pervades a painting.[119]

To a significant if still limited degree, Asperger was also more attentive to autistic responses to literature than his successors in scientific autism research have been.

Asperger (1944) reported the responses of four child patients to fictional narratives. Varying in amounts of detail, these summaries accumulatively suggest that, overall, autistic engagement with stories was less indicative of talent than responses to maths tests. If considered in this cursory way, Asperger's paper seemingly supports the subsequently familiar assumption that autistic people are less likely to enjoy fiction. However, one of his main case studies provides evidence firmly and clearly to the contrary. Prior to his 1944 paper, Asperger and his colleagues observed over 200 children who showed signs of autism. Asperger then focused on four boys as 'prototypical' autism cases.[120] 'Harro L.' is the second child profiled. Overlooked in later autism narratives, Asperger's summary of Harro's reading skills deserves quotation:

> one could notice clearly that he read for meaning and that the content of the story interested him. As this observation suggests his *reading comprehension* was excellent. . . . he could say what the moral of a story was even though the moral was not explicitly presented (emphasis in original).[121]

Harro's reading skills thus showed clear alertness to non-literal, symbolic language. As with the summary of autistic responses to paintings then, Asperger's comments testify to how the condition does not necessarily preclude imaginative engagement with the arts. It is regrettable that even with consideration of his possible political agenda behind the 1944 article, such observations by Asperger have received so little acknowledgement in later scientific discourse.

Asperger reports that Harro 'told long, fantastic stories', though these became 'strange and incoherent'.[122] As Frith notes, it is sad that further details were not given and that, similarly, Kanner did not present examples of the stories told by one of his own first patients, Donald.[123] Yet such omissions make these incomplete details doubly insightful. First, they testify that in two of the very first individuals identified as autistic on different continents, aptitude for interpreting and creating fictional narratives was evident. But, second, the absence of any detail regarding these individuals' storytelling in both Kanner's and Asperger's case studies indicates how, from the outset, scientific research has seemingly been less attuned to imagination as a property within autistic subjectivity.

Harro refused to join in games with other children in Asperger's ward, preferring to sit reading books in a corner, appearing 'oblivious' to his surroundings.[124] He was not a savant. His reading was prone to errors, as were his 'original methods' in arithmetic.[125] But Harro was, nonetheless, *present*. His expressions shaped Asperger's research and, thus, the possible meanings of the name 'autism'. What Harro showed Asperger – and shows us – is not just the evidence of autistic imagination but the fact that autistic ability can manifest in diverse ways, outside the dominant expectations. And one of the greatest values of Asperger's early research is that there *were* no such dominant expectations.

After Asperger's death in 1980, various autism researchers would later suggest that Asperger himself had the very syndrome that would later be named after him.[126] If an appropriately scientific study was to convincingly conclude that Asperger was indeed autistic, it would add a fascinating layer to discussions of autism and empathy deficiency. But how reliable and relevant are Asperger's comments on autistic responses to art and literature? Scientific researchers of autism ever since have neglected to acknowledge these (let alone discuss them). Are Asperger's assertions of artistic sensibilities within autism problematic because they complicate the hypotheses and conclusions of bounteously funded research into autism and STEM subjects? In stressing the value of autism to society in 1944, it's possible that Asperger may have exaggerated the creative talents he saw in the condition. Certainly, his summaries of responses to paintings and stories provide a more rounded profile of autistic intelligence than his reports of mathematical and scientific aptitude alone would have done. However, to dismiss Asperger's observations on autism and the arts by attributing them to the period's political context would similarly implicate his more extensive, more influential, emphasis on autism and what we now call STEM skills. Could Asperger have stressed those abilities above artistic talents because they present more obviously utilitarian functions within society?

Asperger wrote in 1944 that numerous 'distinguished scientists' appeared autistic.[127] The first of his four case studies in the paper, 'Fritz V.', became a professor of astronomy who, Feinstein reports, 'solved an error in Sir

Isaac Newton's work which he had previously noticed as a child'.[128] Fritz's achievements indicate that Asperger did not exaggerate autistic talent in scientific work. I strongly sense that the same reliability applies to his portrayal of Harro's literary awareness and, furthermore, to Asperger's implication that this gift was not highly unusual in autism. A six-year-old Austrian girl referred to Asperger in 1952 was Elfriede Jelinek. In 2004, Jelinek – a 58-year-old novelist, poet and playwright – won the Nobel Prize for literature. Asperger did not diagnose Elfriede Jelinek as autistic in the end.[129] She remains a refreshingly private public figure. However, in 1995, Jelinek commented: 'Yes, I was an Asperger patient. Not an Asperger autistic though indeed not far off'.[130] Autistic tendencies and talents are both complex and diverse. But it is not the condition of autism itself that impairs or dismembers imagination: it is only narratives of culture and science that have done so.

Writing in the profoundly fraught political context of Europe in the early 1940s, Asperger asserted at length the various talents seen in many autistic children, evidencing his will to stress the value of autism itself to society. However, it is necessary here to critically acknowledge emerging research which interprets some of Asperger's other decisions in the early 1940s as complicit with the bleakest of political orders. Speculations that Asperger was a Nazi sympathizer have been inevitable, given his increasing professional eminence in Austria under Hitler's regime.[131] Unlike most of his medical peers in Vienna at the time, Asperger was never a member of the Nazi party. Most researchers concur that he was fundamentally opposed to Nazism.[132] Asperger would have been obliged to keep such views private at the time – and this means that any conclusive evidence that he was *not* a Nazi sympathizer is unlikely to appear. Most disturbingly, however, John Donvan and Caren Zucker's journalistic history *In a Different Key: The Story of Autism* (2016) alleges that Asperger knowingly complied with Nazi policies that led to the deaths of children.[133]

Donvan and Zucker – citing unpublished research by historian Herwig Czech – state that in 1942, Asperger served on a panel of seven advisors commissioned to classify the status of 210 children in an unnamed Austrian psychiatric hospital.[134] The panel decided that 35 of the children were not 'educable' – a decision which, as Czech alleges Asperger knew, condemned them to euthanasia.[135] As Silberman (2016) points out, Donvan and Zucker do not explore the possibility that Asperger may still have used his position 'to save as many children as possible'.[136] Nonetheless, Czech's archival research also uncovered the deeply distressing information (later verified by Silberman) that in 1941, Asperger signed a referral for an infant girl with encephalitis – Herta Schreiber – to be admitted to Vienna's Am Spiegelgrund clinic. This was one of the most notorious sites in the Nazis' euthanizing of disabled children. On 2 September 1941, Herta died at the Spiegelgrund clinic, a day after her third birthday.[137]

Reflecting on Donvan and Zucker's iconoclastic though clearly important revaluation of Asperger in relation to Nazism, Silberman implores: 'The most important lesson is not that brutal regimes like the Third Reich enable evil men to do evil, but that they are able to compel even well-intentioned people to do monstrous things.'[138] Czech's research on Asperger's alleged links to Nazism is still to be published, and the contents of the relevant documents privately owned by Czech have yet to be clearly disclosed.[139] However, in addition to the terrible lesson as articulated in Silberman's measured response, it will remain vital that any ambiguities around Asperger's stance or actions in the 1940s do not distract any of us from the risks of our own era – particularly in the context of the new eugenic fixations discussed in 'Autism and the Machine'.

SILBERMAN'S *NEUROTRIBES*: SCIENCE, SCIENCE FICTION AND AUTISM

Steve Silberman's 2015 book *Neurotribes* – a widely and rightly acclaimed 534-page history of autism, and a sequel to his 2001 'Geek Syndrome' article – states that the

> curious fascination that many autistic people have for quantifiable data, highly organized systems, and complex machines runs like a half-hidden thread through the fabric of autism research.[140]

The accuracy of Silberman's point is undeniable. Yet I am struck by something further: much of the preceding quotation actually seems more immediately relevant to many autism researchers than to autistic people. One such researcher is Silberman himself.

The limitation of Silberman's *Neurotribes* narrative is that, overall, it reinforces equations of autism with STEM subjects as popularized by its author's own 'Geek Syndrome' piece (2001). *Neurotribes* establishes the profile of the adult autist as a science genius by focusing in the first chapter on the lifestyle and achievements of physicist Henry Cavendish (1731–1810). Like Oliver Sacks (2001) and, more substantially, Ioan James (2003, 2006), Silberman theorizes that Cavendish was what we now would call autistic.[141] Silberman then similarly profiles mathematician Paul Dirac – also suggested by James (2003) as autistic.[142] However, unlike James (2003, 2006), but similarly to Baron-Cohen (2012), Silberman's narrative tends to not include artistic

ability in the discussion. *Neurotribes* emphasizes autistic talent, achievement and (implicitly) potential, but almost exclusively in STEM traditions.
Silberman's archival research into Asperger's work is fascinatingly detailed.
Yet *Neurotribes* mentions Harro only to remark that as well as performing
'complex mathematical operations in his head', he 'was an avid reader who
had a vivid and original way of talking about things'.[143] Nevertheless, there
is one group of readers whose Aspergic connections *Neurotribes* asserts:
science fiction fans. Unsurprisingly, Silberman stresses the *science* element
in the said genre when discussing its possible appeal to autistic minds.

Neurotribes cites reflections on a link between autistic experience and the
consolations of science fiction from one of its major historians (and critics),
Gary Westfahl. In 2006, Dr Westfahl conjectured that prior to the historical
recognition of autism, the 'lonely adventurers on solitary quests to distant
planets' in science fiction must have valuably appealed to readers 'then
regarded only as "reclusive" or "eccentric", who we would now classify as
cases of undiagnosed Asperger's Syndrome'.[144] Westfahl identifies as having
undiagnosed Asperger Syndrome himself, and additional comments (not presented by Silberman) from his 2006 *Locus* magazine article are also relevant:

> A person with this condition always feels like an alien being in an alien world:
> why are all these people able to relax and have fun at this party while I am feel-
> ing so uneasy and uncomfortable? . . . to a teenager in the 1930s with Asperger's
> Syndrome, a story about an astronaut encountering aliens on Mars might have
> had an air of comforting familiarity.[145]

Clearly, Westfahl's Asperger status does not prevent him from writing inci-
sively about fiction, nor imaginatively about readers. He proceeds to argue
that conventions within science fiction have developed in ways that may
leave it less pertinent to autistic perspectives, outlining how, since the 1930s,
the genre has

> adjusted to place a greater emphasis on conventional, well-adjusted characters
> who happily function in social situations.[146]

Westfahl's many academic publications include a 2007 study of science
fiction author, publisher and editor Hugo Gernsback (1884–1967).[147] *Neurotribes* references Westfahl's support for Silberman's assertion that Gernsback could have met the diagnostic criteria for adult Asperger syndrome.[148]

Silberman's own commentaries on science fiction are less critically obser-
vant (or perhaps just less autistic) than Westfahl's. Of cheap 'potboiler'
science fiction favoured and published by Gernsback (whom Silberman is
portraying as autistic) in the 1930s, Silberman summarizes that 'technology took precedence over psychology, and plot, and character'.[149] Yet these

three qualities were similarly observed as lacking throughout potboiler fiction at large in the era, including crime and sex novels.[150] More pertinent is Silberman's discussion of how Canadian author A. E. van Vogt's novel *Slan* (1940) inspired a subculture of fans. Silberman details how, in the 1940s, self-proclaimed Slan Fans – identifying with the eponymous mutants, as well as Vogt's novel itself – established shared houses ('Slan Shacks'), with the ideal that in these they could focus on reading science fiction and creating related magazines to the exclusion of all else.[151] Expanding on Westfahl's conjectures regarding the appeal of science fiction to undiagnosed autists in the mid-20th century, Silberman suggests that eponymous 'slans' of Vogt's novel had 'special resonance' with such readers because they saw something 'of their own predicament in this tale of superintelligent, supersensitive, and profoundly misunderstood mutants struggling to survive in a world not built for them'.[152] To quote Westfahl's summary of Vogt's novel, slans are 'a race of hyperintelligent mutants with psychic powers who live among, and are persecuted by, "normal" human beings'.[153]

Neurotribes brings its discussion of autistic science fiction fans up to date by profiling John Ordover and Carol Greenburg, a married autistic couple who met as teenagers at a *Star Trek* convention. Silberman introduces Greenburg as finding in *Star Trek* 'a metaphor for an inclusive society' and quotes her describing how

> there was no one who was left out in the *Star Trek* universe, no one who was ostracized, no one who was too weird. . . . That was a lifesaving message for a kid who got bullied for being different.[154]

Once again, this shows imaginative engagement with fictional realms from an autistic perspective. Greenburg's literary achievements are notable too: she and Ordover became contributing co-editors of the *Star Trek* franchise of novels and short stories. Moreover, the couple have emerged as prominent writers on autism rights and policies through the valuable website *Thinking Person's Guide to Autism*, on which Greenburg serves as an editorial consultant.[155]

Given the intense appeal of science fiction to some autistic readers, it is ironic that the genre is often derided for (in effect) involving *excessive* imagination, in which settings become so unearthly that such fictions seem to overrule meaningful commentary on human experience.[156] Not to all readers, though. The quotations from Westfahl and Greenburg indicate how the other-worldly scenarios of science fiction are precisely what *chimes* via metaphor with some autistic experiences of loneliness and separation from a neurotypically dominated society. Yet, in view of the hostility or snobbery towards science fiction as 'genre fiction' rather than 'literature', Silberman's positioning of autistic readers as primarily fans of narratives in which (as in his dismissal of Gernsback's work) there is scant 'psychology', 'plot' or 'character' insinuates another literary exclusion of autistics. I therefore close this chapter by revisiting Atwood's 2003 usage of autism in *Oryx and Crake* and relating it to her own divisive views on science fiction, before comparing critical responses to Atwood's novel from within the autism community.

WORD PERSONS OF THE AUTISTIC WORLD UNITE: CRITICAL RESPONSES TO ATWOOD'S *ORYX AND CRAKE*

Discussing *Oryx and Crake*, Atwood rejects the term 'science fiction', describing this novel as 'speculative' fiction.[157] She explains elsewhere: 'Science fiction has monsters and spaceships; speculative fiction could really happen'.[158] This does not preclude shared tropes between the genres, as shown by Atwood's broad and perhaps coincidental inversion of Vogt's science fiction plot in *Slan*, presenting humans out to destroy mutant others in their midst.[159] In Atwood's novel, as summarized earlier, the autistic Crake and his colleagues at 'Asperger's' University engineer the near-total erasure of humanity and create the post-human 'Crakers', who are incapable of symbolic thinking. But the trouble with Atwood's naming of her novel as *speculative* is that if we read its depiction of Asperger syndrome within such terms, *Oryx and Crake* implies that autism can potentially become a threat to humanity. The obvious oversight is that autistic people are actually far more vulnerable to the actions of neurotypicals than vice versa. In 2005, the massive U.S. charity 'Autism Speaks' was founded, with an aim that was effectively the mirror opposite of *Oryx and Crake*'s scenario. For the past decade, the 'charity' – which took until 2015 to invite two autistic people onto its board – has pumped billions of dollars into seeking scientific means towards a cure for and the 'prevention' of autism.[160] It takes neither speculation nor fiction to see that this agenda potentially implies the disappearance of autistic people from the world.

Atwood's Crake is autistic and also a scientist – notably an amoral one, motivated by money. Ultimately, the advancement of corporate greed and genetic engineering is more pertinent than the powers of 'demi-autistic' intelligence as butts of *Oryx and Crake*'s satire, and I'm sure Atwood intended no insult to autistic people by utilizing the condition as a narrative prosthetic. But the novel's portrayal of STEM-bound autistic adults who oppose the very existence of fiction seems to have been composed under assumptions that people diagnosed with autism are perhaps unlikely to read speculative (*not science*) fiction as embodied by *Oryx and Crake*. However, individuals from the online autistic community have asserted various critical responses to *Oryx and Crake*, including its portrayal of their own diagnostic condition. In different ways, these commentaries highlight the problems inherent in Atwood's use of autism as a metaphor, at the expense of recognizing Asperger syndrome as a subjectivity and identity in its own right or reality.

Autist's Corner blog – whose author (listed only as Lindsay) holds degrees in both biochemistry and English literature – features a valuable essay titled 'Metaphor at the Expense of Characterization: Autism in Margaret Atwood's *Oryx and Crake*' (2008). In particular, Lindsay criticizes Atwood's portrayal of 'Asperger's U.' students, whose

> obsessive singlemindedness and lack of the normal human need for social interaction or R&R makes them immensely valuable to the biotech corporations queuing up to hire them fresh out of college. Just typing that really brings home to me how profoundly unrealistic a scenario it is, not only in terms of the kind of worker employers tend to value, but also in its crude understanding of autism. . . . I believe Atwood concocted this version of 'autism' to stand as a personification of everything she is trying to criticize about biotechnology, agribusiness and consumer culture.[161]

Similarly, while praising Atwood's novel as 'very interesting and entertaining', a post on autism forum *Wrong Planet* by Mysticaria asserts that *Oryx and Crake*

> portrayed people with Aspergers as cold, self-absorbed, immoral, idea-driven people who lost touch with their 'humanity' and were only concerned with advancement and structure. Basically, mad geniuses. And this seems to be a highly stereotypical view . . . because although, some people with Aspergers may appear to be that way, and think in a highly logical manner . . . they are still people with feelings as well.[162]

Nonetheless, of the numerous *Wrong Planet* comments on *Oryx and Crake*, most are favourable. A post asking if members would recommend the novel received three positive replies, though again, these are critically nuanced, as exemplified by the following from SleepyDragon, who observes that Atwood's novel makes

> no attempt to define, explicitly, what it means to be Asperger's, or to paint a detailed portrait of anyone who is, beyond what is necessary to serve the narrative. Doing so would not have served the narrative in any case, in my view; it is Jimmy's very normality which makes him the odd one out in this situation. I found this an immensely satisfying reversal from the usual scenario where the so-called 'normal' people are the dominant ones.[163]

These quite different responses from the autism community challenge dominant viewpoints that autists do not enjoy reading fiction or struggle to engage with plot, metaphor and character. As such, they present important demonstrations of autistic critical agency – autistic *literary* critical agency, no less.

Within Atwood's plot of the autistic Crake destroying human civilization and creating a species to his own specifications, we can discern a tendency observed much earlier by Paul Longmore in a 1985 critique of screen representations of disability: the implication that 'disabled people resent the nondisabled and would, if they could, destroy them'.[164] Yet there is an important complexity to note here: in Atwood's novel, Asperger syndrome is not a disability. This marks a sometimes liberating, sometimes problematic development in both scientific and cultural narratives of autism addressed in the following chapters.

CONCLUSION: THE SYSTEMIZING FOCUS AND ITS IMPLICATIONS FOR AUTISTIC DIVERSITY

The main texts addressed in this chapter, both from science and from literature, have one thing in common: in different ways, they reinforce associations of adult autism with STEM talent, often to the exclusion of recognizing autistic literary sensibilities or, indeed, autistic imagination. Scientifically, diagnostically and perhaps also culturally, the most influential of these narratives have been those of Baron-Cohen and the University of Cambridge's Autism Research Centre. To end the chapter, and to extend the framework for this book's further discussions, I will critically revisit UCARC's name for what it regards as the dominant process in autistic subjectivity: systemizing. Let us look again at that name and focus largely on four letters contained within it: sySTEMizing.

SySTEMizing. I present this typographically ungainly nomenclature not to signify autistic thinking itself but the distorted, distorting ways in which influential scientific and cultural narratives have conceptualized autistic minds from outside. It is apposite that 'systemizing' contains the acronym for science, technology, engineering and mathematics, but it is also coincidental. If we keep on looking at sySTEMizing with priority to one part (however essential), the fuller meanings of systemizing itself are lost. As I pedantically stated earlier, without small details, we cannot *have* the whole picture. Thus, my point here is that the repeated association of adult autists with STEM talent risks disregarding or even denying the wider reaches of autistic thought and feeling.

UCARC's website defines systemizing as 'the drive to analyse or construct a system. A system is anything that follows rules'.[165] The centre states:

We have found that people with autism or Asperger Syndrome may have unusual talents at systemizing (e.g., in physics), that people who are gifted mathematicians may be more likely to have a diagnosis of autism or Asperger Syndrome.[166]

Strengthened by the results of the massive *PLOS ONE*/Channel 4 survey (2015), the UCARC's two decades of research devoted to proving such hypotheses have repeatedly yielded findings which consistently indicate a link too interesting to dismiss. Yet, as detailed earlier, UCARC's foundational late 1990s' conclusions on autism and sySTEMizing were not without ambiguity. Still more complicating is the fact that the unaltered 2001 AQ questionnaire (used for the *PLOS ONE*/Channel 4 survey) was originally designed not only to measure autistic traits in adults but also to further support UCARC's ongoing hypothesis on sySTEMizing. My concern is that the UCARC's own sySTEMizing focus has detracted scientifically, culturally and diagnostically from the recognition and *appreciation* that many other autistic people can, and do, have valuable strengths in wider areas.

Despite UCARC's stated associations, *all* academic work depends to some degree on systemizing. This applies to the study (as well as the creation) of literature. Take a sonnet, for example. There are many different kinds, but nearly all adhere to – or involve awareness of – different systems of interrelating rules and patterns, including how many syllables per line, the positioning of rhymes at particular points, the sequencing of stressed and unstressed syllables and a good deal more besides. More vastly, *poetry* is a system of tradition and experiment: two qualities it shares with science. But poetry is also more intimately conducive and *gratifying* to autistic senses and sensibilities than tends to be recognized. Reading, speaking and writing it can create a kind of verbal stimming – a sort of dance between the mouth and mind. Not unlike autism itself, poetry can flourish outside of the norms of linguistic expression. And, as later chapters will consider, poetry – including poems written by autistic authors – is a system which creates and enables discussion, understanding and *experience* of both imagination and emotion. Language itself is also a system: one that shapes our perceptions – and, for the conceivable future, one that is crucial to the definitions, and the diagnosis, of autism.

When systemizing is allowed to be informed by emotion, we have critical thinking. Yet another problem of UCARC's sySTEMizing of autism is that in concentrating exclusively on abilities to engage with abstract or material dimensions of the world, the model reinforces suppositions (and expectations) that autistic people are devoid of interest in others rather than considering that we may simply express such feelings in more subtle or less orthodox ways.

In her ground-breaking study of the gendered rhetoric surrounding autism, Jordynn Jack (2014) critiques how influential non-fiction texts, including *Time* magazine's 1994 Bill Gates profile and Silberman's 2001 'Geek Syndrome' piece, are essentially synecdochal.[167] Jack discusses the synecdoche as a rhetorical trope through which reference points are misleadingly positioned as if to 'epitomize a larger whole'.[168] Summarizing the synecdoche of male autistic ICT workers, Jack warns that such profiling risks

> presenting autism via stock characters that turn into stereotypes, deflecting attention away from a wider range of actual autistic individuals, not all of whom are computer geeks.[169]

Jack's observation here is also pertinent to wider processes. Indeed, sySTEM-izing as manifest in UCARC's research findings and its AQ questionnaire is a synecdochal process, ultimately creating an incomplete portrait, however compelling it may be. But it is also worth considering the deeper commonality between the scientific and fictional narratives of autism.

SySTEMizing as performed by Baron-Cohen and his UCARC colleagues is apparent in Coupland's *Microserfs* and Atwood's *Oryx and Crake*, as well as in Silberman's article 'The Geek Syndrome' and its expansion in *Neurotribes*. That these scientific, fictional and journalistic narratives were composed independently from one another seems to legitimize each, thus strengthening the impression that autism is more prevalent, or at least more visible, in adults who devote themselves to STEM careers. Yet the scientific and literary narratives of autism critiqued have more in common than the mere repetition and dissemination of the STEM association. In essence, what these particular selections from both forms of autism discourse share is an element of fiction itself. I emphasize the term 'fiction' *critically* here: that is, I hope, open-mindedly. My point is that the dominant contemporary narratives of autism from Baron-Cohen and Silberman are based on extensively researched *facts* – yet facts themselves are abstracts, drawn from a wider, infinitely complex (perhaps ultimately unknowable) reality. These factual accounts, like the fictional narratives discussed, do not present an automatically false or fantastical set of circumstances, but a concentrated, meaningful and indeed illuminating distillation of human experience. Nonetheless, the problem with these factual narratives, as also with the literary ones, lies less in what is emphasized than what (and who) amid this process is denied. Thus, in arguing that UCARC's narratives of autism and STEM are most insightful if read with similar critical awareness to that which we grant fiction, I am by no means asserting some postmodernist contention that all science is ultimately fiction. I am simply highlighting the limitations of certain influential and still valuable scientific models of adult autism and suggesting that we should continue to critically debate the repetitive emphasis underpinning this collusion of literary and scientific texts.

While Baron-Cohen's definition that 'truth is (pure and simply) repeatable, verifiable patterns' is intentionally concise, its emphasis on repeatability alone as verification both masks and marks how UCARC's sySTEMizing of autism tends to reinforce, rather than expand, constructions of autistic thinking.[170] What similarly troubles me about Baron-Cohen's definition of truth lies in the casually parenthetical phrase 'pure and simply'. Oscar Wilde wrote: 'The truth is rarely pure and never simple. Modern life would be very tedious if it were either, and modern literature a complete impossibility!'[171] As Coupland's critical yet unresolved discussion of autism in *Microserfs* indicates, part of what makes this identity so compelling a subject for literature is its sheer complexity – indeed, mystery – as a way of being. Without doubt, UCARC's narratives on how autistic people's minds work are honourable and in some ways constructive in striving to make autistic subjectivity better understood. The trouble is that the UCARC's quest for (much-publicized) repeated results has tended to *reduce* both medical and cultural conceptions of autistic ability down to a narrow and potentially exclusive set of expectations through the sySTEMizing focus.

The focus and findings of UCARC's research on autistic ability and STEM present a largely persuasive truth, verified through repetition. They appear to be accurate but still mostly incomplete. Hans Asperger, on whose work UCARC draws substantially, suggested that for success *in art*, as well as science, a dash of autism is essential. Asperger also reported that many autistic individuals showed engagement – in effect, imaginative engagement – with art and literature, particularly Harro: one of the key case studies Asperger presented to introduce *different*, as well as shared, facets of autism. Therefore, against UCARC's repeated conclusions of a link between autism and STEM, Paul Feyerabend's more radical but also more ambitious philosophy of science becomes indispensable. Feyerabend asserted that the duplication of 'well-confirmed theories' risks impairing the critical power of scientific research and, moreover, that such uniformity 'endangers the free development of the individual' in terms of the scientist herself and, potentially, the human beings who are the subjects of scientific research.[172] The kind of dangers against which Feyerabend warned are encapsulated in the scoring of UCARC's AQ 2001 questionnaire, currently being used to shape a national survey of autistic traits, and still utilized by various clinical services as a diagnostic screening tool. According to UCARC's scoring system, a capacity for numeracy and science-based work is classified as an autistic trait, while being capable of imagination (as embodied by the scoring of statements relating to fiction) is deemed beyond the reaches of the autistic mind. Such assumptions have ramifications not just for scientific research on autism but for recognition (or not) of the *diversities* of autistic ability within academia and culture more broadly.

As the media-pleasing mainstream of scientific discourse continues interpellating people (including, crucially, autists themselves) that autistic subjectivities can flourish only within STEM parameters, we face an increasing risk of streamlining the further education and careers of younger generations who have autistic tendencies or diagnoses. This process risks implicating autistic individuals in something approaching a scientifically endorsed narrative process of cultural and economic eugenics. It is not just a matter of possibly impairing and disabling autistic communities by discouraging individuals within them from pursuing arts, humanities or social science subjects (all of which can add to and deepen understandings of autism). It is also a matter of impoverishing culture at large by indirectly marginalizing autistic voices from spheres including politics, literature and journalism, as well as academia itself. And it scarcely needs emphasizing here that although progression is evident, authentic autistic voices remain severely marginalized from the public sphere as it is.

At times, the dominant emphasis on systemizing as the foundation of autistic subjectivity seems to say more about medical science – and how scientists construct autistic thinking according to their own values – than it does about the realities and varieties of autism. In 'Proverbs of Hell' (1793), William Blake states: 'A fool sees not the same tree that a wise man sees'.[173] But then, nor do *two* wise people see the same tree – not if they're gazing from different neurological perspectives or, indeed, standing in different academic positions. Thus, my conclusion to this chapter is ultimately a question. If autism research remains dominated almost exclusively by scientists – and mostly neurotypical scientists at that – then how can the sum of academic knowledge on autism ever approach anything like completeness?

NOTES

1 Autism Research Centre, 'Systemizing in Autism Spectrum Conditions'.
2 Autism Research Centre, 'Systemizing in Autism Spectrum Conditions'.
3 Eagleton, *'Zero Degrees of Empathy*: Review' (accessed 12 August 2016). See also Eagleton, T. *The Event of Literature* (New Haven: Yale University Press, 2012), 61.
4 Shelley, *A Defence of Poetry and Other Essays*, 31.
5 Titchener, *Lectures on the Experimental Psychology of the Thought Processes*.
6 Wing and Gould, 'Severe Impairments', 16, 27.
7 Wing and Gould, 'Severe Impairments', 16.
8 Wing, 'Asperger's Syndrome', 117, 123.
9 Tantam, 'Asperger Syndrome in Adulthood', 160–61, 179.
10 Feinstein, *A History of Autism*, 152, cf. 201–2.
11 See Baron-Cohen, *Zero Degrees of Empathy*, 69–78.
12 Baron-Cohen et al., 'The Autism-Spectrum Quotient', 5–17, 6–7, 15–16.
13 Milton, 'On the Ontological Status of Autism', 883–87.
14 Milton, 'On the Ontological Status of Autism', 886.

15   See Alderson, 'Why Aren't We Trying to Cure Autism?' Alderson's leaning in favour of finding an autism 'cure' (a 'four-letter word') is by no means unproblematic, though I find his candour on such a sensitive subject commendable. However, in calling for common ground to be found between neurodiversity movements that campaign for acceptance rather than normalization and, at the other extreme, 'Autism Speaks', Alderson perhaps underestimates the imbalance of power between autism advocacy groups such as GRASP and the world's most prominent autism organization. Moreover, Alderson's commentary on the evolving perspectives on autistic imagination since Wing and Gould's article 'Severe Impairments of Social Interaction and Associated Abnormalities in Children: Epidemiology and Classification' indirectly highlights the historical subjectivity of key premises regarding the condition (see Alderson, *Challenging the Myths*). However, this subjectivity is, paradoxically, one reason why his ideals of curing autism may be premature.

16   Alderson, *Challenging the Myths of Autism*, location 2757. Kindle edition.

17   Loftis, *Imagining Autism*, 17. Kindle edition.

18   Baron-Cohen et al., 'A Mathematician, a Physicist, and a Computer Scientist with Asperger Syndrome', 475–83. 'Folk psychology' and 'folk physics' were Baron-Cohen's earlier terms for what he subsequently frames as empathizing and systemizing, respectively.

19   Sacks, *The Man Who Mistook His Wife for a Hat*, 203–33. Referring to George and Charles as 'John' and 'Michael', respectively, Oliver Sacks provides the most detailed account of the Flinn brothers' lives. See also Silberman, *Neurotribes*, 39.

20   Sacks, *The Man Who Mistook His Wife for a Hat*, 203–4.

21   IMDb, 'The Real Superhumans and the Quest for the Future Fantastic'; Fryer, 'The Human Calculator'.

22   Matthews, *X+Y*.

23   Murray, *Representing Autism*, 87–92.

24   Murray, *Representing Autism*, 92.

25   Murray, *Representing Autism*, 68.

26   Murray, *Representing Autism*, 68.

27   Tilton, *The Everything Parent's Guide to Children with Autism*, 189.

28   Shaul, *Our Brains Are Like Computers!*

29   Autism Research Centre, 'Fetal Steroid Hormones'.

30   Baron-Cohen et al., 'Elevated Fetal Steroidogenic Activity in Autism', 369.

31   Baron-Cohen et al., 'Elevated Fetal Steroidogenic Activity in Autism', 374.

32   Baron-Cohen et al., 'Elevated Fetal Steroidogenic Activity in Autism', 374. The authors clearly state their ethical stance against the brief, withdrawn and 'inappropriate' introduction of the androgen-blocking drug Lupron to 'treat' autistic children. Baron-Cohen's most extensive commentaries on autism, ethics and science to date occur in his detailed and humane review of Deborah R. Barnbaum's *The Ethics of Autism* (Bloomington: Indiana University Press, 2009). See Baron-Cohen, 'Does Autism Need a Cure?'. *The Lancet* 373 (2009): 1595–96.

33   Ne'eman, 'Screening Sperm Donors for Autism?'.

34   Huxley, *Brave New World*, location 766. Kindle edition.

35   Jack, *Autism and Gender*, 111.

36 *Time*, 'Diagnosing Bill Gates'. See Jack, *Autism and Gender*, 111–14, for an insightful critique of the article.

37 Silberman, *Neurotribes*, 449.

38 Coupland, 'Microserfs', *Wired*, 1 January 1994 (accessed 9 August 2016). http://www.wired.com/1994/01/microserfs/.

39 Coupland, *Microserfs*, 159. Original emphasis.

40 See Silberman, *Neurotribes*, 18; Watson, 'In Silicon Valley, Young White Males Are Stealing the Future from Everyone Else'.

41 See Coupland, *Microserfs*, 159.

42 Folmar, 'Channelling the Lives of Silicon Valley in Person'; Snider, 'The X-Man'.

43 Coupland, *Microserfs*, 183.

44 Coupland, *Microserfs*, 355.

45 Coupland, *Marshall McLuhan*, 48–51.

46 Blincoe, 'Feeling Frail'; Ferguson, 'Profile'.

47 See Atwood, *Oryx and Crake*, 22, 27, 292–93.

48 See Atwood, *MaddAddam*, 288.

49 See Atwood, *Year of the Flood*, 175–76, 271–72.

50 Atwood, *Oryx and Crake*, 79.

51 Atwood, *Oryx and Crake*, 97, 198.

52 Atwood, *Oryx and Crake*, 203.

53 Atwood, *Oryx and Crake*, 228.

54 Atwood, *Year of the Flood*, 176, 271, 376.

55 Atwood, *Year of the Flood*, 8, 191.

56 Atwood, *Oryx and Crake*, 239.

57 OED Online, 'Neurotypical adj. and n.'

58 Atwood, *Oryx and Crake*, 228.

59 Mitchell and Snyder, *Narrative Prosthesis*.

60 Atwood, *Oryx and Crake*, 419–20.

61 Atwood, *Oryx and Crake*, 46.

62 Fitzgerald, *The Genesis of Artistic Creativity*, 241.

63 Baron-Cohen, 'Autism and Minds Wired for Science'.

64 See Baron-Cohen, 'Autism and Minds Wired for Science.'

65 Isaac Newton (1642–1727), Henry Cavendish (1731–1810), Marie Curie (1867–1934), Albert Einstein (1879–1955), Irène Joliot-Curie (1897–1956) and Paul Dirac (1902–1984).

66 Morton, 'Think Different?'.

67 James, 'Singular Scientists'.

68 James, 'Singular Scientists'.

69 Baron-Cohen, 'Autism and Minds Wired For Science'.

70 Asperger, 'Problems of Infantile Autism', 45–52.

71 James, *Asperger's Syndrome and High Achievement*.

72 Asperger, 'Problems of Infantile Autism', 58.

73 Baron-Cohen et al, 'The Autism-Spectrum Quotient', 16.

74 Baron-Cohen et al., 'Is There a Link between Engineering and Autism', 104.

75 Baron-Cohen et al., 'Engineering and Autism', 98.

76 Wolff, 'Letters to the Editors', 97.

77 Baron-Cohen et al., 'Autism Occurs More Often in Families of Physicists, Engineers, and Mathematicians', 296–301. For the findings cited, see 297–99.

78 Baron-Cohen et al., 'The Autism-Spectrum Quotient', 5.

79 Baron-Cohen et al., 'The Autism-Spectrum Quotient', 5, 15. In the first trial, adults already diagnosed with Asperger Syndrome or 'high-functioning' autism had a mean AQ of 35.8 on a scale of 50 (or 71.6%), while the mean AQ of randomly selected controls was 16.4 (or 32.8%). An AQ of 32+ (64%+) is the suggested cut-off marking 'clinically significant levels of autistic traits', though diagnostic assessment is recommended for individuals in this category *only* if they are 'suffering some distress'.

80 See Baron-Cohen et al., 'The Autism-Spectrum Quotient', 7 for a breakdown of which answers score positively as autistic traits.

81 Ruzich et al., 'Sex and STEM Occupation'.

82 Ruzich et al., 'Sex and STEM Occupation', 12.

83 Ruzich et al., 'Sex and STEM Occupation', 1.

84 Baron-Cohen et al., 'The Autism-Spectrum Quotient', 6.

85 Baron-Cohen et al., 'The Autism-Spectrum Quotient', 7.

86 *Wired* Staff, 'Take the AQ Test'.

87 Baron-Cohen et al., 'The Autism-Spectrum Quotient', 5.

88 See Baron-Cohen et al., 'The Autism-Spectrum Quotient', 7.

89 Woodbury-Smith et al., 'Screening Adults for Asperger Syndrome', 335.

90 See The National Autistic Society, 'Information for General Practitioners'.

91 Baron-Cohen et al., 'The Autism-Spectrum Quotient', 15–16. See statements 19, 9, 29, 49'.

92 Baron-Cohen et al., 'The Autism-Spectrum Quotient', 15–16. See statements 8, 14, 20, 21'.

93 Baron-Cohen et al., 'The Autism-Spectrum Quotient', 10.

94 Baron-Cohen et al., 'The Autism-Spectrum Quotient', 5.

95 Baron-Cohen et al., 'The Autism-Spectrum Quotient', 10.

96 Baron-Cohen et al., 'The Autism-Spectrum Quotient', 5.

97 Baron-Cohen, *Zero Degrees of Empathy*, 75.

98 Feyerabend, *Against Method*, 35.

99 See Sokal and Bricmont, *Intellectual Impostures*, 73–79. For more extensive debates on Feyerabend's legacy, see Preston et al., *The Worst Enemy of Science?*

100 *Telegraph Men*, 'Are You on the Autism Spectrum? Take the Test'.

101 National Autistic Society, '11 Shocking Statistics about Autism and Employment'.

102 Davies, *Neo-Victorian Freakery*.

103 Mitchell, *History and Cultural Memory in Neo-Victorian Fiction*, 7, 37.

104 Davies, *Neo-Victorian Freakery*, 8.

105 OED Online, 'Dismember, v'.

106 Davies, *Neo-Victorian Freakery*, 16–19.

107 See Feinstein, *A History of Autism*, 15–17; Silberman, *Neurotribes*, 127–29, 216.

108 Wing, 'Asperger's Syndrome', 116, 118, 119, 121, 126, 128.

109 Wing, 'Asperger's Syndrome', 124. Cf. Kanner, 'Autistic Disturbances of Affective Contact'.

110 Wing, 'Asperger's Syndrome', 123–24.

111 Wing, 'Asperger's Syndrome', 122. See Asperger, 49, 55, 88, for his comments on autism and mathematics.

112 Asperger, 'Problems of Infantile Autism', quoted in Wing, 'Asperger's Syndrome', 115–29.

113 Wing, 'Asperger's Syndrome', 117.

114 Wing, 'Asperger's Syndrome', 118. Wing later expanded on such points, though with only slight modifications. See Wing, Lorna. *The Autism Spectrum* (London: Robinson, 1996) Location 847, Kindle edition.

115 Hawkes, 'Why a Dash of Autism May Be Key to Success'.

116 Einstein, *On Cosmic Religion and Other Opinions and Aphorisms*, 97.

117 See Baron-Cohen et al., 'A Mathematician, a Physicist, and a Computer Scientist with Asperger Syndrome'; 'The Autism-Spectrum Quotient'.

118 Asperger, 'Problems of Infantile Autism', 45–52.

119 Asperger, ' "Autistic Psychopathy" in Childhood', 72–73.

120 Asperger, ' "Autistic Psychopathy" in Childhood', 39, 84.

121 Asperger, ' "Autistic Psychopathy" in Childhood', 55.

122 Asperger, ' "Autistic Psychopathy" in Childhood', 51.

123 Frith, *Autism and Asperger Syndrome*, 51. For an extensive account of Donald Triplett's life, see Donvan and Zuncker, *In a Different Key*.

124 Asperger, ' "Autistic Psychopathy" in Childhood', 56.

125 Asperger, ' "Autistic Psychopathy" in Childhood', 56.

126 See Feinstein, *A History of Autism*, 9. See also Clayton Behavioural, 'Did Hans Asperger Have Asperger's Syndrome?'.

127 Asperger, 'Autistic Psychopathy in Childhood', 74.

128 Feinstein, *A History of Autism*, 30.

129 See Feinstein, *A History of Autism*, 30.

130 Feinstein, *A History of Autism*, 30.

131 See Donvan and Zucker, *In a Different Key*, 328–31.

132 See Feinstein, *A History of Autism*, 15–17; Silberman, *Neurotribes*, 127–29, 216.

133 See Donvan and Zucker, *In a Different Key*, 339–40.

134 Donvan and Zucker, *In a Different Key*, 340.

135 Donvan and Zucker, *In a Different Key*, 340.

136 Silberman, 'Was Dr. Asperger a Nazi?'

137 Donvan and Zucker, *In a Different Key*, 339; Silberman, 'Was Dr. Asperger a Nazi?'.

138 Silberman, 'Was Dr. Asperger a Nazi?'

139 Unspecified documents shared by Czech are the main source for the account of Asperger's possible links to Nazism in Donvan and Zucker's book. Donvan and Zucker also cite an unpublished paper that Czech submitted to *Molecular Autism* in 2015. See Donvan and Zucker, *In a Different Key*, 590.

140 Silberman, *Neurotribes*, 233.

141 Silberman, *Neurotribes*, 19–34.

142 Silberman, *Neurotribes*, 35–38.

143 Westfahl '*Homo Aspergerus*', quoted in Silberman, *Neurotribes*, 101.

144 See Silberman, *Neurotribes*, 239.

145 Westfahl, '*Homo Aspergerus*'.

146 Westfahl, '*Homo Aspergerus*'.

147 Westfahl, *Hugo Gernsback and the Century of Science Fiction*.

148 Silberman, *Neurotribes*, 241–43.

149 Silberman, *Neurotribes*, 235.

150 See Hoggart, *The Uses of Literacy*, 223–44.

151 Silberman, *Neurotribes*, 236–39.

152 Silberman, *Neurotribes*, 236.

153 Westfahl, '*Homo Aspergerus*'.

154 Silberman, *Neurotribes*, 466.

155 'Thinking Person's Guide to Autism'.

156 See Krystal, 'It's Genre'.

157 Atwood, *Writing with Intent*, 285. See also Atwood, *In Other Worlds*. Kindle location 1–6.

158 Potts, 'Profile'.

159 See Atwood, *In Other Worlds*. As an essayist on science fiction, *Oryx and Crake*'s author may or may not have been alluding to the similarities with *Slan* in naming her central character 'Jimmy' (Vogt's main character is 'Jommy').

160 See Autism Speaks, 'Mission'. On the new appointments, see Autism Speaks, 'Autism Speaks Welcomes Three New Board Members'. For autistic perspectives on this development, see Autism Self Advocacy Network. 'Statements on Autism Speaks Board'.

161 Autist's Corner, 'Metaphor at the Expense of Characterization: Autism in Margaret Atwood's "Oryx and Crake"'.

162 Wrong Planet, 'Oryx and Crake'.

163 Wrong Planet, 'Oryx and Crake (No Spoilers)'.

164 Longmore, *Why I Burned My Book and Other Essays on Disability*, 134.

165 Autism Research Centre, 'Systemizing in Autism Spectrum Conditions'.

166 Autism Research Centre, 'Systemizing in Autism Spectrum Conditions'.

167 See Jack, *Autism and Gender*, 115–20.

168 Jack, *Autism and Gender*, 112.

169 Jack, *Autism and Gender*, 114.

170 Baron-Cohen, *Zero Degrees of Empathy*, 75.

171 Wilde, *The Importance of Being Earnest*, 362.

172 Feyerabend, *Against Method*, 35.

173 Blake, *The Marriage of Heaven and Hell*, 31.

Chapter 2

Metaphors and mirrors: The otherness of adult autism

Online searches for information regarding autism and pregnancy almost overwhelmingly bring up speculative theories and counter-theories around what causes autism. There is contrastingly little public recognition that the *experience* of pregnancy (and the lifestyle changes it creates) may present particular sensory (and other) adjustments for women with autism or Asperger syndrome.[1] Similarly, quests to find advice for autistic teachers or academics almost invariably lead to resources on how to work with autistic youngsters. The possibility (and evidence) that some autistic schoolchildren or university students can eventually *become* teachers or academics continues to elude recognition in the public sphere.[2] These patterns encapsulate two increasingly serious problems in how autism is conceptualized. The neglected fact here is that while autistic youngsters will always be autistic, they will not always be young. The *adult* thus remains the most socially and professionally marginalized of all autistic identities.

Eight decades after the first scientific definitions of autism emerged, knowledge of the condition is still in its medical and cultural infancy. It is therefore unwittingly apt that the figure of the child remains the presiding cultural signifier of autism (and, problematically, this is usually the white male child).[3] This tendency is especially striking in charity appeals. Children, particularly autistic children, are vulnerable: thus, as Murray (2008) discusses, the image of a child is more likely to elicit charitable support.[4] It remains imperative that childhood autism is given further social and educational recognition because there are more children diagnosed with autism now than ever before.[5] However, what will become increasingly oppressive is the relative social, cultural and professional sidelining of autistic adults: not in relation to autistic children but in relation to all other adults. A society and culture that presumes to be attentive to autism but focuses only on children threatens to diminish the recognition and agency of autistic adults (which these children will become). This book thus prioritizes narratives and portrayals of adult autism, but in order to highlight the complexities of this identity, the present chapter gives particular attention to cultural and scientific texts addressing transitions from childhood *into* adulthood. Social and emotional vulnerability does not always lessen with age in autism. In early adulthood especially, new challenges and pressures emerge at precisely the point where independence is expected and where professional support lessens drastically or is withdrawn entirely.

This chapter critiques how autism itself is socially, medically and culturally conceptualized as 'other' and how the tendency for the condition to be associated mainly with childhood doubly marginalizes autistic adults. However, this does not mean that I adopt, in a reductive sense, a purely social model of autism. Philosopher Ian Hacking – who extensively and often innovatively writes of autism to expose the hollowness of 'social construction' theories in the broadest sense – valuably emphasizes that while autism is a socially given name, it still refers to a biological reality, however incomplete its definitions might remain.[6] Hacking thus contemplates autism as an *interactive* identity, 'a labyrinth of interlocking alleys' between the social and the biological.[7] And as Tom Shakespeare points out in firm alliance with Hacking's view, to regard disability as wholly a 'social construct' risks undermining the physical and mental struggles faced *within* the 'disabled' body (including the mind).[8] I strongly concur with Hacking and Shakespeare. However, the reason why this chapter primarily critiques how autism has been theorized and narrated (and in those ways constructed) is that social, medical and cultural realms can potentially be reshaped to create more progressive and accepting approaches to autism.

Many facets of experience and identity as confronted in this chapter are made more disabling for autistic adults by the ways in which these are *otherized*. Autism is (to adopt Hacking's term) *interactive*, in the sense that while presenting genuine neurological and thus physical 'difference', cultural forces shape not only how autism is regarded from outside but also how autistic people are expected to view themselves. In identifying such processes, I recurrently turn to a metaphor (and object) which has held intriguing presence in portrayals of autism, both from autists and from neurotypicals, both in literature and in science: the mirror.

Medical knowledge of autism remains seriously incomplete, and as will be discussed, the prevalence of metaphor in the related scientific discourse frequently correlates with areas of mystery (and speculation). This chapter also contemplates autism in relation to a more immediate point of metaphor, mystery and speculation: I refer to the spectrally vague, inherently subjective and sometimes frankly terrifying suppositions of 'normal', against which autism is defined.

PICKING UP THE MIRROR: ENFREAKING NORMALCY

What *is* 'normal'? In an indispensable contribution to disability studies, *Enforcing Normalcy* (1995), Lennard J. Davis critiques the emergence and power of normal as a concept. He identifies how, in word usage at least, 'the coming into consciousness in English of an idea of "the norm"' dates back only to ca. 1840–1860.[9] Davis examines the then new role of medical statistics in constructing ideas of normal bodies – which, he notes, 'are perhaps not unrelated to the standardized movements of the body demanded in factory work' in the 19th century.[10] Furthermore, Davis's etymological analysis of normal also yields the following insight: prior to 1840, 'norm' referred to a carpenter's measurement square.[11] The origins of normal thus derive from a *tool* – an inanimate prosthetic (which is how human beings were increasingly regarded during the Industrial Revolution). But normal, as an idea, can itself be regarded as a tool: a means of promoting and reinforcing conformity. And, by the same lines of logic, so can certain notions of disability – in particular, autism. To be called *autistic* – clinically, casually or even jokingly – is to be called by a name which, in both medicine and culture, is still predominantly associated with impairment, deficiency and, of course, abnormality.

Autism acts as a conceptual mirror to normalcy in a vast and evolving series of ways. Infants are expected to 'mirror' those around them by gazing back and then smiling back. Then there is the verbal mirroring: the learning, via vocal and often visual mimicry, of how to make and repeat certain sounds, forming words. A key sign of autism in infants is the absence of such reciprocation – or, at least, the absence of what passes as reciprocation in the anticipated ways, which derive from comparison with 'typically' developing children. Autism, then, is not a mirror of neurotypical behaviours. But autism is a mirror of neurotypical *expectations*. This does not end with childhood. If we briefly reconsider the Cambridge Autism Research Centre's current 'Adult Autism-Quotient Test' as a reflection of what constitutes *neurotypicality* instead of autism, we have a 50-statement index (or checklist) of supposedly normal behaviours. Preferring company over solitude, going to parties more often than libraries and favouring chit-chat over deep or detailed conversation: these are all scored in the test as signs and confirmations that you are socially and medically normal. In an historical era when conformity is rewarded – and is good for the economy (or, at least, that of the rich) – there all too easily emerges an expectation of recognizing facets of oneself, if not sameness at large, wherever one looks. Disability disrupts this expectation of a mirror-like image. And, in the past two decades, autism has become arguably the most prominent and sensationalized of all disabilities across literature, television, cinema and popular science.

Few might deny that to be autistic is to experience a genuine and sometimes painful distinction from the majority of people. Even if we reject the term 'impairment', autism still involves a set of *differences*. However, in various cultural narratives, the types of attention promoted towards autism – or, more insidiously, towards certain popular *signifiers* of autism – may further marginalize autistic adults by accentuating such differences and exaggerating their significance, hence this chapter's concern with how autism is *otherized* in society, culture and politics.

In the following discussions, I confront 'otherness' in social, historical and cultural configurations of autism (rather than referring to the 'other' in psychoanalytical terms of those, or that, from which the self is separate). Othering is a process of narrative (and therefore power) through which a group is positioned as inferior or threatening to an implied norm. An otherized population is depicted as deviant from the centre, yet, simultaneously, these 'others' are often portrayed as uniformly indistinguishable from one another. The texts critiqued in chapter 1 exemplified this through their implications that autistic people, by definition, lack imagination. Otherizing people into a homogenous mass denies their individuality and, thus, their humanity. Otherizing the population or rulers of a nation makes it easier to elicit support for invasion or colonization, the killing or maiming of innocent people in the process.[12] In this way, otherizing the autistic population makes it easier to talk of 'curing' them. The chapter later discusses the rhetoric of 'curing' autism as endorsed in various powerful charity organizations, also embodied in the U.S. Combatting Autism Act (2006).[13]

Yet, as a means of seemingly justifying certain policies and actions, othering often elicits projection. Projection allows a dominant group to deny what it dislikes in itself by defining such traits as attributes of the *other*. More broadly, othering enables hegemony to rule over two groups: the other, but, simultaneously, the normal subjects. Showing otherized traits in oneself brings the risk of being treated as an outsider, a traitor or even an enemy of normalcy. Emphasizing the otherness of 'them' also acts as a social and political sticking agent, bonding 'us' together by the virtue of our not being them. However, dominant groups are also *dependent* on the presence of otherness. In order for one group to become 'superior', an other group is necessary and needs to be cast as inferior. Thus, without negative yet reassuring notions of otherness, normalcy itself cannot be sustained.

As will be shown in this chapter, ableist narratives sometimes *use* autism as another form of mirror. Normalcy cannot maintain its power unless it has corresponding notions of otherness. Autism has proven an unusually compelling notion of such otherness. Autism is much more than mere social difference: it is cerebral, it is sensory and it is physical. Often, however, it is towards *social* difference that normalcy looks in order to confirm – and groom – its own identity. Through the following discussions, aided by narratives from within autism communities, I want to metaphorically pick up the mirror, stand behind it and hold it back up to some of the values questionably projected onto autism.

THE INFANTILIZING OF ADULT AUTISM IN DIAGNOSTIC OBSERVATIONS

Supposed norms regarding youth and age – the ongoing *development* of a person – are integral to how autism is otherized. The speech and interests of some autistic children are often viewed as prematurely or somehow inappropriately 'adult'. Although advanced or even savant skills in autistic children are culturally celebrated, other expressions of maturity are sometimes discouraged, most conspicuously where speech is concerned. Despite suggesting the potential to excel in literacy, 'adult-like' speech in autistic children tends not to be rewarded (unlike numeracy skills). For instance, in 2012, a New York child psychiatrist describing traits of Asperger syndrome in a news article remarked of a nine-year-old patient:

> There was something very strange about him. He would walk into my office, shake my hand, say 'Hello, Dr Klein, how are you?' Pseudo-adult. Mechanical.[14]

Why this constitutes 'strange' or even problematic behaviour is intriguing: sophisticated speech from children to adults implies equality and thus potentially unsettles authority. What, then, of autistic adults and notions of age-typical behaviour? Given the greater social and political agency that usually comes with adulthood, it is sometimes shocking to see and experience how adult autism is infantilized in psychiatric procedures. Moreover, the notions (or *expectations*) behind some tests risk further displacing what is already a neurologically 'different' subjectivity.

Adults being tested for autism in a range of countries (and languages) are increasingly being presented at evaluation meetings with children's toys including dolls and miniature cars, as well as picture books for preschool children. The purpose is to enable clinicians to observe how these may prompt interactions (or not) with the professionals present. Yet there are such things as adult 'toys': stress balls, for instance. Why not use ornaments (which often share features with toys) – or other household objects? Surely an alarm clock, a pen and a jar of coffee would initiate (or not) the kind of interactions that clinicians need to test. A complication presented by the use of children's toys in adult psychiatric assessments is that patients who are parents may be accustomed to interacting via these, while adults with no children may not have handled such objects for decades.

Similarly, adult autism assessments are increasingly using books to prompt comments on the content: children's books. In this clinical canon, the classic is David Wiesner's minimally worded picture book, *Tuesday* (1991). Various adults tested for autism in the UK have expressed a mixture of bewilderment and derision at the use of this in autism assessments.[15] Wiesner's book portrays a day in the life of frogs that can fly. *Kirkus Reviews*, a U.S. publishing periodical, classed *Tuesday* as a book suitable for age three and upwards.[16] But might a newspaper story or magazine photospread not be more relevant to the lifestyle, normative or otherwise, of adults being assessed? Another problem with expecting adults to interact with clinicians via children's toys and books is that some clients might assume – wrongly, one would hope – that their parenting (or *potential* parenting) skills are being assessed. In voicing such thoughts, I am not criticizing individual clinics that present adults with children's toys and books as one part of autism assessment. I am, however, criticizing the restrictive selection of *children's* artefacts for use in the procedure. In doing so, I also wish to highlight the wider and deeper otherizing of adult autism which such practices express (and reinforce).

The reason – at least, the immediate reason – behind the children's artefacts specified earlier being used so widely in autism testing is that these (including a copy of Wiesner's *Tuesday*) are made commercially available to clinics as part of the *Autism Diagnostic Observation Schedule*™ package.[17] Conceptualized by Catherine Lord et al. (1989) and provided by California-based Western Psychological Services, an updated second edition appeared in 2012 (*ADOS*™-2). The schedule provides a 'standardized' though semi-structured model of assessment procedures.[18] *ADOS*™-2 may be used only by qualified professionals, who receive training in how to observe and score clients based on responses to the accessories as prompts. Although clinics use the schedule only as one part of the assessment, it can be decisive of the diagnostic outcome. *ADOS*™-2 allows professionals 'to accurately assess and diagnose' autism 'from 12 months through adulthood'.[19] But the unstated yet obvious problem is this: although four 'modules' of guidelines are presented for assessment of different age groups (module 4 being adolescents and above), the same bundle of accessories, consisting solely of objects and books designed for children, is used for *all* ages of people being observed. Thus, the same cultural items used in childhood autism consultations are also (potentially crucial) 'tools' for the adult equivalent. The trouble here is that autistic children and adults, like neurotypical children and adults, are *not* necessarily equivalents. Behind this standardized Observation Schedule™ is an older, comparably standardized idea: that autism is somehow predominantly and most urgently a condition affecting children.

Presenting a grown-up with a toy or a text designed for children conveys a message (if not an assumption) that to be an autistic adult is still somehow to resemble a child. It is possible that I might be interpreting the usage of children's artefacts in adult psychiatry too 'literally', but that does not prevent me from doing so *critically*. The content of *ADOS™-2* re-implicates the 1940s' equations from Kanner and Asperger that autism itself is predominantly linked with childhood. Since both of those nominal pioneers of autism definitions were paediatricians, that was perhaps inevitable. Yet the tacitly infantilizing attitudes encoded in the diagnostic practices critiqued earlier indicate a more pervasive element of 21st-century conceptions of autism. To society (including psychiatry), adult autistic identities – and responses to them – remain a point of much uncertainty. There is not yet a cultural or medical space in which to acknowledge adult autism as an entity or identity in its own right. In its own way, the infantilization of autistic adults is a form of normalization: to liken us to children is to expect our subservience. And children have less social and political agency than adults.

AUTISM AND DISORDER: FOUCAULT, CONFINEMENT AND CULTURAL FEAR

The name 'autism disorder' was introduced to the American Psychiatric Association's revised *Diagnostic and Statistical Manual of Mental Disorders* (*DSM-III*) in 1987, replacing the term 'infantile autism' and acknowledging a lifelong condition.[20] The fifth edition of the *Manual* (2013) uses the heading 'Autism Spectrum Disorder'.[21] But what does the naming of autism – and other neurological differences – in terms of 'disorder' say about the desirability of *order* in a wider, political sense? And why is autism sometimes characterized as an association one should seek, in one's conduct, to avoid? To begin contemplating such questions, Foucault's genealogy of mental illness as a changing concept through *Madness and Civilization* (1964) is enabling to the present age.

Foucault elucidates how 'madness' did not become significantly reviled as an identity in the West until the Middle Ages, when it succeeded leprosy as the most feared illness. Foucault's critique of this process indicates how the existence of an ostracized yet fascinating *other* served a need in European societies to refine and maintain dominant power structures. In the Renaissance period, some people deemed mad would be exiled from the land itself onto a 'ship of fools'. These took inhabitants to shrines where miraculous healings had been reported, but most of the time such ships were in transit – reducing the presence of madness in society, and creating greater conformity and thus political stability.[22] By the 17th century, societal responses to madness were shifting from expulsion to 'confinement' and control: people deemed insane were being placed in hospitals and, during the next two centuries in England and France, these institutions became places where the public could pay to watch, taunt and manipulate the inhabitants.[23] Madness was thus held up to 'civilization' as a public spectacle of otherness. Aspects of this continue into the 21st century through the naming of autism.

In February 2015, it was announced on the front page of the American newspaper *USA Today* that Russian president Vladimir Putin met the criteria for Asperger syndrome. The American researchers behind this conclusion (who had never met Putin and simply observed moving images of him) were working for the Pentagon. This 'assessment' – or conclusion, it rather seems – was commissioned in 2008 by the Bush administration amid escalating tensions between America and Russia. Putin was 'diagnosed' by Brenda Connors: an expert in movement-pattern analysis, but not autism. Why the Pentagon did not recruit a qualified autism specialist to 'diagnose' Putin is an interesting question. Invoking archaic notions of trauma as the cause of autism (discussed later in this chapter), the diagnostic report made the Bettelheim-like assumption that Putin's 'neurological development was significantly interrupted in infancy'.[24] In addition to seriously misrepresenting the entire diagnostic process of autism, the whole farcical episode had chilling implications. In effect, the Pentagon appears to have been treating the name of autism as a potential political *weapon*.

As Nadesan points out, autism is – among much else – 'a nominal category useful for grouping heterogeneous people all sharing communication practices deviating significantly from the expectations of normalcy'.[25] Foucault critiques how 'madness' entails *conceptual* confinement of individuals who demonstrate politically undesirable difference. And, over the past three decades, no other form of neurological difference has been subjected to as much cultural attention as autism. Various defining patterns critiqued in Foucault's account of madness and civilization remain evident in the positioning of autism against an implicit yet dominant norm. Autism is a lifelong condition, understood to be biogenetically caused – and it is precisely this that renders the social significance of the name so unusually potent. To call a person autistic is to position his or her identity as fundamentally and unalterably deviant from the supposed norm and thus the imagined majority of fellow human beings. Therefore, the power of the name, and how it is used, should not be underestimated.

Susan Sontag's *Illness as Metaphor* (1979) and *AIDS and its Metaphors* (1991), respectively, critique how cultural narratives surrounding cancer and AIDS parallel the sense of horror once accorded to leprosy. Sontag, herself recovering from cancer while writing her 1979 essay, observes:

> Nothing is more punitive than to give a disease a meaning – that meaning being invariably a moralistic one. Any important disease whose causality is murky, and for which treatment is ineffectual, tends to be awash in significance. . . . The disease itself becomes a metaphor. Then, in the name of the disease (that is, using it as a metaphor), that horror is imposed on other things. The disease becomes adjectival.[26]

Examining narrative parallels between cancer in the 20th century and tuberculosis in the previous two centuries, Sontag shows how diseases 'thought to be multi-determined' and thus regarded as 'mysterious' have 'the widest possibilities as metaphors for what is felt to be socially or morally wrong'.[27] The very term 'disease', as Scully (2004) demonstrates, remains a vague, ambiguous word both medically and socially.[28] With the occasional exceptions of rhetoric emphasizing the need to find a 'cure', autism has rarely been named as a disease in the 21st century.[29] However, Sontag's examinations of disease and metaphor enable us to see how the name of autism has been implicated in the very processes that she identifies – and how it thus becomes a disease in the sense of its cultural function as a locus of otherness. The major indication of this has been the tendency for certain *associations* with autism to be cast in popular culture as traits to be either avoided or disguised.

What Sontag critiques as the 'adjectival' significance of mysterious diseases to connote what is regarded as socially or even morally 'wrong' was especially striking in cultural references to autism during the 1990s and early 2000s, as Asperger syndrome became an increasingly prominent topic in media and culture. One association with autism that attracted unusual derision was the notion of 'special interests'. For example, in a 2002 autobiographical essay on being a music fan, poet Simon Armitage wrote that he had resisted acquiring a complete collection of albums by Bob Dylan (over 40 had been released by then) partly because

> to find myself in possession of the entire works of Bob Dylan, like owning every copy of the *National Geographic* or a complete set of Pokemon cards, suggests to me a kind of autism that, for most of my adult life, I've been attempting to avoid.[30]

This apparent confession bears a tension between self-deprecation and a fear of the name 'autism'. Considered in the context of Armitage's other publications of this period, however, this mention of autism, while possibly ironic, is not a casual or one-off occurrence. Male autistic children are portrayed in Armitage's novel *Little Green Man* (2001) and the poem 'The Stone Beach' (2002). As Murray (2008) points out, the presence of an autistic son in Armitage's novel serves to humanize the boy's immature father; thus, autism is present in *Little Green Man* more as a device for 'plot mobility' than an identity recognized in its own right.[31] In 'The Stone Beach', the figure of a three-year-old autistic boy comparably serves to shift the narrative; the poem ends with speaker following this child's gaze and experiencing a moment of quiet revelation.[32] More affectingly than *Little Green Man*, Armitage's poem presents a touching reach towards engagement with another subjectivity. However, Armitage's quoted musing on collecting certain cultural artefacts invokes a harsher idea of autism. The difference here is that the name of autism is being linked to *adulthood*. Naming autism as an interpellation to 'avoid', Armitage's comment reflects a wider cultural tendency for autism – or for traits associated with this term – to be regarded as socially wrong, even in their slightest deviations from the average and the bland.

As well as being a neurological and physical way of being, autism is a social classification. It thus incurs confinement in terms of how a person is regarded by peers. Like madness as historicized by Foucault, the presence of autism – and the casualness with which the name is used adjectivally – presents a powerful lesson to the neurotypical population (and to undiagnosed autistics): if you do not conform, your identity may risk becoming confined to a name and concept placed on you from outside; a name that, both medically and culturally, is narrated in predominantly negative, even dehumanizing terms.*

THE SCREEN AS MIRROR: RICKY GERVAIS'S
THE OFFICE (UK) AND THE NEUROTYPICAL GAZE

Increasingly through the 20th century, offices became not just signifiers of conformity but concentrations of it. And, amid heightened conformity, otherness

---

* **'Peculiar'**

   Peculiar: this adjective stems from the classical Latin *pecūliāris*, referring to that which belongs to a person and is 'one's own, personal, private' (OED). In its looser, current sense, 'peculiar' refers to a quality, feature or custom 'that characterizes, distinguishes, or belongs to a person, thing, or place' (OED). Yet my own particular (if not peculiar) experiences of this adjective as an interpellation during childhood in the English Midlands invoke a direct, almost synonymous relationship to what was at the time becoming medically recognized as Asperger syndrome. *Don't keep flapping your hands, people will think you're peculiar!* and *You should've stopped walking on your tiptoes years ago. It looks peculiar!* These interpellations from adult family members may sound harsh, but though I was unable to obey them (and uninterested in trying to), my memory presents the quotations (and similar warnings) in a manner I recall as loving and concerned. The message I interpret by delay here is: For your own sake, I don't want people to otherize you.

becomes accentuated. A fixture of the sensationally popular, well-observed UK mock-documentary television comedy *The Office* (2001–2003) was the bullying of a managerial assistant, Gareth, by two fractionally lower-ranking colleagues, Tim and Dawn.[33] I would not call the quietly victimized Gareth a serious portrayal of adult autism: his hapless character mainly serves to satirize micro-management. Yet his comedy value and cartoonish social ugliness depend conspicuously on four social traits associated with autism: tactlessness, pedantry, difficulty reading facial expressions and inability to tell when others are joking. Gareth's very confusion at his peers' shared humour renders him their target. At one point, Tim goads Gareth by calling him a 'special needs child'.[34] As Dawn and Tim's friendship grows strained by their unresolved attraction to each other, 'winding up Gareth' becomes one of few scenarios in which the two co-workers can feel relaxed together. Making a minority of Gareth is seminal to the bonding of his two peers. Tim and Dawn further otherize Gareth by prompting him to make politically offensive statements, confirming their moral superiority. Yet the comedy itself otherizes Gareth by encouraging the audience to join in viewing him as a spectacle of lightweight and liminal neurological disorder. Tim and Dawn are the audience's most obvious points of identification in *The Office*. They express dissatisfaction not just with work but with their lives, prompting empathy. For that reason, their fondness for aggravating and socially preying on a colleague's autistic vulnerabilities is unsettling. Dawn and Tim are not crudely glamorous by television standards. Their likeability is entwined with their conventionality, almost rendering the latter attribute a virtue in itself. Crucial to reinforcing their normalcy is Gareth's otherness, and certain traits of autism are essential to his role.

As is reflected in the earlier quotation from Armitage, overtly specialist interests (especially those involving collecting) had become both popularly and negatively associated with autism by the early 2000s. In *The Office*'s second series (2002), Gareth attempts to impress a woman to whom he is attracted by boasting of his recall for facts about 'Monster Trucks' culled from his sets of collectable information cards aimed at children.[35] The audience is shown how the woman's face registers her derision and, of course, Gareth is reliably unable to recognize this. While using a stereotypical post-*Rain Man* trope of autism – the combination of eidetic memory and a love of facts – this scene takes Gareth's lack of self-awareness to a new level, implying that this mostly contemptible figure is demonstrating a culturally recognizable trait of autism and does not even know it.

Everything Gareth says to his boss reeks of sycophancy: *not* a trait usually associated with autism. And yet, as a text, this television comedy itself plays ingratiatingly to an implied authority: the ableist gaze. Critiquing the mis-representation of disability in cinema, Longmore in 1985 asserted: 'As with popular portrayals of other minorities, the unacknowledged hostile fantasies of the stigmatizers are transferred to the stigmatized'.[36] In *The Office*, it is the associations of autism that are configured as undesirable –not the comfortable unwillingness of assembled neurotypicals to respect these. Gareth is otherized to the point of superficially appearing to *deserve* being bullied. In a cloyingly safe way, the series is able to position traits of autism as points of mockery because, first, Gareth's 'special needs' are a *joke* and not a diagnosis and, second, he is too insensitive to understand that he is being mocked.[37] In venturing these observations, I am not suggesting that comedy should refrain from mocking autism, nor anything else. Whether through irony, 'irony' or outright hostility, ableism in comedy can mirror and therefore expose elements of the social climate in which it meets success. Comedy can confront and challenge us with our own prejudices. However, it can also reward and exploit them.

It remains problematic that ableist comedy can reinforce cultural (and social) marginalization because so much that would in any other context be called prejudice or even hate speech can be justified as 'just a joke'. This is the conventional defence wielded to the point of cliché both in the school playground and on the lucrative stage of high-profile comedy. It is also a riposte which positions any targets who express offence as the humourless ones in the wrong. Yet for some autistic people, the re-interpellation of ableism as just a joke can be doubly oppressive, since it incurs the widespread (but drastically simplistic) notion that autism is characterized by the absence of any sense of humour.

In view of the entertainment value of autistic traits – and, increasingly, of autism itself – Foucault's study of the mutually intensifying relationship between confinement and public spectacle grows newly pertinent. In 18th-century Paris (prior to the revolution) and in London at Bethlehem Hospital ('Bedlam') until around 1815, the public could pay to tease and torment people institutionalized as insane; the spectacle of neurological otherness thus became a commodity.[38] When we view autism as a nominal and conceptual confinement which has become a cultural fixation, it becomes possible to see elements of such processes continuing. A difference between the present and the 18th century is the availability and multiplicity of mass media. And we can be more comfortably entertained by neurological difference if we are gazing at a *text* (fictional or otherwise) rather than an actual person. The 'representation' of autism for the neurotypical gaze often creates a lucrative spectacle – and it is easier for culture industries to manipulate guilt-free gazes at autism if the focus aligns with adulthood, as in the case of *The Office*. Yet, in (too) many cases in popular culture, what tends to be overlooked – or simply disregarded – is the virtual certainty that autistic adults will be gazing at the same text, too.

POST-*CURIOUS*: ADULT AUTISM AS CULTURAL SPECTACLE IN *BIG BANG THEORY* AND *THE ACCOUNTANT*

Events in cultural history are seldom reducible to linear patterns or narratives: there are too many factors in play, all progressing and regressing in different directions at varying paces. Inevitably, the same is true in the history of autism portrayals. Nonetheless, it is notable that Armitage's valuably honest-seeming 2002 remark on wishing to avoid supposedly autistic instincts in himself coincides with the uses of autistic associations to otherize, and make mockable, the figure of Gareth in *The Office* (2001–2003). In hindsight, such texts suggest how the period 2001–2003 marks an unusually harsh moment in adjectival namings of, or allusions to, adult autism. The commonplace notions of adult autism in Margaret Atwood's *Oryx and Crake* (2003) discussed in chapter 1 comparably exemplify the otherizing of such an identity. In these examples, the significance of autism is *peripheral* to wider themes and, in this sense, functions as (to return to Mitchell and Snyder's term) narrative prosthesis. Yet part of what makes these configurations of autism appear dated now is the contrast they present with the most popular and influential portrayal of autism to emerge in this period: Mark Haddon's novel *The Curious Incident of the Dog in the Night-Time* (2003). Haddon provided the first British text to receive widespread cultural attention with autism at the *centre*. Through the fictional 15-year-old Christopher Boone, Haddon's novel invoked a vulnerable and *likeable* human figure with whom audiences could empathize. However, as various critiques have stressed – particularly those from within autism communities – Haddon's depiction of Asperger syndrome depended on, and reinforced, pre-existing neurotypical ideas of autism (not least through Christopher's similarity to *Rain Man's* Raymond).[39] As Murray (2008) dissects, the success of Haddon's novel prompted a series of autism portrayals in which similar tropes were used – most obviously, the association with mathematics.[40] As such, *Curious Incident* created a blockage in the linearity of autism 'representations' in the sense of limiting genuine progression (though as chapter 3 will show, various lesser-known autism fictions have transcended its shadow).

In 2009, *Slate* magazine asked: 'Is the world ready for an Asperger's sitcom?'.[41] The answer was evidently 'yes'. The U.S. sitcom in question, *Big Bang Theory* (2007–), had become one of the most commercially (and critically) popular television series of its era. *Slate* pointed out that while autism is not named in the script, the show's four young, male academics – all researching STEM areas – clearly demonstrate traits of Asperger syndrome. In other words, the expectations surrounding autistic identities by the post-*Curious* late 2000s are conveyed so bluntly that the autism spectrum does not *need* to be named. As so often in fictional portrayals, a single character is otherized as more overtly (and comically) autistic than those around him: Sheldon Cooper, a theoretical physicist. But though the namelessness of autism within *Big Bang Theory* itself correlates with a series of stereotypes in order for the condition to be recognized, Sheldon, like Haddon's Christopher, is foregrounded as a likeable figure. Whether Sheldon appeals to audiences as an autistic character or an autistic cliché (or both), one thing is clear: commonplace and comfortable ideas regarding autistic adult otherness are central to the humour of this show. Some autistic viewers praise *Big Bang Theory* for mirroring not just their recognizable experiences but the sometimes bewildered yet benign responses of neurotypical others to autistic social traits.[42] Unfortunately however, the presence of autistic people as audience members still appears to be a matter of scant consideration in the most lucrative area of screen culture: Hollywood.

The anti-hero of Gavin O'Connor's action-thriller film *The Accountant* (2016) is Chris Wolff (Ben Affleck), an autistic man with a grudge against humanity, who specializes in forensic accountancy for criminal organizations. Predictably, much of the humour lands on Chris's disregard for social niceties. However, this disregard quickly extends to a tendency to shoot people's heads off when he is not solving spectacularly complex mathematical problems. O'Connor claims that *The Accountant* is 'about a protagonist that you've never seen before in film'.[43] Presumably, he is referring here to previous portrayals of accountants, because this film's central 'character' of a glamorous white autistic male with savant mathematical skills is as clichéd as the director's first claim of authority on neurodiversity: 'My wife's best friend's son has autism'.[44] O'Connor describes how, in preparing *The Accountant*, he and Affleck started to 'watch documentaries, listen to podcasts and read books on autism' before meeting with 'educators and specialists' and, finally, meeting with men who were 'high-functioning autistic Asperger'. The process then 'became about grabbing different behavioral details from different people to create our character', O'Connor states.[45]

Stories from directors and actors about spending time with autistic people before portraying the condition on screen became commonplace following Dustin Hoffman's description of doing just that for *Rain Man*.[46] But the 1980s was a relatively innocent – if pivotal – time in cultural depictions of autism. Three decades later, *The Accountant* underlines the lowest point so far in the use of such claims for promotional ends. The consultation of autistic people in the production of screen portrayals *is* important – so long as the publicized encounters are not merely about observation. But the obvious problem with 'grabbing different behavioural details' from different autistic people is that it leads to a *composite* performance, veering dangerously close to stereotype. In selecting only the autistic behaviours deemed most interesting for cinema or television settings, the result is often a Frankenstein's monster version of autism: parts of various people stitched together in such a way that the character ceases to resemble a human being. Unsubtly enough, Chris Wolff is recruited by a company named 'Living Robotics'.

Against the ridiculous promotional boasts that *The Accountant* gives an 'honest' portrayal of autism, Alexandra Haagaard (2016), writing for *The Establishment*, responds that it is an honest depiction only of how autism is sometimes seen by people who are not themselves autistic, rendering 'a character who is constantly and explicitly signified as Other'.[47] Stating her own autistic identity in the same piece, Haagaard's review articulates how it felt to view not just *The Accountant* but its manipulation of a complicit audience:

> I cringed when the audience laughed as Chris inadvertently insulted a client with his blunt manner, . . . when they laughed as he awkwardly attempted to converse with . . . a love interest . . . when they laughed at Chris' brother angrily calling him, 'you weird fuck'. . . . This was not the friendly laughter that happens once you recognize you've done something a bit odd. . . . This was the laughter of the kids in the schoolyard. . . . This was the laughter of the mob clamoring.[48]

Texts as varied as *The Office* and Atwood's *Oryx and Crake* have in different ways depended on autism as an otherized identity in order to satirize wider social and political patterns. Chillingly, however, *The Accountant* relies on caricature notions of autism for mere audience gratification. Not unlike the exhibiting of 'mad' people for public amusement in the 18th and early 19th century as chronicled by Foucault, the 21st-century cultural fixation with autism is a lucrative business.

Foucault's paradigm-altering studies of madness (1964), criminality (1975) and sexuality (1976, 1984) highlight the historical subjectivity of social attitudes to otherness.[49] It therefore remains dangerously easy for us to otherize previous (though ancestral) eras by falsely believing that repressive and abusive treatments of neurodivergence are now confined to the distant past. To remind ourselves of how the mentally ill were treated in Bedlam during the 18th and early 19th centuries is to risk congratulating ourselves on – and overestimating – the superiority of our own, supposedly enlightened attitudes and responses to mental difference. At the same time, however, an era in which autism is a point of cultural fixation is simultaneously an era in which the expectations surrounding it can be subverted.

CONJECTURING OTHERNESS: AUTISM, METAPHOR AND METONYMY

The enigmas that autism presents to science, society and culture – and, thus, to many people with the diagnosis – is such that the condition is extensively narrated by figurative, non-literal language. *The Office*, for instance, uses certain metonyms of autism to otherize Gareth and, more obliquely, uses his autistic traits as metonyms for the obsessiveness of micro-management. Such patterns *suggest* autism in place of naming it – and in doing so they tend to evade deeper engagement with the meanings of autism as subjectivity or identity. However, this (increasingly prevalent) type of metonymic process will be more closely addressed in chapter 3. In the present discussion, I focus primarily on certain metaphors that surround (and often distort) meanings of autism in both science and culture. Metaphor is a pervasive narrative process by which autism is otherized. What is often key to the influence of metaphors in scientific discourse is their very subtlety, which sometimes risks their being mistaken (and reported in the media) as facts.

'Unfortunately, metaphor is ubiquitous in the field of autism', writes Douglas Biklen (2005).[50] He critiques how a range of established scientific terms including 'mindblindness' and 'central coherence' as supposed explanations of autism are ultimately metaphors, since no laboratory (or other) means of explaining these features of autism have yet been identified.[51] In what follows, I explore how specific examples of metaphor signify major gaps in not just clinical narratives but clinical *knowledge* of autism. An oppressive pattern will become apparent: when theories concerning autism are least certain, the metaphors used tend to otherize autistic people and their families in the most negative terms.

Clinical (and neurotypical) interpellations that autistic people often misunderstand metaphor in conversation are at least as old as Kanner's 1943 article, which emphasized the *literalness* with which autistic children interpret requests and questions.[52] Kanner expanded on this in his lesser-known but more empathic 1946 article 'Irrelevant and Metaphorical Language in Early Infantile Autism'. The 'irrelevant' language describes how autistic children would repeat learned phrases with seemingly little appreciation of context.[53] Kanner's 1946 comments on metaphor, meanwhile, reiterate his view of their 'literal' interpretation. (And yet the title of Kanner's article is worth taking literally – or deconstructing – to point out that to some autistic subjectivities, metaphor itself is irrelevant language). Happé (1991) helpfully observes that autistic adults do receive and use figurative language creatively via similes but again reports that metaphor tends not to be understood (in the expected ways at least) by autistic adults.[54] But the source of perhaps the most widely read equation of autistic thinking with misunderstandings of metaphor is Haddon's *Curious Incident of the Dog* (2003). The second of two reasons why Christopher finds people 'confusing' is that 'they often talk using metaphors' (the first reason being that single body language gestures can mean multiple things).[55] And though, like 'Harro L.' in Asperger's 1944 paper (see chapter 1), I can discern metaphor in written fictional narratives, it can still confuse me in conversation. In my case, this mainly has to do with *speed*: I can read, re-read and reflect at my own pace. By contrast, conversation usually demands rapid alternations of interpreting and responding. However, I must stress here (because it is rarely considered in clinical accounts of autism) that to take a metaphor literally still involves imagination, as well as subjectivity and therefore individuality. Sometimes, even neurotypical ideas of autistics interpreting statements literally border on metaphor. If you say 'It's raining cats and dogs', some autistic people might imagine that for some reason these animals are falling to the ground; others might just think you are weird. Furthermore, misinterpretations do not wholly mean a failure to *recognize* metaphors (or cliché) in conversation.[†]

Instructive advice on how best to communicate with autistic adults (especially in workplaces) often recommends avoidance of non-literal language.[56] It is thus indicative of how autism is predominantly conceptualized from *outside* – by neurotypicals – that metaphor is, in Biklen's phrase, 'ubiquitous' in autism discourse, not least in science. I do not suggest that metaphors in autism discourse from neurotypicals should be avoided, however. On the contrary, when read critically, they can subversively reflect wider patterns at play in how autism is regarded and thus conceptualized.

What *is* metaphor? Elizabeth Ashton (1997) evaluates how definitions of metaphor and its purposes have remained somewhat contested since the period of Aristotle's *Poetics* in the third century BCE. Most pertinent here, however, is Ashton's discussion of how positivist philosophers have distrusted metaphor when it is put in service of seemingly proving a fact. The positivist notion that 'anything which can only be expressed through metaphor is merely conjectural' is, Ashton argues, 'persuasive, although flawed'.[57] However, in the case of neurotypically dominated autism rhetoric, metaphor really *is*, in most instances, 'conjectural' because so much remains unknown. For this chapter's concerns, two effects of metaphor are often problematic.

---

† **On Taking 'Literally' Too Literally**

When I was undertaking voluntary work in a busy drop-in centre, the co-ordinator instructed me to go for my break. In a somewhat flustered state, mid-multitasking, I tried to finish unpacking a box of donated tins of food into order on a shelf before leaving for my break (because I was worried that someone might trip over the box if I left it unattended). Several minutes later, I was still sorting the soup from the spaghetti when my supervisor (who I'll call Lionel) returned and told me again to go for my break, or he would 'break my legs'. Slightly shocked, I later asked a co-worker if he had heard what Lionel had said to me, about breaking my legs. Perhaps having sensed my (then undiagnosed) autism for other reasons – he had asked me that morning if I had heard of Haddon's novel – the co-worker replied that Lionel was only joking and 'didn't mean it *literally*'. However, I already knew that. I was not worried that Lionel might break my legs. But I *was* worried that he must have been extremely angry with me, rather than just making a point. Although that is a true story, I offer it here as a metaphor.

First, metaphor often displaces factuality by invoking two properties to make a statement about just *one* of these.[58] Metaphor is, by definition, a form of *redefinition*. Second, metaphor often functions as interpellation. Loftis (2015) notices that metaphors around autism often function with similar effect to stereotypes. Whether empowering or repressive, stereotypes and metaphors 'have a profound effect on public perceptions of autism and especially on questions of identity and self-construction within the autism community itself'.[59] Moreover, stereotypes and metaphors can *become* each other.

A rhetorical purpose of metaphor is to render something easier to understand via a point of comparison. Metaphors surrounding autism imply means of enabling society and culture to better empathize with this subjectivity from outside. This is a noble, necessary aim, but the problem is that metaphors invoke autism *as something it is actually not*. For this reason, it is essential to treat neurotypically authored metaphors for autism critically. What if the metaphor that supposedly takes all of us closer to understanding autism is actually misinterpreting or even manipulating the reality, pushing autism and neurotypicality further apart? Moreover, while metaphors around autism are usually intended to enhance understanding, these frequently emphasize and dramatize autistic otherness.

The word 'autism' itself is a metaphor, marking certain speculations, if not judgements on how this way of being has been viewed from outside. 'Autism' carries no etymological properties outside of *autos:* the Greek term for 'self'. The suffix '-ism' can refer to action, prejudice, peculiarity, pathology and ideology, but with each of these, *autism* implies the self as the insular limit of the person's awareness. This is misleading, given the intensity with which external factors can impact on autistic subjectivity, from the sensory to the social. 'Autism' remains, like any name, contestable and redefinable by those with whom it is associated (and the suffix '-ism' can also signify a political movement). However, I state these literalist observations to highlight certain processes in how the supposed nature of this condition continues to be conceptualized in the prevailing discourses. It is ironic that a name pertaining to 'self' remains so otherized. I am often asked, 'What it is *like* to be autistic?'. While I can answer on what it is 'like' to be *diagnosed* autistic (see chapter 4), explaining what this subjectivity itself is like presents a philosophical conundrum, since I have never been anything else. However, given the otherizing from outside as manifest in the adjectival name 'autistic' (and in so much further discourse around the condition), it is telling that various autistic people have used the drastic but revealing metaphor of the alien.

In 1993, Temple Grandin famously gave to Oliver Sacks the simile that being autistic felt like being 'An Anthropologist on Mars'.[60] This became the title of Sacks's 1995 book on neurological conditions, including cerebral achromatopsia (colour-blindness), amnesia, Tourette syndrome and, most extensively, autism (culminating with a detailed profile of Grandin). It is important to note that Grandin likened her perspective to being *on* Mars, not *from* there. Yet it is poignantly telling that many autistic people – or, at least, many autistic authors – have likened the condition to being an alien. Alicia A. Broderick and Ari Ne'eman (2008) expressed concerns about this from their own autistic viewpoints.[61] There are now more published examples of this metaphor from autistic people than from neurotypicals. In particular, it has occurred in book titles, for instance, Clare Sainsbury's *Martian in the Playground* (2010) and Joshua Muggleton's *Raising Martians* (2011).[62] 'Wrong Planet' is the name of a major online autism forum; its logo is a green, antennae-bearing cartoon creature.[63] The name, however, carries more than just a metaphor of estrangement and minority: it is the planet on which autistic people are made to feel estranged and minoritized that is wrong.

Uses of the alien metaphor by autistic people sometimes imply an internalization, if not acceptance, of being socially and culturally otherized. Nonetheless, this metaphor can expose the marginalization within which autistic people are culturally encouraged to conceive of themselves. Surveying various cultural associations between autism and aliens, Hacking (2009) comments, 'Friend or foe, aliens are definitely not us. However, we seem to hold up aliens as mirrors to teach what is best and worst in us or in the human condition'.[64] The mirror of dominant social mores presented by autism reveals, more starkly than anything else, the value placed on ideas of normalcy. Such ideas are ill-defined and elusive – but the presence of autism as something *not* normal helps to give these some embodiment. It is not normal to focus extensively on one object, idea or task at the expense of others; it is deviant to prefer solitude to company; and if a person is oblivious or (more subversively) indifferent to social convention, a pathological diagnostic explanation may be expected. What is also mirrored in the autist as 'alien' metaphor is the existence of ableism and its inability to fully accept neurodiversity as yet. To quote the empowering clarity of autistic blogger and journalist Caro Narby: 'We're not aliens, but we certainly are *alienated* by a culture that refuses to accept that we live, love, and relate to the world and to our communities as human beings'.[65]

LOST IN THE MIRROR METAPHOR: CHALLENGING THE MYTH OF AUTISTIC NARCISSISM

'The Child Is Father of the Man', wrote William Wordsworth.[66] The legacy of childhood is of course widely emphasized throughout psychiatric discourse, but is unusually formative to autism assessment. Diagnostic procedures for adult autism can bring forth the spectral influence of childhood to such a point that it becomes something like a third parental presence. Since autism is understood as a congenital, lifelong state, it is necessary for assessments in adulthood to focus closely on available records and accounts of a person's childhood to ascertain whether traits she or he is presenting have always been there in some sense. But there can be an additional way in which childhood might create a vivid presence in autistic adulthood. Controlled interviews with autistic adults have suggested what Crane and Goddard (2008) term an 'autobiographical memory deficit'.[67] However, a more ambitious study by Zamoscik et al. (2016) – in which participants freely submitted responses online – indicates that the ability of autistic adults to remember childhood experiences often *surpasses* that of non-autistics.[68] Certainly, a wealth of memoirs by autistic adults suggest multitudinous ways in which childhood experiences can be recalled with great intensity. Autobiographies which extensively demonstrate this include those of Temple Grandin (with Margaret M. Scariano, 1987), Donna Williams (1992), John Elder Robison (2008) and Tito Rajarshi Mukhopadhyay (2008).[69] And what is sometimes remarkable is the degree to which narratives by autistic adults of their own childhood experiences present very different – and diverse – perspectives in comparison with how childhood autism continues to be theorized and interpellated by professionals. In view of this discordance, it becomes seriously problematic that psychiatric discourse continues to marginalize (if not wholly ignore) the alternate perspectives provided from within autism communities.

The metaphor of the mirror occurs in various autism discourses. It is insightful to consider certain distances in how autistic responses to mirrors as physical objects have been narrated from outside (in psychiatric discourse) and inside (through autistic autobiographies). In an article titled 'Autism: Lost in the Mirror?' published in the *Journal of Psychology and Clinical Psychiatry*, Alison Barry (2015) describes how, while working on applied behavioural analysis with preschool autistic children, she sensed that many would complete tasks 'primarily' (in her view) for the reward of being allowed to look into a mirror. These children appeared 'fully satisfied', gazing at 'their own' images.[70] A psychoanalytical psychotherapist, Barry hypothesizes that what may 'give rise' to autism is a 'failure' at what Jacques Lacan theorized as the mirror stage of development. In one of Barry's key sources, Lacan (1949) theorized this as the process through which – by progressively recognizing the self in the mirror between the ages of 6 and 18 months – infants conceive of their full bodies and how these render them distinct from the mother.[71] In a most drastic conjecture, Barry states that until the mirror stage, 'the child's body is in an autistic state'.[72] Casually implying that *all* humans are born autistic – but some fail to progress beyond this via the mirror stage – Barry uses Lacanian theory to present one of the most wildly infantilizing speculations about autistic identity to have appeared in decades. Barry (2015) acknowledges no autism research from later than the 1990s. Nor does she cite any autistic authors.

Barry refers to her professional observations to assert that autistic responses to the mirror, 'rather like the myth of narcissus', signify 'an entrapment in their own mirrored ideal ego'.[73] This presents a variant on outside assumptions that autistic people inherently lack imagination, as critiqued in chapter 1. Yet Barry's adult neurotypical perspective on what the autistic infant might see in a mirror is contradicted by accounts of childhood from autistic adult perspectives – which, in turn, differ interestingly from each other. South Indian author and poet Tito Rajarshi Mukhopadhyay (2008) writes as a 19-year-old of how mirrors brought him a sense of peace in childhood. Mukhopadhyay narrates how he loved to stand before a mirror in his house as an infant not to see his reflection, but for much more subtly perceptive (and imaginative) reasons:

> I believed that the mirror wanted to tell me a story because I wanted to tell *it* a story. . . . I realized that the mirror would absorb all the colors within its own stretch of self. The blue sky behind the window would look bluer in the mirror.[74]

Mukhopadhyay describes how his mother would follow him with a handheld mirror to engage his attention – but he 'had no way to make her understand that the mirror upstairs was different'.[75] Being before his favourite mirror, he writes, still 'helps secure my scattered senses'.[76] Asked by Biklen (2005) whether his relationship to the mirror was 'a metaphor for some experience in [his] actual life', or 'a daydream, a wished-for world', Mukhopadhyay replied:

> The world inside the mirror looked silent to me because the real world was too complex to cope with . . . my power of imagination also helped me a great deal to make my own convenient escape inside the world of the mirror.[77]

The role of imagination (and individuality) in autistic mirror-gazing is also conveyed by Donna Williams. As a child, Williams once enjoyed playing with an older girl, Carol, but never saw her again.[78] Williams details how she then pretended that her own reflection was Carol. 'I would cry and look desperately into Carol's eyes reflected in the mirror, wanting to know the answers to the way out of my mental prison'.[79] Williams's narrative starkly articulates how a mirror can be a scene of imagination and wonder, but also a confirmation of loneliness. Notably, Mukhopadhyay and Williams's diverging accounts of mirror-gazing both substantially contradict prevailing assumptions from outside regarding autistic narcissism.‡

THE BROKEN METAPHOR: 'MIRROR NEURON' THEORY AND THE NORMATIVE STARE

Every mirror presents an alternate version of this world, created by this world. Through the otherizing of autism by and against dominant social values, it is unsurprising that the mirror has become an abiding metaphor in the discourse, as scientific and cultural narratives explored here will show. Barry's conjectures on narcissism add to a tradition in which theories of autism from outsiders, however well-intentioned, can still drastically under-estimate the diversity of autism as both entity and identity. What often seems to be the problem here is that, while autism is constructed as a deviation from norms, the ways in which it is narrated from outside remain *bound* by those norms, thus reinforcing them. The section 'The infantilizing of adult autism in diagnostic observations' concluded by stressing the uncertainty surround-ing how to acknowledge (and respect) autistic adulthood. Such uncertainties frequently lead to the cultural positioning of adult autism as an identity onto which undesirable social traits or associations are cast from outside – often from implicitly ableist positions.

Scientific discourse recurrently utilizes metaphor to seemingly explain the causes and nature of autism – or, at least, to simplify (and popularize) certain theories regarding these. Unfortunately, such metaphors tend to dramatize autistic otherness and often imply its inferiority. A recent example is the so-called broken mirror theory of autism, which attracted considerable atten-tion through the 2000s with scientific articles by Williams (2001), Iacoboni and Dapretto (2006) and, in particular, Oberman and Ramachandran (2007).[80] In slightly different ways, all three studies posited that the ostensible absence of reciprocation seen in autistic children could be explained by a (metaphori-cally named) 'mirror neuron system' (MNS) at the frontal cortex within the brains of humans and monkeys. In effect, this 'broken mirror' theory of autism

---

‡ **The Mirror Down the Garden**
    In certain childhood phases, I spent more time staring into a mirror than playing with other chil-dren. But the mirror was not about my own reflection – at least not that of my body; my mirror-twin only got in the way. I found 'my own reflection' in a different sense: the world of familiar rooms made oblique and untouchable. The further I tried to gaze into the reflection's edges, the more alluring it was – especially the grandfather clock, telling the symmetrical time. I once unhung an antique mirror from my grandparents' front room wall and carefully carried it into the garden. On placing the mirror against an outdoor wall, it was frustrating to realize that it could stay balanced only if at a certain, unsatisfying angle. Yet what I saw was still enough: another lawn, another shed. Another whole outside world. As an adult, I sometimes find a similar sense of peaceful curiosity in the act of writing.

rests on earlier theories that imitation and reciprocation involve activation of the same neurons in two individuals: hence the name 'mirror neuron'.[81] However, none of these articles actually used the metaphor of a broken mirror to refer to autism. It was instead unveiled by Ramachandran and Oberman ahead of their journal article in a piece for the popular magazine *Scientific American* (2006), announcing that studies of mirror neurons 'may explain how autism arises' and lead to 'better ways to diagnose and successfully treat the disorder'.[82] Showing a remarkable lack of empathy, Ramachandran and Oberman's magazine effort embodies one of the most offensively otherizing and dehumanizing assumptions about autistic adults: that none of us will seek and read publications on our condition. After characterizing autism with grimly familiar rhetoric of a terrible affliction, the authors uncritically imply that the 'broken' MNS in autism marks some kind of evolutionary throwback. They hypothesize 'that cross-domain [neurological] mapping may have originally developed to aid primates in complex motor-tasks' but 'eventually evolved into an ability to create metaphors': an ability which, Ramachandran and Oberman remind us, is often lacking in autistic people.[83] By evolving to enable recognition of metaphor, they continue, 'mirror neurons allowed humans to reach for the stars, instead of mere peanuts'.[84] It is clear what the authors were insinuating about autism and evolution with that metaphorical flourish.

The broken mirror theory (and its exposition in the popular media) was strongly criticized by Southgate and Hamilton (2008), who emphasized two points of caution. First, 'successful imitation goes beyond simply matching actions across bodies' (it involves multiple neurological processes). Second, 'a dysfunctional MNS should be expected to manifest in problems other than imitation' – the authors assert, for instance, that autistic people tend not to have difficulties in predicting actions (or patterns): processes that are also associated with what is known as the MNS, broken or otherwise.[85] In partial response to Southgate and Hamilton's critique, two initial pioneers of MNS research, Rizzolatti and Fabbri-Destro (2010), presented a more nuanced consideration of how it may still be relevant to autism, but this remains heavily speculative.[86] Southgate and Hamilton's 2008 summary remains pertinent: available data to scientifically support the theory fails to 'paint a clear picture of MNS activity in autism, being either difficult to interpret or contradictory'.[87] The most recent comparisons of MNS activity between autistic and neurotypical adults, by Schunke et al. (2016), suggest that imitative differences between the two groups are not attributable to this particular neuron system.[88]

The centrality of imitation (or lack thereof) to MNS theories reflects how social expectations of reciprocation – and thus, conformity and predictability – are encoded in the positioning of autism as *other* and 'broken'. Social mirroring performs and reinforces social norms. Gestures that demand responses are interpellations. This means that two (or more) brains are involved in the presence of autistic otherness – as are a series of social conventions and expectations. Imitation is a form of reciprocation, as are compliance and subordination. Considered in this way, when an autistic person does not reciprocate with the anticipated gestures, the process is not reducible to his or her MNS, for the pattern also implicates the observer.[89] The fact that such concerns remain almost entirely absent from the dominant scientific discourse remains problematic, for the oversight excuses expectations of 'normalcy' from any role in how autism may present (and be experienced) as an impairment.

OTHERIZING AUTISM PARENTS: REFRIGERATOR PSYCHIATRISTS AND THEIR 21ST-CENTURY SPECTRES

Autistic people themselves are not the only ones to have been oppressed by pseudo-scientific metaphors. In the 1950s and 1960s especially, the absence of any identifiable cause of autism led to parents being accused of having somehow triggered the condition unconsciously. This claim was wholly speculative. Again however, metaphor was essential to the spread and sensationalism of this theory via the trope of the 'refrigerator' mother. Although this theory has been challenged, revoked and discarded in orthodox autism psychiatry since the late 1960s, its legacy lingers into the present day – most conspicuously, in popular culture, as this discussion will expose.

In contrast with the later broken mirror theory, the most prominent, damning and damaging theories (and metaphors) surrounding autism in the 1950s and 1960s implied that imitative processes initially functioned all too acutely in autistic children prior to the onset of detectable traits. Kanner and subsequently, Bruno Bettelheim announced in both medical research papers and the mainstream media that autistic children were in effect mirroring unconscious emotional rejection from their parents. In 1956, Kanner (with Eisenberg) first used the refrigerator metaphor for autism parents.[90] Kanner elaborated on this in 1960 when profiled in *Time* magazine as a leading child psychiatrist. The feature culminates in a report that

> there is one type of child to whom even Dr. Kanner cannot get close. All too often this child is the offspring of highly organized, professional parents, cold and rational – the type that Dr. Kanner describes as 'just happening to defrost enough to produce a child'.[91]

Kanner emphatically renounced this theory on autism parenting in 1969.[92] However, in the meantime, his theories from the 1950s had been adapted and further popularized by Bettelheim. Although Bettelheim did not use the 'refrigerator parent' metaphor, he positioned the mother–child relationship as the cause of autism, expounding this belief in broadcast and print media, as well as his book *The Empty Fortress: Infantile Autism and the Birth of the Self* (first published 1967). In the much-publicized book's title, autism again becomes subjected to metaphor and anticipates two rhetorical features of 21st-century campaigns for 'cures'. The 'fortress' implies a battle; and, in the subtitle, autism is separated from the idea of a self.[93] But what also (sadly) remains pertinent is the cultural legacy of Bettelheim's otherizing of autism parents: his central premise throughout *The Empty Fortress* is a 'belief that the precipitating factor in infantile autism is the parent's wish that his child should not exist'.[94] Although Bettelheim's wording there alludes to fathers, this is more a mark of the book's essentially patriarchal stance, from which the responsibility of a child's development is pinned to the mother.[95] However, to quote the words of Uta Frith (in 2000): '*This theory was speculative and not based on evidence*' (my emphasis).[96] A wide array of observations and experiments (particularly studies on twins) have discredited the blaming of parents, as theorized by Kanner and Bettelheim.[97] Yet the refrigerator parent model persists in cultural portrayals of autism parents well into the 21st century. Here, the parent-blaming theory introduced by Kanner resurfaces metonymically, by implicit associations.

It remains telling that early medical narratives surrounding autism foregrounded metaphors (refrigerator parents; a child trapped in a fortress) because these theories were ultimately speculations which did not resolve the massive gaps in scientific understandings of autism but in hindsight, merely *marked* them. Not unlike metaphor itself, the narratives of the mid-period Kanner and (more extensively) Bettelheim sought to explain autism by relocating the focus, onto parents. The cultural persistence of such theories via metonymy points not just to the continuing mystery of how autism is caused but to patches of ignorance regarding how autism research has advanced since the 1960s.

Unfortunately – and avoidably – fictions of adult autism in which parents are peripheral continue to uncritically perpetuate Bettelheim-like assumptions in 21st-century popular culture. British television comedy-drama *Doc Martin* (2004–2017) foregrounds the autistic social traits of Martin, a 40-something general practitioner. It is no surprise when a psychiatrist neighbour casually mentions Martin's 'Asperger Syndrome'.[98] It would be more accurate to say that Martin (a superlatively intelligent but socially clumsy man) embodies the media's favourite ideas of Asperger syndrome. Although the series has involved numerous directors and writers, all periodically reinforce the same suggestion: Martin's autism was caused by his mother, Margaret. In the three episodes to feature Margaret (2005, 2013), she is cast as coldness personified. Her skeletally pallid complexion and minimal physical movements suggest a corpse. She explicitly tells Martin that the timing of his birth ruined her life.[99] In later appearances, Margaret is accused by a relative of having 'damaged' Martin during his childhood (a suggestion to which she is indifferent).[100] Martin is told by his aunt that she remembers him as a 'sensitive' infant 'shut down' because of 'the remoteness of his father and the coldness of his mother'.[101]

The UK is not the only region in which Bettelheim-style portrayals of parents persist in fictions of adult autism, particularly in television. In the third series of Swedish-Danish detective drama *The Bridge* (2014), the mother of the (otherwise) convincingly and powerfully presented autistic detective Saga Norén is revealed as having been neglectful and controlling towards her daughter. In addition, it is suggested that Saga's mother had Münchausen syndrome by proxy, which led to the death of Saga's sister.[102] (A variation on Münchausen by proxy is also latent in the prevalent suggestions that parents falsely insist their child is autistic to acquire extra school services, addressed in chapter 5). Although the portrayal of an autism mother in *The Bridge* is more complex and subtle than in *Doc Martin*, in both, the limited appearances of autism mothers invoke few characteristics *except* the bleak combination of implied emotional neglect in the past alongside continuing indifference to their grown-up children's feelings. The effect is thus to further – yet very misleadingly – reinforce that the foregrounded characters are autistic by resorting to outdated and widely criticized theories which unfortunately persist as clichéd metonyms. It is conspicuous, however, that these recent popular cultural dalliances with parent-blaming occur in fictions of *adult* autism, while screen portrayals of parents to autistic children have progressed.

The 2016 British television drama *The A Word* – adapted from the Israeli series *Yellow Peppers* (2010–2014) – depicts the parents of a young autistic son as loving and responsible, as well as convincingly concerned about his diagnosis and future. It is as if in television fictions of *adult* autism – invoking mothers born when parent-blaming was still rife – outdated and offensive tropes are still deemed acceptable. This further suggests assumptions that adult autists are somehow absent from the audience – or else, that culture industries consider us as such a minority that our feelings are worthless. Amid all this, a major consequence, rarely addressed even in clinical histories of autism, becomes exposed. Archaic but culturally lingering theories (or judgements) that autism is caused by parents' emotional rejection can be every bit as devastating to autistic children and adults as to their parents.

*   *   *

Half a century after the height of mother-blaming in autism discourse, the influence of parenting on an autistic child's development has gained renewed focus among some researchers and practitioners. This presents a deeply complex and sensitive series of considerations, as Mitzi Waltz (2013) confronts in her social and medical history of autism. Waltz quotes Canadian autism activist and researcher Michelle Dawson (2003), who uses a haunting metaphor to identify a problem rarely acknowledged in mainstream media coverage of adult autism:

> Bettelheim's worst and most enduring crime was to create an extreme: to push the pendulum up so high on one side that after its release it swung with a vengeance to the opposite extreme and stuck there. . . . A catastrophic view of autism means that any scrutiny of the parents' claims is not only unlikely, it is assumed to be reprehensible.[103]

The 'catastrophic view' named by Dawson refers to how parents – especially those emphasizing only devastation as a consequence of autism – have become some of the most culturally prominent spokespeople on the condition, creating the effect of removing autistics themselves 'from the vicinity of any important discussions or decisions'.[104] Thanks to a diverse group of autism advocates including Dawson herself, this marginalization of autistic voices may be gradually lessening. Yet Dawson's 2003 observations remain pertinent for further reasons. Bettelheim's legacy – including his discrediting – means that almost any suggestion that parenting can impact on an autistic child's development has become potentially reprehensible. Among the many problems here is an implication that to be autistic is to be outside of psychological, social or medical influence of any environmental factors: a dehumanizing notion that wrongly equates autistic subjectivity with a uniform, unchanging state. Autistic people will always be autistic, but this does not mean that our subjectivities and identities are fixed, nor that our experiences cannot be as formative as for *all* people. Another oppressive tendency incurred by Bettelheim's legacy is the sense that for autistic adults to acknowledge difficulties in relations with parents – which, in neurotypical lives, are accepted as an inevitable part of being human – is to risk reigniting connotations of blame. My experiences as a patient and also a researcher of autism psychiatry suggest to me that any such misinterpretations from professionals are now rare in the UK. It is, instead, contemporary culture that presents a repressive environment, in which to disclose any non-normative family experiences is to risk being misunderstood. Nevertheless, an effect of the vague, elusive notions of normalcy against which autism is conceptualized is that realities of autism parenting, in all their diversities and complexities, are still prone to trivialization via metaphors that invoke extremities. What also becomes suppressed in the same narrative process is recognition that *having* (as well as losing) parents is no less complex in an autistic life than in any other human life.

Recent changes in the framing of scientific hypotheses appear to be stirring a shift from the discredited belief that only poor parenting can cause (or explain) autism towards implications that only perfect parenting can offer hope for autistic children and their futures. In October 2016, the lead item on the BBC's UK News website announced: '"Super-parenting" Improves Autism' and carried the byline: 'Training Mums and Dads as "Super Parents" Can Dramatically Improve a Child's Autism, a Study Shows'.[105] The study, published hours earlier in *The Lancet*, is a report on the Preschool Autism Communication Trial (PACT), an 'intervention' programme in which clinicians observe parents interacting with their preschool-age autistic children and offer advice via techniques including filming and reviewing various situations.[106] The report claims that by enhancing parents' awareness of specific, subtle aspects of an individual autistic child's behaviours, 'improvements' – a persistent word in the *Lancet* article – will emerge in the child's social skills. Less is said in the report of how this marks an achievement on the part of the children, as well as the clinicians or parents. However, *The Lancet*'s article never uses the exact term 'super-parenting'. The phrase is actually presented by the BBC's reporter, expanding on a comment from one of the PACT report's co-authors:

> We're taking the parent's interaction with the child and taking it to a 'super' level, these children need something more than 'good enough', they need something exceptional.[107]

The story's positioning as the BBC's headline news reflects an ongoing fixation with autism on the part of the media, if not the public. Its wording, meanwhile, illustrates the continuing role of metaphor in narrating autism, and it is important to call 'super-parenting' just that: a metaphor, and yet another example of how this process can so easily disable, rather than enable, understandings of autism. The prefix 'super' derives from a Latin term meaning 'above or beyond'.[108] Not unlike 'normalcy', 'super' is evasive enough as a definition, let alone a reality. The dangerous implication of PACT's rhetoric is that it could condemn anything less than super-parenting as somehow a failure. This presents a grotesque irony, given that most autism parents are *already* 'super-parents' in the sense of meeting commitments far beyond those known or imaginable to most others. The PACT programme embodies super-parenting in the sense that clinicians, *alongside* a parent or parents, are working to help the child: there are multiple persons in this 'parenting'. At present, PACT (a trial programme) is a service that remains above and beyond those accessible to the majority of autism families.

The ongoing cultural focus on autism parents – including parents of autistic adults – is an extension of how autism itself is otherized and how there is an assumed need for it to be explained, if not 'treated'. Metaphor and metonymy continue to distort, distract from and displace the immeasurable spectrum of realities involved in autistic identities and in autism parenting. However, the complexities and mysteries surrounding autism have also led to the condition – or sometimes just the name – being used as a cultural metaphor for a range of wider social patterns and forces.

THE WHO'S *TOMMY* (1969) AND THE CULTURAL ONSET OF METAPHORICAL AUTISM

Foucault's illustration of the historical subjectivity (and thus changeability) inherent in social and medical reactions to mental difference should remind us of the dangers involved in assuming present attitudes to be more enlightened than those of the past. The recent medical and cultural discourses around autism parents appraised in the section 'Otherizing autism parents: refrigerator psychiatrists and their 21st-century spectres' exemplify how, between the 1960s and the 2010s, presumptions that chronology equates with genuine progress must always be critically interrogated. The following discussion demonstrates how one particular cultural text from the late 1960s actually presents a more substantial and crucially more *questioning* narrative of autism – and autism parenting – than the recent portrayals addressed earlier.

An early, extensive and (in hindsight) prescient positioning of autism itself as a cultural metaphor is The Who's 1969 double-album rock opera *Tommy*, conceived by the band's songwriter and guitarist, Pete Townshend. British film director Ken Russell's mesmerizingly disturbing cinematic adaptation appeared to acclaim in 1975 (starring The Who's singer Roger Daltrey as Tommy). Reflecting the gradual cultural recognition of autism, the condition did not become widely mentioned in relation to Townshend's narrative until the 1990s, when *Tommy* became a Broadway musical, directed by Des McAnuff (1992). Autism is never named in these three versions: Tommy is (to quote the recurring lyrical motif) 'deaf, dumb and blind'. Yet, *Newsweek* critic Jack Kroll casually praised the opening scenes of the 1992 musical for poignantly depicting 'an autistic child'.[109] Uta Frith (2003), while noting that additional themes are 'superimposed' onto autism in *Tommy*, hails the 1969 album as one of the first portrayals to address the sensory aspects of the condition. In Frith's 2003 view, Townshend's own (albeit retrospective) comments on *Tommy* provide 'direct evidence' of 'the phenomenon of autism contributing to art and culture'.[110] Since the 1990s, Townshend has increasingly referred to Tommy as 'autistic'.[111] In 2013, he stated that in a 'revelation' while writing the songs, he decided that the ' "deaf, dumb and blind" hero could actually be – in effect – autistic; he would not be physically disabled at all'.[112] Townshend's first published references to Tommy as autistic appeared in 1977 – eight years after the album's release but more than a decade before the success of *Rain Man* (1988) demonstrated the condition's cultural allure.[113] I therefore use this rock album to illustrate that while popular culture (including *Tommy*) has often sensationalized autism, this does not always exclude critical engagement with the meanings of autism in relation to wider social values and forces. Metaphors (though inconsistent across the songs) are key to how *Tommy* achieves this and, as will be shown, instrumental music itself enables one of the narrative's most evocative portrayals of autistic experience.

Metaphor is an interactive process: it can be as much an act of interpretation as of authorship. Autism becomes consistently identifiable as a motif on The Who's 1969 album when we view the figure of Tommy using some – but only some – degree of metaphor. Tommy is born an apparently typical baby but as an infant he loses speech and (seemingly) hearing and sight. The song evoking this transition, 'Amazing Journey', focuses on Tommy's inner subjectivity, omnisciently narrated as a state of transfixed detachment. He is also 'amazing' to those around him, and this is conveyed in a manner anticipating later fascinations with autistic otherness as a focus of speculation and projection from outside. 'Sickness', states the lyric, can take human thought 'Where minds can't usually go'.[114] Deaf, 'dumb' and blind, Tommy has multiple impairments which – as is the case in different ways in autism – intersect. These impairments, again as in autism, involve the mind and the senses and therefore the body. They also drastically impair his communication. As if in an extreme dramatization of autism, Tommy's loss of hearing, sight and speech makes him seemingly unreachable to his family and to doctors.

Townshend later called *Tommy*'s configurations of disability 'daft, flawed and muddled'.[115] That may remain true. Nonetheless, Townshend's choice of Deaf-blindness as a metaphor enables a thought-provoking contemplation of autism, which still bears a resonance with how the condition continues to be narrated five decades later. But it also remains necessary to acknowledge how *Tommy*'s narrative of Deaf-blindness as a metaphor is unfortunately misleading. Deaf-blindness has never meant that the person appears (as Tommy does to his doctor) 'completely unreceptive'.[116] The lives and work of countless Deaf-blind individuals including Laura Bridgman, Georgia Griffith, Haben Girma and, most famously, Helen Keller (who died in 1968, the year before *Tommy*'s release) demonstrate that this identity does not equate with inability to communicate. But then, nor is any autistic person 'completely unreceptive'. I labour these emphases here not to suggest that *Tommy* irresponsibly misrepresents impairment but to point again to how metaphors surrounding disability often obstruct knowledge and understanding. In other ways, though, metaphors both through and surrounding autism across *Tommy* recognize aspects of this way of being in a depth that was peerless in late 1960s' popular culture.

Tommy's lyrics are eloquent and impassioned, but equally essential to the album's invocation of autism is the music itself. More extensively than through the words, the subjectivity of a preverbal child, adolescent and young adult is signified by two instrumentals, 'Sparks' and 'Underture'. These tracks present variations around the same guitar riffs but differ in length. 'Sparks' (the album's fifth track) lasts two minutes; 'Underture', three songs later, is by some way *Tommy*'s longest piece, lasting just under ten minutes. 'Underture' (a term seemingly invented by Townshend, or *Tommy*'s musically ambitious producer Kit Lambert) contrasts with the album's opening 'Overture' in more than name. 'Overture' presents a medley of the album's subsequently recurrent melodies before a sung introduction. As such, 'Overture' is characterized by musical transition, as well as lyrical omniscience. However, it is 'Underture' – symmetrically closing the album's first half – that most boldly subverts conventional expectations of popular music, including those followed elsewhere on *Tommy*.

While most of the album's lyrics narrate Tommy's disability from outside, the ten-minute 'Underture' musically invites a more complex imagining of his inner state. Like 'Sparks', this instrumental interlude revolves around a guitar sequence of A minor to G major to F major to E major. As songwriter and guitarist Paul Wheeler points out, a very similar sequence underpins numerous popular songs of the 1960s, including The Beach Boys' 'Good Vibrations' (1966) as well as The Who's own 'Pinball Wizard', later on *Tommy*.[117] The harmonic essence of 'Underture' is thus relatively conventional for its time. It is the exposed *repetition* of its refrain that makes this piece audacious. Presenting listeners with something like a musical maze, 'Underture' removes a visual component: there are no longer any verbal images. Returning to the guitar-led refrain of the earlier, shorter 'Sparks', the long and repetitious 'Underture' continually defeats expectations of hearing sung *words*, suggesting both the disappearance of Tommy's speech and his inability to decipher that of others. Vocals are sporadically featured, but are wordless, repeating the same sound: an extended, monotone 'Ahhh' (not unlike a meditative *OM*). I must acknowledge here that as a verbal, non-Deaf and non-blind person, my observations regarding 'Underture' and the absence of language, sight or hearing are profoundly limited. However, I do wish to emphasize here the potency of 'Underture' as a musical metaphor for autism. Key to this is the wordless track's repetitiveness within its unusual length. The Who omitted 'Underture' from their otherwise near-complete live performances of *Tommy* in 1969–1970, perhaps because its only minimally progressive refrains risked boring the audience (and the musicians). There is, however, an important quality to hear and contemplate in the recording: the seemingly cyclic acoustic guitar-led refrains are underscored throughout by a series of subtle variations. Thus, I am emphasizing here an obviousness that I have long hoped, and failed, to find recognized in autism discourse: within repetition and 'sameness', the subtlest *differences* present extraordinarily rewarding points of fascination.§

*   *   *

Although Tommy's parents and peers assume him to be 'deaf, dumb and blind', a doctor eventually declares that Tommy *can* see and hear, but has some mysterious 'inner block', for which there is no 'operation' nor any other 'chance' of a cure.[118] What the doctor calls the 'inner block' ostensibly isolating Tommy from others resembles Bettelheim's metaphor of autism in the title *The Empty Fortress* (1967). The most dated aspect of *Tommy* is thus the suggestion of emotional trauma as the cause of autism. As an infant, Tommy becomes 'deaf, dumb and blind' after witnessing the murder of his stepfather by the boy's own biological father. At the climax of the song '1921', Tommy's parents repeat to him that he didn't 'hear' or 'see' this incident and must 'say nothing' of what has happened to his stepfather and, indeed, to him.[119] Responding literally to his parents, Tommy ceases talking and becomes so unresponsive that he passes as being blind and deaf. As Pinchevski (2011) states, Tommy 'rehearses' Bettelheim's now rejected theory of autism as 'an extreme response to extreme circumstances, typically caused by the parents'.[120] Townshend states that he 'began to do some serious research on autism' and found Bettelheim's *The Empty Fortress*.[121] Unfortunately, Townshend's comments on autism even in 2013 do not suggest familiarity with developments in how autism is understood post-Bettelheim. Nevertheless, *Tommy* also narrates autism in what, with hindsight, were remarkably progressive ways. This 1969 album presents a more creative, critical treatment of

---

§ **'You try so hard but still don't understand'**

It is worth momentarily returning to Armitage's comments on how owning the entire works of Bob Dylan would suggest 'a kind of autism'. In 2016, Columbia Records released a 36-disc CD boxed set of Dylan's complete live recordings from his 1966 tour. This promises recordings of 18 performances of mostly identical setlists, in mostly the same order, performed by the same musicians. I can easily imagine how my purchasing this commodity might seem to reaffirm neurotypical ideas of my own autistic love of 'collections' and 'sameness'. Yet to me, the appeal of this set is for the very opposite reason: I cherish the *differences* within each performance, from night to night. The root of this excitement, in my 'case' at least, is sensory: I hear – or, at least, find fascination in – subtle differences, which most others apparently do not. None of which, of course, prevents me from being within the ideals of Columbia's marketing department.

the Kanner-Bettelheim model than is attempted or provided in the television fictions from the 2010s, discussed in the section 'Otherizing autism parents: refrigerator psychiatrists and their 21st-century spectres'. Diverging from Bettelheim's implicitly patriarchal speculations, Townshend does not position the mother as the cause of the trauma. Tommy's parents both remain loving constants throughout the narrative.

'Christmas', the seventh track, shows Tommy sitting alone and seemingly 'unaware' while other children eagerly open their presents.[122] The excitably up-tempo verses are then interrupted by the father (whose lines are sung by Townshend) despairingly asking Tommy if he can hear him. However, the later recurrence of this refrain in 'Christmas' suggests that it is the father who cannot 'hear' his autistic son. For between the father's two refrains comes the slow, falsetto (and thus childlike) refrain pleading 'See me . . . feel me'. Singing in a different key, Tommy's father does not seem to hear this, and the lyric proceeds to invoke a parent's attempts to interact with an autistic child in just the ways that other parents seem to do with other children. But the 'Christmas' lyric incurs an additional, interpellative force, boldly addressing the intersection of disability and religion to raise a heavy and highly emotive question. Tommy's father wonders how his preverbal child can be 'saved' from damnation if he does not 'know' Christ or the Gospel. The possible distress that such a thought might present to some autism families is a delicate matter. Yet the apparently fundamentalist Christianity of Tommy's father seems to assume an ableist, occidental and colonialist Christ, whose message is limited to literal, culturally exclusive, verbal language.

Townshend's 1969 lyrics anticipate what would become two key focal points in mainstream 21st-century autism rhetoric: spectacular talent (on pinball machines) and the socially encouraged search to 'cure' his condition. In different ways, processes of otherizing autism manifest both celebrations of talent and calls for a cure. Their combination makes *Tommy* unusual, since celebrations of autistic talent often undermine emphases on impairment and thus the desirability of a 'cure'. Tommy, the 'deaf, dumb and blind kid', becomes a pinball champion ('Pinball Wizard').[123] Here again is a precursor to subsequent associations: pinball machines, popular in amusement arcades and cafés in the mid-20th century, were cultural antecedents to computerized games. However, in Townshend's 1969 lyrics and more so in Russell's 1975 film adaptation, what makes the adult Tommy a subject of media fascination – and in the songs 'Miracle Cure' and 'Sensation', a Christ-like figure attracting followers and 'disciples' – is his sudden and complete recovery from apparent autism. This means that in the final quarter of the narrative, Tommy's experiences largely cease to resonate with the condition. Yet the epiphanic importance placed on his transformation – narrated as a cure from outside rather than growth via his own natural agency – prefigures the present-day focus of cultural, scientific and political missions to effectively normalize autistic people.

The image used to reinforce Tommy's autism in the lyrics and which becomes crucial to his metaphorical transition out of this subjectivity, is a mirror. Describing how he 'began to do some serious research on autism' while writing *Tommy*, Townshend elaborated in 2013: 'Somewhere I read about an autistic child who had stared constantly into a mirror, as though he was the only person in the world'.[124] He may have meant 'Charles N.', one of 11 children described by Kanner (1943). Charles's mother described to Kanner how her son was currently 'interested in reflecting light from mirrors and catching reflections', adding: 'When he is interested in a thing, you cannot change it. He would pay no attention to me and show no recognition of me if I enter the room'.[125] In perspective and sentiment, the quotation closely resembles the mother's narrative in Townshend's 'Smash the Mirror': the pivotal lyric on *Tommy*.

In 'Go to the Mirror!', a doctor establishes that Tommy *can* see when the young adult, considered blind, becomes transfixed with his own reflection. In the subsequent 'Smash the Mirror', Tommy's mother angrily chastises him because he seems to see only himself and not her. The mirror here invokes the notion of autism as an intense and limiting focus on *the self*. As such, the lyric takes the notion of autism – which, as the section 'Conjecturing otherness: autism, metaphor and metonymy' considered, is partially a metaphor – literally. Tommy's 'miracle cure' occurs when his mother smashes the mirror. The brutality of destroying an autistic person's point of fascination is not a concern implied within the lyrics. Instead, the disappearance of Tommy's reflection (musically evoked through the fading half of a sustained piano chord) symbolizes surrender of the self to enable spiritual growth: a principle variously common to Buddhism, Islam and Christianity. However, Townshend's lyrics were more influenced by the teachings of his Irani-Indian spiritual master, Meher Baba (1894–1969). In 1977, the lyricist stated that when writing *Tommy*, he conceived of an 'analogy' between 'the autistic child' and what Meher Baba taught was the unenlightened 'illusion' of life without consciousness of God. Townshend elaborated: 'The device was that when [Tommy] came out of his autism and became *normal*' (my emphasis), this presented such a 'miracle' that he acquired 'a sort of Saintlihood' because 'his experience in that state was quite unique'.[126] Townshend's use of autism as a metaphor for lack of spiritual consciousness bluntly exemplifies narrative prosthesis, as his talk of analogy and metaphorical 'device' indicate.[127]

Narrative prosthesis as critiqued by Mitchell and Snyder (2000) incurs both dependence on and exploitation of disability to serve a range of rhetorical purposes. But such aspects of *Tommy* do not preclude the narrative's engage-ment with social, emotional, cultural and political matters in relation to autism. The cultural fixation on the 'cured' Tommy as a saint-like figure ('Miracle Cure', 'Sensation') obliquely exposes the elevation of normalcy itself. The same songs also present ominous imaginings of how – should indi-viduals ever be 'cured' of autism – such identities might come to dominate cultural expectations regarding the condition.

*   *   *

Unusually, even by 21st-century standards of autism portrayals from outside, Tommy's identity is never defined simply by disability but by disability at the intersection of much broader social influences and experiences. As well as religion and spirituality, these include alternative healing ('Eyesight to the Blind'); bullying ('Cousin Kevin'), sexual initiation and drugs ('The Acid Queen'); sexual abuse ('Fiddle About' and, more ambiguously, '1921'); leisure ('Pinball Wizard'); psychiatry ('Go to the Mirror!'); media ('Miracle Cure'); and, of course, the implicit yet constant centrality of normalcy. Positioned in relation to each of these forces, Tommy becomes a symbol of vulnerability. While he is otherized through multiple impairments, these intensify themes of human innocence and experience. Again, this entails a prosthetic use of autism in the narrative, but *Tommy* nonetheless points to how, while autistic identity may be pervasive, no autistic person's identity is *reducible* to the condition because it is always converging with other social patterns and identities.

Using facets of autism as a metaphorical means of addressing broader social forces, The Who's 1969 *Tommy* is a precursor to a scale of com-mentary more common to literary novels in later decades, as exemplified in texts addressed elsewhere in this book including Douglas Coupland's *Microserfs* (1995) and Margaret Atwood's *Oryx and Crake* (2003). Like these and other later texts, *Tommy* uses disability as narrative prosthesis, and as with the novels, Townshend's lyrics reflect medical and cultural associations of autism that were dominant in its time. Between Townsh-end's *Tommy* in 1969 and, for instance, *The Bridge* (2011–2017), we see a shift in association of autism from multiple disabilities – the 'deaf, dumb and blind' trope – to a (very) high-functioning identity. To compare these portrayals, decades apart, is to be reminded of the subjectivity of how autism has been conceptualized in its brief, formal history from the late 1930s to the present.

Yet what remains constant is the accentuated otherizing of autistic sub-jectivities, traits and identities. Parents, too, continue to be recipients of this. Again, it is cautionary to adopt a Foucaultian emphasis that chronological progress does not in any simple way ensure or yield more humane perspectives on medical otherness. In much-publicized histories of autism up to the present day, such as Silberman's *Neurotribes* (2015) and Donvan and Zucker's *In a Different Key* (2016), chronologically linear narratives culminate by (rightly) emphasizing the emergence of Neurodiversity and Autism Rights movements. However, accounts of overt parent-blaming during the 1950s and 1960s are largely confined to the middle chapters as if signifying an anomalously unenlightened age in autism history from which we have now recovered. To give just one example of how this is not the case, dominant treatments for autism in France (often involving Lacanian psychotherapy) remain highly controversial and were the subject of a 33-page complaint report from Autism-Europe (2002).[128] Such 'therapies' for autistic families in France were also critically exposed in Sophie Roberts's (subsequently banned) documentary *Le Mur* (*The Wall*) in 2011.[129] Of particular concern is the use in France of 'packing', in which naked autistic children are tightly wrapped in towels which have been refrigerated.[130] Another problem (especially but not exclusively) in France is the mother-blaming still inherent in certain psychoanalytical views of autism. Barry (2015), researching in Ireland, uncritically quotes the view of fellow Lacanian, Françoise Dolto (from 1984), that autism is caused by a 'rupture' in the mother–infant relationship.[131] Thus, while progress is undoubtedly apparent in the growing Autism Rights movements, it remains important not to be complacent and to continually consider why we *need* such movements.

Tommy's 'cure' in adulthood leaves the final quarter of The Who's 1969 album relevant to autism only in the hypothetical sense that an ostensibly post-autistic figure becomes the subject of mass media fixation and a cult-like following. Through the disappearance of disability, *Tommy* implicates the cultural uncertainty surrounding the figure of the autistic adult. Although this chapter has so far considered various fictions in which adult autism is either named directly or established via stereotypes, The Who's album is the only outside narrative to progressively contemplate autistic experience beneath the surface of the spectacle. Therefore, I will end this chapter by focusing on the work of two autistic authors who confront the anxieties of adult autistic identity without compromise, through poetry.

AUTISM AND THE PERSON: LES MURRAY'S 'IT ALLOWS A PORTRAIT IN LINE SCAN AT FIFTEEN'

A tender and troubled depiction of autism at the onset of adulthood is Australian author Les Murray's poem 'It Allows a Portrait in Line Scan at Fifteen' (1994), written about his then teenage son.[132] In various interviews, Murray has described himself as 'mildly autistic'.[133] He conveyed this allusively in 'Portrait of the Autist as a New-World Driver' (1977), published before his son's birth and, more overtly, in the 2006 poem 'The Tune on Your Mind' (discussed in chapter 5). However, Murray's 1994 portrait of his son presents a person for whom the condition is more disabling. The poem was published in three literary periodicals in 1994 and then in Murray's volume *Subhuman Redneck Poems* (1996); it has since been included in numerous poetry anthologies and later selections of Murray's work. Of four subtly different versions of the text and title, I prioritize the most recent, as featured in Murray's *New Collected Poems* (2003) and then subsequent publications.[134] 'It Allows a Portrait in Line Scan at Fifteen' is perhaps the best-known work by one of Australia's most widely read and translated poets, and rarely goes unmentioned in media profiles of Murray. Such prominence reflects the intrigue surrounding the subject of autism, yet the poem is extraordinary in its own right among cultural narratives of the condition. Unlike many textbook profiles or fictional portrayals, 'Portrait in Line Scan' is not didactic in the sense of reductively explaining autism by presenting a composite personification. Based on one individual, it instead offers something more enlightening by prompting questions rather than offering answers.

Within Murray's title, 'line scan' suggests properties of poetry; line scan is also the function by which certain types of cameras capture images, one tiny 'line' of input at a time. With this metaphor, Murray's 'Portrait in Line Scan' of his son acknowledges that an individual is being depicted via another's subjectivity. Line scan (as distinct from area scan) is also the most effective technology for creating still images of rapid movement. This theme of elusiveness, and of the potential distortion in a still depiction of a moving subject, is integral to Murray's lines. Not unlike a line scan photograph, this poem – rich in visual imagery – identifies details of the person portrayed one line at a time, forming a single piece of text.

Comprising one stanza built of 60 statement-like sentences over 42 lines in varying lengths, Murray's free verse 'It Allows a Portrait in Line Scan at Fifteen' is more sombre, less linguistically playful than many of his poems. Piecing together the poem's multitudinous motifs and facets is a bit like being presented with a Picasso portrait in jigsaw form. The sequencing of events and details is only fragmentally chronological. To see the subtle consistencies across the poem's almost cubist disjointedness is to suspend any conclusions: a process perhaps not dissimilar to that required when seeking to empathize with cognitive otherness. The fragmented nature of the poem's chronology also invokes both the vividness and complexities of memory as a dimension of autistic consciousness. Two particularly heavy memories recalled in the poem – one by the father, one by the son – concern interpellation: the naming of autism.

With no clear indication of disability in the enigmatic title, 'It Allows a Portrait in Line Scan at Fifteen' begins by describing an unusually troubled and talented boy. While indications of autism increase with successive details (more strongly two decades on, in an era of such greater attention to the condition), it is not until the 13th line that autism is mentioned:

> Giggling, he climbed all over the dim Freudian psychiatrist who told us how autism resulted from 'refrigerator' parents.[135]

This detail was added when the poem was published in Murray's *Subhuman Redneck Poems* (1996). The 1994 version introduced autism much more ambiguously (later, at line 28), with the following question, seemingly but not exclusively signifying the son's voice via italics: '*Is that very autistic, to play video games all day?*'.[136] This remained in the 1996 version, along with the 'Freudian psychiatrist' line. In Murray's 2001 volume *Learning Human: New Selected Poems* and subsequent publications, the 'video games' question was omitted. Although the poem was published in four subtly different versions from 1994 to 2003, Murray's only changes to the text involved when, and how, autism is directly named. Constant through every version of the poem, however, is the following detail (six lines before the end):

> *Don't say word!* when he was eight forbade the word 'autistic' in his presence.[137]

The (original) italics signifying the son's voice, this line quietly unveils the poem's own politics of naming 'It' and affirms the son's agency as the portrait's subject. Hence, for most of the poem, from the title downwards, the name of autism is simply 'It'. But 'It Allows a Portrait in Line Scan at Fifteen' is simultaneously a poem about 'us' as a whole family – and with the added interpellation from the callous (or refrigerator) Freudian psychiatrist in the 1996 version, the poem gains a bleaker layer, as parents, too, become oppressed by others' ignorance.

Although Sigmund Freud (1856–1939) never wrote about autism, the influence of Freudian psychoanalysis in the mid-20th century was such that various influential psychologists conjectured autism's cause as psychogenic, rather than innate or genetic as is now understood. Yet the sometimes dubious word 'innate' is crucial here: as Feinstein points out, the Austrian-born Kanner was writing not only in the era and aftermath of the Third Reich, but in a period when eugenic ideas held high currency in America, where he was researching.[138] In July 1942, the American Psychiatric Association's official journal debated whether children with 'feeble-mindedness' over the age of five should be given 'euthanasia' both for their own sake and that of their parents.[139] Considered in this context, Kanner's parent-blaming can, with some speculative generosity, be regarded as a misguided effort to protect autism from eugenic debates. But it is Bettelheim, whose conjectures on autism were strongly influenced by Freud's models of the anal and phallic stages of personality development, who remains the most extensive and notorious protagonist in blaming autism on parents.[140] However, Bettelheim's cultural prominence in the 1960s should not detract from the fact that others influentially took comparable lines in blaming parents. For instance, in the 1970s, psychoanalyst Donald Meltzer's post-Freudian *Explorations in Autism* (1975) was less overtly negative about autism than Bettelheim's narratives had been, and Meltzer's conviction that autism is rooted in mothering is more measured in expression. Nonetheless, Meltzer reinforces the mother-blaming angle, and the 1975 book was reissued in 2008.[141]

In Murray's poem, the arresting, haunting presence of the psychiatrist's scare-quoted refrigerator interpellation suggests how, in a deeply unfortunate transference, unempathic professionals could enact a variant on the very accusation aimed at parents in psychogenic autism theories. As such, the psychiatrist's interpellation in the poem is comparable to the rupture in parent-child relationships as speculated by Bettelheim in the damage it could wreak. As the section 'Otherizing autism parents: refrigerator psychiatrists and their 21st-century spectres' discussed, the refrigerator parent theory of autism still persists in various 21st-century narratives.[142] However, Murray's naming of the theory in 'Portrait in Line Scan' (from the 1996 version onwards) differs importantly from these. First, Murray refers to the theory critically, and from the perspective *of* an autism parent. Second, Murray's poem opposes the refrigerator supposition throughout. It does so through its loving attentiveness to the son as portrayed but also through the details – even in just one line – of how the psychiatrist is depicted. In a benevolent gesture of agency and defiance, the son undermines medical authority insofar as it is represented in the poem, giggling as he climbs 'all over the dim Freudian psychiatrist'.

* * *

Murray's 'It Allows a Portrait in Line Scan at Fifteen' invokes various contrasts but is less a poem of binaries than hybridities: between childhood and adulthood, nature and society, other and self, silence and speech, impairment and disability. But the most complex tension is between autism itself and a son's growth as a person, between *It* and *he*. At certain moments in the poem as discussed below, *It* appears to somehow separate the boy from his own will, if not his very self. More frequently, however, the lines present autism as something that distinguishes – and, often, distances – the 15-year-old from *others*. Through its complex configurations of autism, others and the self,

Murray's 'Portrait in Line Scan' becomes especially compelling in relation to semantic (and political) debates about whether we should refer to the 'person with autism' or the 'autistic person'.

Following Jim Sinclair's essential article 'Don't Mourn for Us' (first published 1993), many autistic authors (myself included) have increasingly favoured 'autistic person' (or 'Autistic person') over 'person with autism'. Nonetheless, as a parent's perspective, 'It Allows a Portrait in Line Scan at Fifteen' points towards how and why the person-first naming carries an important honesty. Both philosophically and experientially, the person-first definition is *lived* by many individuals and their families. In a literal sense, for self and for others, the person is present *before* the diagnosis because autism is rarely identifiable before the points at which developmental 'milestones' are expected as babyhood moves into infancy. From the 1996 version onwards, Murray's poem mirrors this process by withholding the first mention of autism until the 13th line, which also presents the psychiatrist's singular appearance. Yet 'It Allows a Portrait in Line Scan' also confronts how autism is much more than just a name or diagnosis, through disparately sequenced declarations including:

'He no longer hugs to disarm. It is gradually allowing him affection.'
'He'd begun to talk, then returned to babble, then silence. It withdrew speech for years.'
'*Eye contact, Mum!* means he truly wants attention. It dislikes I-contact.'[143]

Murray's lines go on to address ways in which to be autistic is – increasingly, as adulthood approaches – to be disabled in a social sense. But more starkly, the poem recognizes a way of being, which, for the teenager portrayed, is limiting (if not impairing) in a more immediate, intimate sense, affecting much in the son's interactions with his family. 'It requires rulings', and the quoted examples typify how the poem's statement-like lines recurrently address what *It* allows and forbids, almost to the extent that autism is personified as *other* to the boy's own self. In the earlier lines especially, *It* is positioned as both a force and obstacle between the son and other people. Only 'gradually' is *It* 'allowing him' affection. *It* 'withdrew speech for years'. When *he* 'truly wants attention' from his mother, *It* dislikes 'I-contact'.

In individual lines – though not as an entire text – Murray's poem might, on the surface, seem to prefigure the rhetoric of the powerful, divisive and misleadingly named charity 'Autism Speaks' (founded 2005). The organization's most widely disseminated interpellations – targeting parents' emotions and thus their charity – personify autism as if a demon possessing a child. A lengthy example of this approach is the sensationally titled documentary *Sounding the Alarm* (2015).[144] The same notion of autism and humanity being somehow separable by science underpins the charity's ominous long-standing mission (nominally retracted only in 2016) of funding 'research into the causes, prevention, treatments and a cure for autism' – procedures that would threaten to obliterate autism itself from the world.[145] However, I address this parallel between facets of 'Portrait in Line Scan' and the agenda of Autism Speaks not to *align* the poem with the controversial charity but to distinguish them, and to highlight how the intensely complex (and emotional) questions felt by autism parents are manipulated by this organization.

Autism does sometimes involve painfully wondering about how different an individual might be (or, worse, might have been) if, in some fantasy, your or my or his or her impairment or difference was not here. Such thoughts can be hard to avoid when autism is so often narrated and interpellated to us in negative terms. The problem is that when (for example) I have been frustrated or embarrassed about being *slower* than most of my peers to meet developmental and lifestyle milestones, I have been internalizing and there-fore reinforcing ableist assumptions that normalcy is meaningful, attainable or desirable. Against such oppression, a gift of Murray's 'Portrait in Line Scan' is that unlike most depictions of autism in novels, films and television, it gives minimal depiction of neurotypical others. This poem thus transcends the stifling essence of ableism: the comparison of an individual with the majority. Nevertheless, Murray directly confronts one of the most emotive, complex and potentially disabling aspects of autism. 'He'd begun to talk'; then 'It withdrew speech for years'. Contrasting profoundly with the rhetori-cal terror of Autism Speaks, Murray's poem does not express or interpellate any emotive judgement on the son's silence. Again, Sinclair's 'Don't Mourn for Us' is pertinent, urging parents:

> You try to relate to your autistic child, and the child doesn't respond. . . . That's the hardest thing to deal with, isn't it? The only thing is, it isn't true. . . . You try to relate as parent to child, using your own understanding of normal children, your own feelings about parenthood, your own experiences and intuitions about relationships. And the child doesn't respond in any way you can recognize as being part of that system. That does not mean the child is incapable of relat-ing *at all*.[146]

Murray's poem shows how a father and son related without two-way verbal communication by simply *being together*. Even so, Sinclair recognizes that the absence of expected reciprocation from a child can be, for many parents, 'the hardest thing to deal with'. When language is restricted for the autis-tic self – and, thus, for others trying to understand the person's needs and subjectivity – the wondering and the worries of a family might become all the more intense. This reality for some families must not be denied; nor must it be intellectually trivialized.

The work of a father with Asperger syndrome portraying a more disabling autism in his teenage son, 'It Allows a Portrait in Line Scan at Fifteen' allows contemplation of relations between the diagnosis and the person without inflicting any superficial sense of *resolution*. The poem is an open, empathic and proud portrait of a son – and fundamental to how it honours him (and honours autism itself) is its recognition of the difficulties he sometimes endures. But before discussing the poem's confrontation of pressures inflicted on autistic people by a society not yet able to accommodate neurological (and social) difference, the nature and experience of autistic distress as narrated in Murray's lines deserve careful consideration.

In vital opposition and resistance to ableist calls for the normalizing of neurological difference, we have neurodiversity movements which themselves are, aptly, diverse in their stances. However, the occasional reduction of autism and other conditions to mere 'labels' (rather than valid and sometimes *enabling* names) in neurodiversity rhetoric can risk downplaying the distresses that may be experienced within the mind and body.[147] 'Portrait in Line Scan' observes a son's many pleasures and fascinations, but to suggest that this poem frames autism as *mere* difference would be to neglect its barest detail of vulnerability:

> It does not allow proportion. Distress is absolute, shrieking, and runs him at frantic speed through crashing doors.[148]

Amid the still increasing cultural emphases (and expectations) that some autistic people can demonstrate superlative talents, the *distress* involved at times with this way of being remains too often overlooked. More subtly, but scarcely less problematically, many fictional representations of autism, as discussed later in this book, tend to foreground autistic special interests in certain topics or pursuits at the expense of fully recognizing their obverse: anxiety. A mind that is capable of utter enthrallment through specific points of interest might also be a mind with the capacity to become similarly overwhelmed by fear and confusion. As Murray's poem states, 'It does not allow proportion'.

In a pioneering 2005 article, Dinah Murray, Mike Lesser and Wenn Lawson – all autistic academics – formulate the term 'monotropism' to deepen understandings of what, in psychiatric orthodoxy, tends to be framed as the 'restricted range of interests' in autism.[149] The authors discuss monotropism as an autistic tendency in which attention becomes preoccupied by certain objects, details or tasks. Through a combination of literature review and personal experience, they also detail the emotions accompanying monotropism, including 'terror, ecstasy, rage and desolation' as well as 'detachment' and 'joy'.[150] Of particular note are the article's various emphases on how 'for many of us diagnosed as being on the spectrum of autism, the demand of having to "pay attention" to so many things, simultaneously, is a nightmare'.[151] In relation to these all too recognizable realities of autistic experience, Les Murray's poem is uniquely effective.

As a whole and through its form, 'It Allows a Portrait in Line Scan at Fifteen' invites – and even offers to enable for readers – a cognitive glimpse of autistic subjectivity. Its lines are unusually long: for centuries, 10 to 14 syllables per line has been the dominant convention for poetry in English. In this poem, some of Murray's lines reach 30 syllables. The term 'line scan' here gains further implications. Each line creates a moment of something akin to a monotropic state through its very length – before each subsequent line disrupts the focus entirely. Through its mass of disjointed detail, Murray's single-stanza portrait confers a reading state akin to both sensory and communication overload: experiences which, for many autistic people, young and aged, are among the most demanding aspects of daily life. Yet while the poem shifts abruptly across different themes and settings, amid all this, the young man's key fascinations – drawing and the study of land and soils – are recurrently invoked, suggesting the continuity they provide within a seemingly disordered outside world. We also have this detail:

> When he ran away constantly it was to the greengrocers to worship stacked fruit.[152]

Across Murray's poem, autistic distress and autistic delight are invoked to mutually intensifying effect. Monotropism can cause 'absolute' distress but can also yield a meditative state of near-religious experience, as with the 'worshipping' of stacked fruit. This detail brings an exquisite hint – from outside – of another dimension of autistic subjectivity: the *sensory*. Again, however, Murray's portrait does not flinch from the complexities and difficulties that this can bring.

The senses are essential to communication and, like language, the senses can link physical and cerebral subjectivity. 'It Allows a Portrait in Line Scan at Fifteen' narrates autistic sensory experience with rare and valuable intimacy. A physical obviousness (and pain) to many autistic people is the under-discussed fact that the senses also operate *inside* the body, daily, through (among much else) the digestive system. 'When he worshipped fruit, he screamed as if poisoned when it was fed to him' and 'It still won't allow him fresh fruit, or orange juice with bits in it'.[153] Murray's poem thus positions autism as a way of being which 'allows' and 'forbids' the body. But what does the neurotypically dominated world allow and forbid – or enable and disable – of autistic identity?

Across Murray's 'Portrait in Line Scan', some of the most impairing aspects of autistic life emerge not from within the self, but from outside, by wider social forces:

> *If they* (that is, he) *are bad the police will put them in hospital.*
> He sometimes drew the farm amid Chinese or Balinese rice terraces.
> When a runaway, he made uproar in the police station, playing at three times adult speed.[154]

Unlike that of the Freudian psychiatrist, the institutional authority of the police is not overridden in the poem. 'Hospital' is threatening to the autistic youngster in a manner connoting prison. Moreover, this ominous encounter is implied as a consequence of the earlier, momentarily glorious depiction of autistic reverie: 'When he ran away constantly it was to the greengrocers to worship stacked fruit'; the 'runaway' then finds himself in the police station. This broken sequence of details illustrates how, while monotropism may be a natural state for autistic individuals, it can present a *social* difference not easily understood or accepted by neurotypical outsiders (hence the necessity for autistic adults themselves to have named and narrated monotropism, as exemplified by Dinah Murray, Lesser and Lawson in 2005). States of reverie through such seemingly (to others) simple stimuli as gazing at fruit are perhaps less accessible to neurotypicals, which is partly why such experiences are socially discouraged and framed by psychiatric orthodoxy as somehow wrong. From the infant who would rather play with a spinning top than meet the eye of a psychiatrist to the unmarried adult who prefers to go home and listen to Glenn Gould over joining in with after-work drinks, it is the social expectation of normalcy (rather than these fascinations themselves) that positions such lives as neurologically different or 'impaired'.

Interpellation, Althusser emphasized, is a process through which individuals internalize dominant ideologies; through interpellation, we become *subjects*. Murray's portrait points towards certain ways in which autistic subjectivity can in some ways, at some times, leave us unusually vulnerable to interpellation. 'Phrases spoken to him he would take as teaching, and repeat' and 'He has forgotten nothing'.[155] This is suggested in the son's italicized repetition of the threat of hospital from the police, but that is only the most literal example. Societal and psychiatric expectations of an adult meeting social-developmental milestones are less rigidly standardized than those placed on children, yet adolescence is fundamentally a state and time of *change* – which, for many autistic people, is the most demanding and challenging inevitability of life. The pressures shown in the poem are not just ableist but heteronormative: 'Bantering questions about girlfriends cause a terrified look and blocked ears'.[156]

As an 'equitable and kind' young man is recognized, Murray's poem ends unsentimentally with images of independence, freedom and fear:

> He surfs, bowls, walks for miles. For many years he hasn't trailed his left arm while running.
> *I gotta get smart!* looking terrified into the years. *I gotta get smart!*[157]

Verbal again after 'It withdrew speech for years', autism is becoming less impairing to the son; how different the effect would be if *It* was still trailing the son's arm, as if holding him back. But what is also emerging is the presence of further expectations from outside as adulthood nears. Ending a poem so rich in details of an individual's knowledge – of soils, 'all the breeds of fowls', 'the counties of Ireland' and more – the final line invokes both verbal stimming and the sense that to be *smart* is to conform to a whole, unknowable set of other, outside values.

NORMATIVITY THROUGH THE LOOKING-GLASS: JOANNE LIMBURG'S *THE AUTISTIC ALICE* (2017)

A rarely addressed experience invaluably voiced by Sonya Freeman Loftis in *Imagining Autism* (2015) is the question of how autistic people may internalize some of the cultural stereotypes associated with them. Loftis critically reflects on this with regard to her own experiences. She begins her introduction by referring to the stereotype that autistics 'lack empathy' and concludes it by musing:

> Maybe the first line of this book, which suggests that I might have some kind of limited capacity for empathy, is merely a sign of my own internalized oppression, of listening to stereotypes, of letting popular representations and constructions tell me how 'autistics' should be.[158]

For me, the keyword in Loftis's recognizable expression here is 'maybe': it is so hard to know how, when and if cultural and medical interpellations are shaping our self-perceptions. And one personal experience into which such questions may become most pertinent is that of looking into a mirror.

In an historical age when capitalism establishes so much value (or expense) on personal, physical appearance, to look at one's mirror reflection can be to feel interpellated by a range of social and cultural expectations. This is true with additional complexities for many disabled adults. Autistic people are frequently interpellated by science and culture that their physical appearance diverges from implicit norms. At the mirror, we may be faced back with eyes that, we are told, too rarely meet for long with those of others, or by memories of discourse declaring differences in the 'emotional' (what other kinds *are* there?) facial expressions of autistic people.[159] Scientists have also expressed unusual interest in the size and shape of our foreheads (especially if these are different to the statistical norms).[160] Meanwhile, sensory and other factors might mean that our skin is often sore or blotched, while repetitive eating habits mean that suitably average weight profiles are elusive to many of us. Noticeably, these last two aspects of autistic physique as experienced by many (not all) adults are rarely represented in screen depictions (since so much importance is attached to glamour in cinema and television, even in the documentary form). This means that few of us resemble the neurotypical actors whose fine faces epitomize autism in many expectant imaginations.

As Snyder and Mitchell (2006) venture, autistic people 'may resist or internalize' implications of the label – and, by extension, its cultural and social baggage. More usually, Snyder and Mitchell continue, autistic people might adopt 'a combination of these two options' of resistance and internalization.[161] While I would add that these 'options' might sometimes be hard to recognize, and harder still to embrace, there is much freedom and agency to be gained for the self – and to be demonstrated to other autistics – by continually *questioning* the cultural interpellations of what it means to be autistic, as Loftis does so laudably. Another publication to do so is UK poet Joanne Limburg's third full-length collection *The Autistic Alice* (2017). Here, the metaphor of the mirror that has glaringly characterized various neurotypical constructions of autism in science and culture is given a different position.

The title sequence of 21 poems in Limburg's *The Autistic Alice* effectively turns a mirror onto the conventions and demands of an ableist and patriarchal society to reveal not just their repressiveness but their absurdity. Bloodaxe Books' press release for Limburg's collection states that the poems explore the author's experiences as a girl and young woman growing up with 'undiagnosed Asperger's'.[162] This detail is important because most poems in the book's title sequence portray situations in family, education and social life in which others seldom attempt to understand or empathize with neurological difference, and instead insist on repressive and ultimately defeated attempts to normalize the individual. What is thus most radical about Limburg's 'Autistic Alice' is the central figure's gradual resistance and eventual rejection of demands (both implicit and explicit) that she should resemble her peers.

Limburg's collection and its press release do not overtly clarify the author's adult diagnostic status. This presents, in its own quiet way, a further resistance of normalization. It is imperative to remember that not all autistic adults need or want psychiatric confirmation of their way of being. Meanwhile, others are unable to access the appropriate diagnostic services, and others still – particularly women – are dismissed by some professionals as non-autistic because they do not conform to the controversial 'extreme male brain' expectation (discussed in chapter 3). Thus, in leaving the medical formalities of the poet's relationship to autism unspecified, Limburg's narratives of *undiagnosed* autism sustain a resonance with an array of identities. Crucial here is the fact that people diagnosed autistic in adulthood have often experienced childhood and adolescence as individuals enduring facets of social disablement without being aware (for worse or better) of their neurological distinction from most peers.

The Autistic Alice stands as a compelling demonstration of autistic literary imagination and, as such, provides another riposte to the reductive equations of autistic talent with mathematics and sciences. In the face of such popular associations as critiqued in chapter 1, it is also striking that Limburg's collection draws directly on the work of a professional mathematician viewed by various 21st-century commentators as having been autistic, and who was also a highly innovative literary author: Lewis Carroll (Charles Dodgson, 1832–1898).[163] Carroll's *Alice's Adventures in Wonderland* (1865) and *Through the Looking-Glass, and What Alice Found There* (1871) satirize social mores by dramatizing the conventional Alice's otherness when she appears in fantastical realms, whose creatures variously regard her as frightening, rude and physically anomalous. The scope for equating Alice's otherness with autistic experience is therefore rich: but as Limburg's sequence implies, this is not a matter of claiming Carroll's Alice herself as autistic but of rewriting her adventures to illuminate the sheer subjectivity – and, often, the absurdity – of what come to be assumed as normal behaviours and aspirations.

The key figure invoked in Limburg's poems alongside Alice is the Red Queen: the impetuous, loquacious and fast-running chess piece of Carroll's tales. In Carroll's *Through the Looking-Glass*, the Queen chastises Alice (who explains that she has 'lost her way'): ' "I don't know what you mean by YOUR way", said the Queen: "all the ways around here belong to ME" '.[164] The Red Queen promises that Alice (whom she orders to move as a chess pawn) will be a queen too when she reaches the eighth square. 'Faster, faster' is her repeated command to Alice.[165] Limburg's 'Alice and the Red Queen' repositions the two eponymous figures as autistic and neurotypical, respectively. But more specifically, Limburg casts the Red Queen as an embodiment of neurotypical *adulthood*: less as a parent or even teacher figure than as the personification of established authority itself, espousing normative ideas of womanhood. This poem, presenting snapshots of Limburg's autistic Alice from infancy to adulthood, centres on *physical* conformity, foregrounding walking, running and dancing.

> Alice takes her first step late;
> before she can grab a second,
> the Red Queen grabs her hand.
> *Stand up straight!* she says,
> *and stop that, whatever it is!*
> *Alice, are you listening?*[166]

The autistic Alice is listening but the neurotypical Queen is not. The Queen is too caught up in her own authority to even register that Alice is talking back to her, let alone to attempt to understand the girl's explanations of how, and why, attempting to keep up with her peers creates such a struggle. When the Queen orders Alice to smile and asks to know why the girl is 'so serious', Alice replies: 'Because it is a serious effort,/ this running to keep pace'. Through verses alternating Alice's subjectivity with the Queen's orders, Limburg's poem expresses autistic experience while also showing its marginalization.

'Alice and the Red Queen' places adolescence as the time of most intense social pressures, as if establishing conformity at this stage is prerequisite for being granted the identity of adulthood itself. Here, conservatively gendered expectations become central to the Queen's interpellations (*'You need a bra! Some heels!'*; *'Get a boyfriend!'*). Almost puppet-like, Alice is commanded to dance by the Queen – and:

> Dancing is worse than running:
> every bit as fast, but now
> there are steps to remember[167]

The social expectation of certain actions or 'steps' is Alice's greatest burden. Others 'can run and speak together' in the sense of simultaneous actions as well as that of creating a social group. Contrastingly, throughout much of Limburg's sequence, Alice lives with intense, sometimes singular, focus. In a preceding poem, 'Alice Between', Limburg swiftly yet perfectly conveys how autistic monotropism brings extremes of anxiety, as well as elation: 'Sometimes, she is petrified/ sometimes, she sublimes'.[168] In 'Alice and the Red Queen', it is not the speed or slowness with which Alice walks, runs and dances that presents any problem for her or for others. Instead, the problem for Alice – and in a different sense, for the Queen – is that the girl is continually compared (and expected to compare herself) with her peers. 'Alice and the Red Queen' hauntingly elucidates how social expectations of independence also tend to function as demands for conformity. Most significant in this poem is the expectation of conforming to dominant outward appearances regardless of inner subjectivity – and doing so in time with others, as in the dancing motif. The Queen's focus is confined to physical, outward appearances; she has no interest in Alice's feelings or inward experiences.

Befitting the cultural reference point of Carroll's *Alice* books, Limburg's 'Autistic Alice' sequence effectively turns a mirror onto dominant conventions that too often go unquestioned. In doing so, Limburg shows how conformity to ableist expectations is ultimately a performance and can therefore be a *choice* – for neurotypicals themselves, as well as autistics. In the final two poems, Limburg addresses autism in the mirror. 'Queen Alice' narrates the protagonist no longer as a girl but now a woman, who has found 'a King' and is the mother of 'a little prince'.[169] But though adulthood is here and brings personal fulfilment, the poem addresses how past interpellations (both personal and cultural) continue to impact on a person's self-perception. In 'Queen Alice', the Red Queen of the earlier poem 'has left instructions' about personal appearance, which Alice continues to recall.

'Queen Alice' ends with a woman questioning whether her younger, 'other, awkward' self was some kind of dream – only to see the same 'unsmiling, sideways stare' in the looking-glass. Against the social acceptance portrayed in the poem, this stare implies a continuing struggle to understand the autistic self in the self in the face of a society which (as starkly reflected throughout Limburg's sequence) is unready to fully acknowledge or accommodate neurodiversity. Yet the autistic Alice's *self*-recognition in the mirror yields an epiphany. The subsequent *Annotated Alice* transforms the narrative in three vital ways. This concluding poem introduces the full emergence of Alice's first-person voice. It is also the first to adopt the past tense and the first to reflect on the *delights* of an autistic childhood. Alice narrates how she 'loved books' and, through *The Annotated Alice* (a 1960 edition of Carroll's *Alice* books with commentary by Martin Gardner) she 'was drawn by/ that other girl with the unsmiling level look'. This encounter with fiction, when she was three years old, marks the autistic Alice's first major connection with another child. Limburg's Alice has more in common with Carroll's fictional Alice than with the children she meets at school. Limburg's poem *The Annotated Alice* also brings the most tender depiction of the girl's relationship with her mother, who 'said I was curious too./ I asked lots of questions'. Following the loaded word 'curious', the tone grows more ominous, intensifying the innocence and vulnerability. When Alice asks her mother 'what would happen if I went through/ the looking-glass', she is told she would

> wake up in hospital, being mended,
> and I was so disappointed. I never meant
> to stay forever on the nonsense side.[170]

Ending Limburg's 21-poem 'Autistic Alice' sequence, the image of having to 'stay forever' outside of the looking-glass continues a sense of estrangement in a world ruled by ableist ideals of normalcy and conformity, as epitomized by the Red Queen. The staying 'forever' also suggests the permanence of autistic subjectivity – an important statement, in an era haunted by lucrative rhetorics of 'curing' autism. Most vitally, Limburg's 'The Autistic Alice', like

Carroll's original tales, highlights the 'nonsense' of so much that becomes elevated as 'normal'. The Queen views difference as something that needs to be normalized (or destroyed), rather than something to be understood. Invoking and then overturning the imbalance between neurotypical and autistic subjectivities in a manner reminiscent of Damian Milton's empowering naming of the 'double-empathy bind', it is the neurotypical Queen whose understanding of others is impaired: not by neurology but by society.[171]

OTHERNESS, AUTISM AND ACCEPTANCE

If we speculatively name other people autistic, can that enable our acceptance of their apparent otherness? Journalist Barbara Jacobson's *Loving Mr Spock: Understanding an Aloof Lover – Could It Be Asperger's Syndrome?* (2006) is a book I read because I imagined the title affectionately referred to a partner who loved *Star Trek*'s Mr Spock – or perhaps loved *something else* almost as much his author partner. *Loving Mr Spock* is in fact a self-help memoir in which Jacobson provides extensive autobiographical evidence that her ex-partner probably has Asperger syndrome. 'Mr Spock' is her retrospective nickname for him. Yet the book, for all that it smacks of an ex's vengeance, is one among many narratives in which individuals research and consider autism as a possible explanation towards a respectful understanding of limitations which they themselves do not face, but are found in another person.

In a 2013 newspaper interview, David Freud, a son of painter Lucian Freud (1922–2011), was quoted as suggesting that for his father (who seldom saw or contacted David), 'ignoring social norms wasn't a style choice' and that he believed the late painter 'had a high-functioning autistic spectrum disorder'. The son continued: 'If you ever met [Lucian Freud], Asperger's would have screamed out at you. . . . My dad was famous for the intensity of his gaze'.[172] Asked to elaborate on his father's possible autism by Phoebe Hoban for her biography *Lucian Freud: Eyes Wide Open* (2014), David Freud described how his father disliked (both passive and active) hugs and explained of the autism suggestion: 'It's speculative on my part. But he looked very intently. . . . I think the *effort* to look had to do with overcoming the ability to look at people'.[173] Hoban includes David Freud's comments in a sequence which otherizes the painter by quoting various emphases on his physical tics, self-absorption and general unpredictability; the book as a whole, meanwhile, is a celebration of Lucian Freud's genius as an artist.[174] Hoban's own, open view on whether the subject of her biography (and possibly his grandfather, Sigmund Freud) was autistic concludes with her comment that whatever the nature of his neurology, 'Lucian clearly perceived the world differently than others'.[175] But even this non-committal stance necessitates deeper questions. Why is it that the compelling individuality of some lives appears to call us, as a culture, to look for explainable pathologies as grand narratives? And is it right that in seeking to understand individuality itself, there is a copiously evidenced cultural inclination to conceptually *group* nonconformist people with eccentric others? Could it be that the alacritous broadsheet reportage of theories that (to just use the most recent example) Emily Brontë may have been autistic appeals not simply to an audience eager to otherize but, more encouragingly, to a readership that may be gladdened to read about lives that reject the vague yet governing forces of social normalcy?[176]

NOTES

1 A notable exception to this (which addresses the scarcity of available resources) is Jeannie Davide-Rivera's 2013 blog post 'Asperger's and Pregnancy; Sensory Issues'. http://aspiewriter.com/2013/01/aspergers-and-pregnancy-sensory-issues.html. In 2016, a small-scale qualitative study in *Nursing for Women's Health* advocated that medical practitioners should be given more training on the issues faced by some women with Asperger Syndrome during pregnancy, childbirth and the early stages of motherhood (Gardner et al., 'Exploratory Study of Childbearing Experiences').

2 Against this tendency, Sonya Freeman Loftis's essay 'Dear Neurodiversity Movement: Put Your Shoes On' addresses various aspects of autism and academia, including sensory experience and clothing. https://www.academia.edu/27111285/Dear_Neurodiversity_Movement_Put_Your_Shoes_On. Also recommended is Dani Alexi's 'Autistic Academic' at https://autisticacademic.com/.

3 See, for instance, the main images on the Internet homepages of the Cambridge University Autism Research Centre, https://www.autismresearchcentre.com/; Ambitious about Autism, https://www.ambitiousaboutautism.org.uk/; and Autism Independent UK, http://www.autismuk.com/.

4 Murray, *Representing Autism*, 139–41.

5 Recent estimates concerning the prevalence of autism vary significantly according to region but also according to the scope (and, possibly, the agendas) of how it is surveyed. In 2014, the Centers for Disease Control and Prevention (CDC) estimated that 1 in 68 *children* in the US had been identified as having an Autism Spectrum Disorder. See http://www.cdc.gov/media/releases/2014/p0327-autism-spectrum-disorder.html (accessed 18 October 2016). However, the UK's National Autistic Society estimates that around 1.1 per cent of the British population *of all ages* 'may have autism'. See http://www.autism.org.uk/about/what-is/myths-facts-stats.aspx (accessed 18 October 2016).

6 Hacking, *The Social Construction of What?*, 114–17.

7 Hacking, *The Social Construction of What?*, 116.

8   Shakespeare, *Disability Rights and Wrongs*, 69–70, Kindle location 1446.

9   Davis, *Enforcing Normalcy*, 24.

10 Davis, *Enforcing Normalcy*, 12. See also 26–30.

11 Davis, *Enforcing Normalcy*, 24.

12 Edward Said, *Orientalism*, 1977. See in particular 20, 26.

13 Bush, 'President's Statement on Combating Autism Act of 2006'.

14 Schwartz, 'Asperger's Ill-Defined'. As with most quotes used in journalism, it is worth considering that the source from which it was extracted may have provided significant additional context.

15 The website 'Autism Teaching Tools™' recommends Wiesner's book as a learning aid for autistic children. http://www.autismteachingtools.com/page/bbbbqj/bbbbgf (accessed 31 October 2016). A 2015 post on The National Autistic Society's Community Discussion Board provides various – mostly critical – responses from adults in whose assessments Wiesner's book was used.

16 *Kirkus Review*, '*Tuesday* by David Wiesner'.

17 See WPSPublish.com, 'Autism Diagnostic Observation Schedule, Second Edition (ADOS®-2)'. For further details, see BestPracticeAutism.com, 'Best Practice Review: The Autism Diagnostic Observation Schedule'.

18 Lord et al., 'Autism Diagnostic Observation Schedule'.

19 WPSPublish.com, 'Autism Diagnostic Observation Schedule, Second Edition (ADOS®-2)'.

20 For a useful commentary on the various formal classifications of autism up to and including *DSM-IV* (1994), see Sponheim, 'Changing Criteria of Autistic Disorders'.

21 American Psychiatric Association, *DSM-5*, 50–59.

22 Foucault, *Madness and Civilization*, 5–10.

23 See Foucault, *Madness and Civilization*, chapter 2.

24 Locker, 'Pentagon 2008 Study'.

25 Nadesan, *Constructing Autism*, 9.

26 Sontag, *Illness as Metaphor*, 59–60.

27 Sontag, *Illness as Metaphor*, 62.

28 Scully, 'What Is a Disease?'.

29 One exception is a sound bite (now retracted) on the website of 'Autism Speaks' on its launch in 2005: 'This disease has taken our children away. It's time to get them back'. Quoted in Murray, *Representing Autism*, 139.

30 Armitage, 'Rock of Ages', 117.

31 See Murray, *Representing Autism*, 159–61. Quote 161.

32 Armitage, 'The Stone Beach'.

33 *The Office*, episode 8, exhibits more overt traits of autism through the appearance of Simon, to whom Dawn refers as Tim's 'favourite computer geek'. Dawn says 'favourite' sarcastically, but the word is also fully apt. Simon is officious, patronizing and smug, but the superiority fix Tim gains while observing him is palpable. Meanwhile, Simon exchanges pedantries with Gareth about go-karting and Bruce Lee, to the amused irritation of Tim and his girlfriend Rachel.

34 *The Office*, episode 2.

35 *The Office*, episode 9.

36 Longmore, *Why I Burnt My Book*, 134.

37 For a discussion of autism, theory of mind and ethics applicable to this point, see Barnbaum, *The Ethics of Autism*, 137–8.

38 Foucault, *Madness and Civilization*, 64–65.

39 See Burks-Abbott, 'Mark Haddon's Popularity'.

40 Murray, *Representing Autism*, 88, 92.

41 Collins, 'Must-Geek TV'.

42 A public discussion of *Big Bang Theory* from an online autism community appears at Wrong Planet.net. http://wrongplanet.net/forums/viewtopic.php?t=81946 (accessed 7 January 2017).

43 Fernandes, 'Director Gavin O'Connor'.

44 Fernandes, 'Director Gavin O'Connor'.

45 Fernandes, 'Director Gavin O'Connor'.

46 See Silberman, *Neurotribes*, 369–70.

47 Haagaard, 'How *The Accountant* Victimizes the Autistic Community'.

48 Haagaard, 'How *The Accountant* Victimizes the Autistic Community'.

49 For some of the most extensive and incisive applications of Foucaultian perspectives to the history and discourse of autism, see McGuire, *War on Autism*, 26–28, 69–73, Kindle edition.

50 Biklen, *Autism and the Myth*, Kindle location 760.

51 See Biklen, *Autism and the Myth*, Kindle locations 813–925.

52 Kanner, 'Autistic Disturbances', 244.

53 For instance, one boy, Paul, said 'Peter eater' whenever he saw a cooking pan, because his mother had dropped a saucepan while once reciting the rhyme 'Peter, Peter, Pumpkin Eater' to him. Kanner, 'Irrelevant and Metaphorical Language', 242.

54 See Happé, 'Autobiographical Writings', 234–8. For an honest, humorous reflection of this from an autistic adult, see Chris Bonnello's blog post 'Taking Things Literally'.

55 Haddon, *Curious Incident*, 19.

56 For instance, The National Autistic Society's *Autism: A Brief Guide for Employers*, 3, 7, 12.

57 Ashton, 'Extending the Scope', 201.

58 Cf. Ashton, 'Extending the Scope', 196.

59 Loftis, *Imagining Autism*, Kindle location 503.

60 Sacks, 'An Anthropologist on Mars'.

61 Broderick and Ne'eman, 'Autism as Metaphor', 463–65.

62 Clare Sainsbury's 2010 factual children's book *Martian in the Playground* offers a series of invaluable inside perspectives on autistic experience in childhood and young adulthood. A different inside narrative is provided in Joshua Muggleton's 2011 manual for parents, *Raising Martians* (2011). My questioning of these titles is not intended as a criticism of the two books' often indispensably wise, informed and constructive content, and I recommend both to readers.

63 Wrong Planet was established by Alex Plank and Dan Grover in 2004. See http://wrongplanet.net/ (accessed 26 September 2016).

64 Hacking 'Humans, Aliens and Autism', 44.

64 Hacking, 'Humans, Aliens and Autism', 45.

65 Narby, 'Double Rainbow'.

66 Wordsworth, 'My Heart Leaps Up When I Behold'.

67 Crane and Goddard, 'Episodic and Semantic Autobiographical Memory', 498

68 Zamoscik et al., 'Early Memories of Autistic Individuals'.

69 See Grandin and Scariano, *Emergence*; Robison, *Look Me in the Eye*; Mukhopadhyay, *How Can I Talk*.

70 Barry, 'Autism', 1. Barry's anecdotal evidence is contradicted by more controlled, scientific experiments (not cited in her article). Cf. Reddy et al., 'Engaging with the Self', 543.

71 Lacan, 'The Mirror Stage', 1–8.

72 Barry, 'Autism', 3.

73 Barry, 'Autism', 1.

74 Mukhopadhyay, *How Can I Talk?*, Kindle locations 140–52.

75 Mukhopadhyay, *How Can I Talk?*, Kindle location 242.

76 Mukhopadhyay, *How Can I Talk?*, Kindle location 1285.

77 Biklen, *Autism and the Myth*, Kindle location 2380.

78 Williams, *Nobody Nowhere*, 20–21.

79 Williams, *Nobody Nowhere*, 23.

80 See Williams 'Imitation, Mirror Neurons and Autism'; Iacoboni and Dapretto, 'The Mirror Neuron System'; Oberman and Ramachandran, 'The Simulating Social Mind'.

81 First reported in 1992 by Di Pellegrino et al., 'Understanding Motor Events'.

82 Ramachandran and Oberman, 'Broken Mirrors', 64.

83 Ramachandran and Oberman, 'Broken Mirrors', 67–68.

84 Ramachandran and Oberman, 'Broken Mirrors', 68.

85 Southgate and Hamilton, 'Unbroken Mirrors', 2–3.

86 See Rizzolatti and Fabbri-Destro, 'Mirror Neurons', 230–33.

87 Southgate and Hamilton, 'Unbroken Mirrors', 3.

88 Schunke et al., 'Mirror Me', 134, 141.

89 For a scintillating critique of such processes from a simultaneously sociological and autistic perspective, see Milton, 'Nature's Answer to Over-Conformity'.

90 See Kanner and Eisenberg, 'Early Infantile Autism', 8–9.

91 *Time*, 'Medicine'.

92 See Feinstein, *A History of Autism*, Kindle locations 2461–71.

93 Cf. Murray, *Representing Autism*, 175.

94 Bettelheim, *Empty Fortress*, 125.

95 For an example of how Bettelheim generalizes on autism mothers via his unsympathetic commentaries on families with whom he had worked, see *Empty Fortress*, 119. Nadesan (2005) and Jack (2014) differently outline the wider, latent tendencies in medicine and culture that enabled Bettelheim's narratives to become so popular, emphasizing how the blaming of mothers was also prominent in psychiatric models of a range of childhood disorders. See Nadesan, *Constructing Autism*, 96–99; Jack, *Autism and Gender*, 35–41.

96 Houston and Frith, *Autism in History*, 102.

97 In a shift that prefigured later autism self-advocacy movements, key pioneers in establishing that autism was not a reflection of parenting were themselves both autism parents and psychologists, including Rimland (1964) and Wing (1971). The first major challenge to parent-blaming appeared in 1964: Bernard Rimland's book *Infantile Autism: The Syndrome and Its Implication for a Neural Theory of Behavior*, to which Kanner (perhaps surprisingly) wrote a foreword. Rimland closely examined each of the bases for claims that autism was caused by parenting and detailed how supporting evidence was seriously lacking. Arguing the case for biological causation, Rimland cited a diverse series of scientific studies. Rimland's 1964 publication remained pertinent enough to warrant a '50th anniversary' edition which (while including several, sometimes critical commentaries from autism researchers in 2014) retains authority in its key premises. Another dignified antidote to parent-blaming was Lorna Wing's book *Autistic Children: A Guide for Parents and Professionals* (1971), written with the triplicate authority of an autism mother, researcher and practitioner.

98 *Doc Martin*, episode 18.

99 *Doc Martin*, episode 12.

100 *Doc Martin*, episode 45.

101 *Doc Martin*, episode 46.

102 *The Bridge*, episode 19.

103 Dawson in Waltz, *Autism: A Social and Medical History*, Kindle locations 2200–2213.

104 Dawson in Waltz, *Autism: A Social and Medical History*, Kindle location 2213.

105 Gallagher, 'Super-parenting'.

106 Pickles et al., 'Parent-mediated Social Communication Therapy'.

107 Gallagher, 'Super-parenting'.

108 OED Online, 'Super-, prefix'.

109 Kroll, 'From the Who to the Whom', 67.

110 Frith, *Autism: Explaining the Enigma*, 25–26.

111 See Ouzounian, 'Pete Townshend Talks'. See also Barnes, *Tommy: The Who*, 22.

112 Barnes, *Tommy: The Who*, 22.

113 Barnes and Townshend, *The Story of Tommy*, 30, 113.

114 The Who, 'Amazing Journey'.

115 Townshend, *Who I Am*, 162.

116 See Deafblind UK, 'About Deafblindness'. Quotation: The Who, 'Go to the Mirror!'

117 My warmest thanks to Paul Wheeler for discussing 'Underture' with me by email (13 Jan 2017).

118 The Who, 'Go to the Mirror!'

119 The Who, '1921'.

120 Pinchevski, 'Bartleby's Autism', 45.

121 Barnes, *Tommy: The Who*, 22.

122 The Who, 'Christmas'.

123   The Who, 'Pinball Wizard'.

124   Barnes, *Tommy: The Who*, 22.

125   Kanner, 'Autistic Disturbances', 236.

126   Barnes and Townshend, *The Story of Tommy*, 30, 113.

127   Townshend's retrospective comments do not present the only way of equating Tommy's autistic-like appearance with Meher Baba's example. Baba himself renounced speech in 1925 (aged 31) and, until his death in 1969, communicated only via an alphabet board.

128   See European Commission for Social Rights. 'International Association of Autism-Europe v France'.

129   For a critique of Roberts's now withdrawn film from both an autistic and Lacanian perspective, see Bond, 'What Autism Can Teach Us'.

130   'Packing' is the subject of a documentary in progress by Alex Plank and Noah Trevino entitled *Shameful*. See http://shamefuldocumentary.com/about.html (accessed 2 November 2016).

131   Dolto in Barry, 'Autism', 3.

132   See Smith, 'A Conversation with Les Murray' for the poet's most detailed comments on his son Alexander in relation to the poem.

133   O'Driscoll, 'Interviews: Les Murray'.

134   The poem appeared identically in Australia's *Quadrant* (June 1994) and the UK's *PN Review* (November–December 1994). In the first of Murray's own books to include the poem (*Subhuman Redneck Poems*, 1996, 42–43), the title was amended to 'It Allows a Portrait in Line Scan at Fifteen'; this saw the first inclusion of the 'Freudian psychiatrist' line. In Murray's *Learning Human: New Selected Poems* (2001), the title is 'It Allows a Portrait in Line-Scan at Fifteen'; the Freudian psychiatrist remains, but the line asking whether playing video games all day is 'very autistic' is omitted here, as also in subsequent publications. Murray's *New Collected Poems* (2003) and later publications return to the unhyphenated title. The 2003 version of the poem can be read online via the Australian Poetry Library's website, although the stanza breaks indicated on the website do not replicate any known print publication of the poem. http://www.poetrylibrary.edu.au/poets/murray-les/it-allows-a-portrait-in-line-scan-at-fifteen-0617122.

135   Murray, *New Collected Poems*, 413.

136   Murray, 'It Allows a Portrait in Line-Scan at Fifteen' (1994 version).

137   Murray, *New Collected Poems*, 414.

138   Feinstein, *A History of Autism*, 33–34, Kindle location 988.

139   See Feinstein, *A History of Autism*, 34, Kindle location 1003.

140   Bettelheim brings these focal points into direct convergence – with particularly harsh speculations on an autism mother – in his 1968 chapter 'Joey: A Machine-Powered Body'. See Bettelheim, *Empty Fortress*, 263.

For the fullest discussion of Bettelheim's influences, including Freud, see Feinstein, *A History of Autism*, Kindle locations 1511–71. See also Severson et al., 'Bruno Bettelheim'.

141   For instance, Meltzer coldly theorized that if 'depression or other disturbance in the mother dries up her attentiveness, warmth, chatter and sensuality toward the baby', the child's 'dismantled' – that is autistic – self 'will tend to float away',

marking an 'arrest in the development'. Meltzer, *Explorations in Autism*, Kindle locations 231–43.

142 Against mainstream medical consensus and the statements of many autism societies, the 'refrigerator' parent theory is unfortunately still upheld by some, as testified in French film-maker Sophie Roberts's (promptly withdrawn) documentary *Le Mur* (*The Wall*), 2011. For reportage on this, see Vitelli, 'The Return of the Refrigerator Parent?'.

143 Murray, *New Collected Poems*, 412–14.

144 Block, *Sounding the Alarm*.

145 Autism Speaks, 'About Us'.

146 Sinclair, 'Don't Mourn for Us'.

147 For instance, the National Symposium on Neurodiversity's post 'What Is Neurodiversity?'.

148 Murray, *New Collected Poems*, 412.

149 Murray, Lesser and Lawson, 'Attention, Monotropism and the Diagnostic Criteria'. The term 'monotropism' was first used in this sense by Dinah Murray in 1992. See Murray, 'Attention Tunnelling'.

150 Murray, Lesser and Lawson, 'Attention, Monotropism and the Diagnostic Criteria', 139, 146, 152.

151 Murray, Lesser and Lawson, 'Attention, Monotropism and the Diagnostic Criteria', 152.

152 Murray, *New Collected Poems*, 413.

153 Murray, *New Collected Poems*, 413.

154 Murray, *New Collected Poems*, 413.

155 Murray, *New Collected Poems*, 413.

156 Murray, *New Collected Poems*, 414.

157 Murray, *New Collected Poems*, 414.

158 Loftis, *Imagining Autism*, Kindle locations 55, 516. See also locations 1309, 1687, 3142.

159 See, for instance, McIntosh et al., 'When the Social Mirror Breaks'.

160 Lainhart et al., 'Head Circumference and Height in Autism'.

161 Snyder and Mitchell, *Cultural Locations of Disability*, 11. Cf. Loftis, *Imagining Autism*, Kindle locations 507, 3448.

162 Bloodaxe Books, 'Joanne Limburg: The Autistic Alice'.

163 Dodgson is among the case studies in Fitzgerald's *Genesis of Artistic Creativity*, 56–65. Further indications that Dodgson was autistic are convincingly evaluated in Brown's *Writers on the Spectrum*, 117–37. For the most extensive discussion of Dodgson and autism, see Waltz's e-book 'Alice's Evidence'.

164 Carroll, *Through the Looking-Glass*, Kindle location 182.

165 Carroll, *Through the Looking-Glass*, Kindle locations 203–17.

166 Limburg, *The Autistic Alice*, 52.

167 Limburg, *The Autistic Alice*, 53.

168 Limburg, *The Autistic Alice*, 39.

169 Limburg, *The Autistic Alice*, 55.

170 Limburg, *The Autistic Alice*, 56.

171 See Milton, 'On the Ontological Status of Autism', 883, 886.

172 Morrison, 'David Freud'.

173 Hoban, *Lucian Freud*, 36–37. For a different viewpoint, which dismisses suggestions that Freud had any particular 'condition', see the comments of his daughter Annie. Hoban, 80–81.

174 See Hoban, *Lucian Freud*, 32–37.

175 Hoban, *Lucian Freud*, 36–37.

176 Cain, Sian. 'Emily Brontë'.

Chapter 3

Against the 'new classic' adult autism: Narratives of gender, intersectionality and progression

What this chapter calls 'the new classic autism' is a repressive narrative feature of the early 21st century and is named as such in order that it might be more clearly identified and interrogated. The new classic autism is essentially a cultural phenomenon rather than a medical one, though the two cross over via media disseminations of certain research projects. I refer here to narrative processes through which distortive and repeated emphasis is placed on hegemonic – and, essentially, *neurotypical* – notions of high achievement in autistic adults. The term 'classic autism' usually refers to Leo Kanner's model of autism as outlined in his 1943 paper.[1] More subtly, classic autism indicates how, prior to the inclusion of Asperger syndrome in the *Diagnostic and Statistical Manual of Mental Disorders-IV* (1994), it was Kanner's observations on impairments in language and intelligence (though mainly in childhood) that dominated diagnostic and cultural understandings of the name 'autism'.[2] However, in the past two decades, the most prominent narratives of adult autism across literature, cinema, television and (worryingly) science have tended to invoke figures who, while finding social situations confusing (often for the amusement of a neurotypical gaze), tend to be verbose, highly intelligent and – most questionably in regard to the realities of opportunities for autistic adults – fulfillingly employed. Accumulatively, such texts perpetuate what amounts to notions of a 'new classic' autism in the sense of not only cultural standardization but also idealization. This is unhelpful and oppressive to adults with the diagnosis who do *not* meet these cultural criteria of near-infallible expertise and sustained, high-ranking employment (in other words, nearly all of us). But this neoliberal phase in autism narratives from outside is most disrespectful of all to individuals who live as 'classically' autistic in the original sense of facing impairments in what society deems as the 'norms' of intelligence and language use. In addition to being compared

127

against 'normally' developing adult identities, these individuals may be further marginalized if they do not conform to the culture industry's favourite ideas regarding autistic adults. In the new classic autism, spectacular achievement becomes inflated in cultural narratives, while attention is deflected from the complexities and diversities of this condition as a disability. In such ways, popular culture risks compounding the social difficulties already faced by autistic people because the assumptions promoted are too often both rigid and unrealistic. Obviously, the idea of anything being 'new' and 'classic' is an oxymoron, and this is just the point: the shallow glamorization of adult autism is widespread and culturally compelling, but as this chapter will demonstrate, it is a relatively recent development (or regression) and it may well be ephemeral. My emphasis, then, is that the cultural fetishizing of the high-achieving white male as the epitome of adult autism is largely based on false constructs, and can therefore be subverted. After critiquing how the University of Cambridge's Autism Research Centre (UCARC) has in effect reinforced the values of capitalism and (especially) patriarchy into autism diagnostic processes, I trace how such hegemonies also define what have been the most popular (and simplistic) autism fictions. However, in adapting but also occasionally challenging Adorno and Horkheimer's critique of culture industries, the chapter then embraces a series of decidedly more progressive literary and screen portrayals of autism. The chapter's purpose thus is ultimately to promote less obvious, more radical recognitions of adult autism. I do so by focusing on a selection of texts which – while not nearly as well known or often debated (yet) as Levinson's *Rain Man* or Haddon's *Curious Incident of the Dog* – offer subversions of the dominant tropes and indicate various new pathways in autism narratives.

PATRIARCHY AND AUTISM: THE CAMBRIDGE AUTISM RESEARCH CENTRE AND THE 'EXTREME MALE BRAIN'

In its October 2016 summary of research on autism and gender, the UK's National Autistic Society critically reported – with concern for the difficulties faced by autistic girls and women in receiving assessment or support – that the male/female gender ratio in autism diagnosis was estimated to be as high as 16:1.[3] The present discussion critiques the possible role of a patriarchal medical gaze in this disproportionately gendered medical pattern. Gould and Ashton-Smith (2011) emphasized the need for diagnosticians to consider how autistic girls and women may present differently to boys and men, and how autism may create different *needs* for females and males.[4] Dale Yaull-Smith (2007), diagnosed aged 41, movingly reflects on how professionals, including doctors and teachers, 'don't expect to find autism in girls because recent research indicates that it is a rarity'. She continues:

> That girls with undiagnosed autism are painstakingly copying some behaviour is not picked up on and therefore any social and communication problems they may be having are also overlooked. This effort of mimicking and repressing their autistic behaviour is exhausting, perhaps resulting in the high statistics of women with mental health problems.[5]

A haunting indication of how gendered stereotypes may unhelpfully mask autism in women – prompting both self-doubt and social isolation – occurs in Liane Holliday Willey's 1999 autobiography of living with undiagnosed Asperger syndrome, *Pretending to be Normal*. Willey describes the distressing and frequent difficulties she experienced in communication with her husband, and women friends, prior to her formal diagnosis (which Willey was in effect forced to initiate herself).[6] Willey writes:

> It was almost as if my husband would begin to speak a foreign language. . . . For years I thought this was the way it was for everyone. After all, isn't this what popular culture and the mass media tell us, that men and women are unable to communicate, that they are wired too differently to ever connect? I came to believe our inability to communicate was the norm. . . . Yet when I would ask other women if they could relate to my experiences, they would tell me they could barely even understand what I was trying to describe to them.[7]

Willey's comments indicate how interpellations of 'female' and 'male' behaviours may misleadingly encourage autistic adults to believe that communication struggles are a natural, unavoidable consequence of gender differences rather than sometimes being the result of a deeper neurological diversity. Willey's reflections point to the pressure of expectations that women are able to easily and reciprocally talk about their feelings with each other.[8] Within four years of Willey publishing her 1999 memoir, it would not only be popular culture promoting the idea that women and men are wired too differently to truly understand each other; the same idea was being propagated by Professor Simon Baron-Cohen, director of one of the world's most prestigious autism science institutions, the UCARC.

Baron-Cohen's *The Essential Difference* (first published 2003) marks a commercial tendency in which a popular science title is promoted as both a comprehensive explanation of intricate theories and a ground-breaking academic intervention. Baron-Cohen asserts the scientific superiority of his book to John Gray's 1992 bestseller *Men Are from Mars, Women Are from Venus*.[9] Yet it is easy to see how the success of Gray's title (and slogan) – and similarly Allan and Barbara Pease's popular *Why Men Don't Listen and Women Can't Read Maps* (1998) – created a bookselling space into which a Cambridge University scientist's views on sex differences slotted all too conveniently.[10] Although the occasional sensationalism of its content suggests a design for the book to be popular ahead of scientific, *The Essential Difference* warrants serious critical attention. In addition to its cultural impact, it is cited as supporting evidence in many of UCARC's own later scientific journal articles as providing both a research hypothesis and a diagnostic model of autism and gender – or, at least, autism and men. Reissued with the contents unaltered under a newly academic-looking cover in 2012, *The Essential Difference* combines – and seeks to link – two of the most sensational subjects in popular science in the early 21st century: sex differences, and autism. First, Baron-Cohen outlines a densely referenced yet quaintly uncritical theory that innate differences between 'the' male and female brains inescapably manifest communication, relationships and abilities between the sexes. Then, in the book's second half, Baron-Cohen summarizes the rudimental features of Asperger syndrome, before detailing his own, now best-known theory: that autism can be defined and understood as the 'extreme male brain'. Despite focusing almost entirely in the book on Asperger syndrome rather than classic autism, Baron-Cohen asserts that autism at large may be synonymous with 'male' neurological traits. The book presents five detailed case studies of Asperger syndrome in men. They are Isaac Newton (1642–1727), Albert Einstein (1879–1955), Cambridge University physics professor Paul Dirac (1902–1984), the 'Arch Code-breaker' Michael Ventris (1922–1956) and a Cambridge University professor of mathematics (at the time), Richard Borcherds (born 1959).[11] Considering that *The Essential Differences* is introduced as a book about autism and averages, these five men create an unusual crew of profiles.[12] But then, they are also featured to reinforce UCARC's additional hypothesis of a link between autism and STEM (science, technology, engineering, mathematics) subjects, which was evaluated in chapter 1.

The Essential Difference briefly confronts the 'delicate' nature of discussing 'essential' differences between the male and female brains, before emphasizing the book's core and marketable premise: '*The female brain is predominantly hard-wired for empathy. The male brain is predominantly hard-wired for understanding and building systems*'.[13] Baron-Cohen concedes that some may fear his theory could present academic ammunition for 'reactionaries' wishing to defend unequal opportunities on gendered terms but asserts that his theory 'can be used progressively'.[14] Quite what is meant by 'progressively' (or 'used') remains much less clear in Baron-Cohen's text, but the quoted words are arresting because *The Essential Difference* presents some of the most imbalanced, socially archaic notions of gender yet committed to publication by an academic this century.

Before addressing Baron-Cohen's research on autism and gender more finely, it is instructive to consider the starting point for his theory. He quotes from Hans Asperger's seminal 1944 article on autism, which opines that the condition presents an 'extreme' form of 'male intelligence'. Asperger adds that among 'normal' children, there are differences in intelligence, and that among autistics, 'male' intelligence is 'exaggerated'.[15]

In view of the context in which Asperger was writing – in Nazi-occupied Vienna – it remains important not to take his comments at face value. Unfortunately, Baron-Cohen's citation of Asperger is unquestioning. In her 1991 translation of Asperger (1944) as used by Baron-Cohen, Frith's footnotes voice more scientific concerns over the validity of Asperger's 'provocative idea' on male intelligence, cautioning that his suppositions regarding gendered abilities were 'very much in accord with cultural stereotypes'.[16] Psychiatrist Jacques Constant notes how Asperger's clearly conservative notions of gender and intellect reinforced then dominant (and propagandized) equations of womanhood with *Kürche, Kirche, Kinder* (Kitchen, Church, Children).[17] Thus, a deeper consideration is whether to interpret Asperger's words as emphasizing maleness, or emphasizing *intelligence*, and thus a future role in society.

Of supposedly 'typical' sex differences, Asperger (1944) suggested that girls have greater aptitude for 'practical', 'tidy' and 'methodical' work, while boys are more inclined towards 'logical ability', 'abstraction', 'precise thinking' and 'scientific investigation'.[18] Here, it is noticeable that he lists the most obviously *profession-orientated* abilities in male intelligence. The penultimate heading in Asperger's paper is 'The Social Value of the Autistic Psychopath' (his unfortunate full name for 'autistic' people, although psychopathy itself is not significantly considered in his 1944 text).[19] As chapter 1 detailed, Asperger's essay (in sections still ignored by Baron-Cohen) also highlights the distinguished creative sensibilities of some male autistic children. Asperger seems to have stressed the diverse talents and potential of his patients above their impairments in order to protect them – and others who may resemble them – from the very serious threat of compulsory euthanasia under the Nazis. Yet despite being supported by various commentators including myself (see chapter 1), this view of Asperger's agenda under Nazism also incurs a deeply unsettling question: why, in that case, did he profile only boys in his study? And why did Asperger explicitly state that although several mothers of his patients showed autistic features, his clinic had yet to meet a girl with 'fully fledged' autism?[20] Such questions imply that in 1944, he did indeed believe autism to be an extreme form of male intelligence.[21] However, in addition to the medical, political and moral complexities faced by Asperger, there is the obviousness that he was working in an era of far less flexible notions of gendered identities, and this is partly what makes Baron-Cohen's uncritical 21st-century citations of Asperger on gender and intelligence problematic.

Asperger's dismissive 1944 view of female autism remains unfortunate because it continues to be demonstrably influential. The legacy of *selected* theories (and statements) on autism from Asperger, as already outlined in chapter 1 in relation to STEM talents, is most prominent in the media-cosy publications of the UCARC. Asperger's conservative views on gender may be partly explicable by historical context, but in the 21st century, it is much harder to excuse the ways in which UCARC parallels Asperger's lack of investigative scientific interest in how autism may affect women. As this discussion will confront, the extreme male brain theory may actually be based less on 'essential' differences between female and male brains than on a series of scientific imbalances.

Simone de Beauvoir's *The Second Sex* (1949) is almost as old as Asperger's formative work on autism, but it is a mark of the archaic subjectivity pervading Baron-Cohen's *The Essential Difference* that Beauvoir's key but vintage feminist text is indispensable here. Her chapter 'The Data of Biology' concerns (among much else) how nature is subject to narrative and how male-dominated scientific discourse implicitly reinforces the subordination of all female species.[22] Beauvoir highlights how the behaviours of female insects, animals and beasts are framed not just as *other* to their male counterparts but as either powerless or dangerous in comparison. Beauvoir observes: 'Females sluggish, eager, artful, stupid, callous, lustful, ferocious, abased – man projects them all at once upon woman'.[23] Thus, 'The Data of Biology' is doubly significant here. First, Beauvoir exposes the role of narrative and thus subjectivity in biology. Second, she discerns how what is now termed the 'male gaze' permeates supposedly objective science. Given that UCARC (while including a number of women scientists) has done much to popularize views that men, as well as autistics, are biologically predisposed to superior skills in STEM areas, Beauvoir's 1949 critique of scientific 'data' remains both cautionary and vital.[24]

The UCARC's equation of autism with maleness rests largely on the notion that this condition is fundamentally characterized by a lack of empathy or 'Theory of Mind'.[25] According to *The Essential Difference* model, empathy is fundamentally the gift of women, while systemizing is the strength of men, hence Baron-Cohen's possibly premature hypothesis of autism as an 'extreme' form of 'maleness'. He details how systemizing is understood to be controlled by the brain's right hemisphere and empathizing by the left. *The Essential Difference* thus equates the right and left brain regions with maleness and femaleness, respectively.[26] In a more nuanced statement, Baron-Cohen clarifies his central claim as being 'only that *more* males' have brains essentially geared towards systemizing.[27] He expands on this by summarizing a series of experiments performed by the UCARC involving prenatal testosterone, but as the review of these will illustrate, the tests – and their results – are riddled with gaps and ambiguities. It is thus a little cheeky for UCARC to name systemizing at large a male predisposition and frankly rude of them to call autism the extreme male brain. The leaps of logic Baron-Cohen formulates here are precisely what renders the 'extreme male brain theory' essentially a *metaphor*. Nor is this metaphor merely a catchy slogan for his 2003 popular science book: he had already announced the 'extreme male brain theory of autism' in scientific journal articles, and *The Essential Difference* was its premature dissemination – and interpellation – to a wider readership.[28]

Here are Baron-Cohen's definitions of 'empathy' and 'systemizing', which he equates with 'average' female and male brains, respectively:

> Empathizing is the drive to identify another person's emotions and thoughts, and to respond to them with an appropriate emotion.
> Systemizing is the drive to analyse, explore and construct a system.[29]

Rather drastically, Baron-Cohen asserts that these qualities are 'wholly different', explaining empathizing as making sense of another person's behaviour and framing systemizing as the means of understanding 'almost everything else'.[30] This presumption of empathizing and systemizing as 'wholly' different processes is problematic for several reasons. It overstates the supposed distinctions between female and male brain types, but also underscores a series of philosophical, methodological and, thus, scientific oversights in the UCARC's model of autism. A fundamental yet unexamined irony within Baron-Cohen's model is that he conceptualizes and measures empathizing according only to quantitative *systems* (including the 'Empathy Quotient' [EQ] questionnaire, discussed later).

Baron-Cohen's commentary on the human brain's two hemispheres reads as unsettlingly reminiscent of how, in the 19th century, 'the East' was otherized and subordinated via the Western narrative processes which Edward Said (1978) critiques as Orientalism. Much as the West was positioned by British colonialists as the implicitly central, normative base against which 'Oriental' colonies were oppressively caricatured, Baron-Cohen's research and its exposition privileges the brain's right, systemizing and male hemisphere.[31] However, his equation of the right brain with systemizing – which he rigidly defines as a predisposition towards science, technology, engineering and mathematics – is itself still only hypothetical. A 2013 study by Nielsen et al. reported no evidence to support the existence of left-brain or right-brain dominance within individual people, nor were sex differences in brain hemisphere activity found.[32] More recently, Aberg, Doell and Schwartz (2016) effectively oppose the CARC's model, supporting long-standing theories that the right brain is responsible for *creativity* (in the sense of 'novel' or 'divergent' neurological processes).[33] Thanks to theories by Nobel Prize–winning neuropsychologist Roger Sperry (1913–1994), whose research, in his lifetime, received cultural prominence comparable to Baron-Cohen's, it was commonplace prior to *The Essential Difference* to oversimplify that analytical thinking was controlled by the brain's *left* hemisphere.[34] Much of the human brain thus remains a source of mystery, and the colonization of public understandings regarding its multitudinous regions remains largely a matter of contesting hypotheses.

Both quantitatively and qualitatively, *The Essential Difference* remains conspicuously asymmetrical in its attention to male and female traits. In a chapter named 'The Evolution of the Male and Female Brain', Baron-Cohen (2003) devotes more than twice as many pages (just under nine) to the evolution of the male human brain in comparison with that of the female (summarized in fewer than four pages). But strangest of all in a recent, non-satirical book are the headings for the strengths that Baron-Cohen attributes to men and women throughout evolutionary history and into the 21st century. When isolated as a series of headings, his asymmetrical list looks like this:

Advantages of the 'male brain'[35]	*Advantages of the 'female brain'*[36]
'Using and making tools'	'Making friends'
'Hunting and tracking'	'Mothering'
'Trading'	'Gossip'
'Power'	'Social mobility'
'Social dominance'	'Reading your partner'
'Expertise'	
'Tolerating solitude'	
'Aggression'	
'Leadership'	

Gossip?! Needless to say – unless discussing Baron-Cohen's research – the supposedly male traits mentioned can all be found diversely in women too. But the aforementioned headings and sections in *The Essential Difference* are not merely a matter of clumsy wording: they are part of a major research project which seeks to equate autism with maleness. Baron-Cohen goes on to assert that more men than women 'choose' to work in 'dominance-orientated' roles. He thus appears to be suggesting that the far greater numbers of men than women in higher-paid professional, political and scientific roles apparently represents not a 'glass ceiling' but the free and happy choices of women and men![37] Since some of the most problematic inequalities faced by women concern opportunities (and pay), it is astounding that 'power', 'expertise' and 'leadership' are not given corresponding sections in Baron-Cohen's discussion of the female brain. He thus not only reinforces but seemingly attempts to *justify* female subordination into domestic associations, culminating in the role of 'Reading your partner' (which has no equivalent in the male strengths list).[38]

In terms of scientific balance and critical awareness, the UCARC's multitudinous publications on autism and gender are surpassed by the book *Asperger's Syndrome for Dummies* (2011). Discussing the heavily male-dominated gender ratio of autism diagnoses, its authors Gina Gomez de la Cuesta and James Mason point out:

> A possible reason for the difficulties in diagnosing women . . . could be the historical fact that initial descriptions of ASCs [autistic spectrum conditions] were of boys. Because more males have a diagnosis than females, researchers and diagnostic experts have had more experience observing boys and men.[39]

Alluding to the UCARC's screening tools, de la Cuesta and Mason point out that these prioritize

> culturally 'male' interests such as computers, trains and cars, and take no account of the more social [*sic*] focus of culturally 'female' interests such as animals, soap operas, fashion or cleaning. So if you're a woman (or a girl), getting a diagnosis is difficult because the diagnostician is looking for 'male' characteristics.[40]

It is instructive here to situate *The Essential Difference*, and its autism-related (and systemizing-seeking) appendices, in the wider context of UCARC's research.

In chapter 1, I critiqued the conflicting agendas of the Baron-Cohen-led Adult Autism-Spectrum Quotient (AQ) questionnaire, finalized in 2001 and still in use in 2017 (with no updates) by many autism diagnosticians internationally. Yet the influential AQ questionnaire – despite being created as a screening tool which may decide whether an adult is referred for more extensive autism assessment – was also designed to support UCARC's hypothesis that autistic traits are more likely to be found in adults working in STEM occupations. In view of the latter purpose, it remains quantitatively unstable that the questionnaire is scored in such a way that every sign of an interest in mathematics or science (and several statements relate to these) counts as an autistic trait, while statements pertaining to an interest in fiction or the arts are automatically scored as signs of neurotypicality. Baron-Cohen's inclusion of the AQ and other UCARC tests for readers to complete as appendices to *The Essential Difference* ends with the caution that these are not by themselves diagnostic and that 'if you have concerns that you might have AS' after completing them *and* 'your concerns predate your filling out these tests', a general practitioner should be consulted.[41] While this is responsible advice, the scoring of the STEM-orientated statements could incur the possibility that the readers of Baron-Cohen's popular book who subsequently receive diagnoses are – albeit minutely – further reinforcing the UCARC's sySTEMizing hypothesis as critiqued earlier. Thus, *The Essential Difference* and its appendices implicitly encourage more men than women to present themselves for autism assessment: a consequence that would only reinforce the UCARC's profile of what it 'means' to be autistic.

Two of the UCARC's subsequent questionnaires used as screening tools for autism are the 'Empathy Quotient' (EQ) and 'Systemizing Quotient' (SQ) tests, both published in 2003.[42] While these have been used for preliminary diagnostic purposes, both questionnaires were also designed to test (if not support) a research hypothesis from Baron-Cohen et al. The journal article in which they were first published was not just a study of systemizing in autistic adults but an investigation (to quote the article's title) into 'normal sex differences'.[43] Again however, the research agenda here may potentially complicate the scientific validity of these questionnaires as diagnostic tools.

A 2003 article in *Philosophical Transactions of the Royal Society* by Baron-Cohen et al. (2003) launched the questionnaires by reporting on two studies – both of which yielded results 'as predicted', reinforcing Baron-Cohen's contention that the male brain is predominantly characterized by systemizing (Study 1), as is also the case with the autistic brain (Study 2). The first study measured the SQ in 278 adults from the 'general population' in order 'to test for predicted sex differences (male superiority) in systemizing'.[44] Seemingly of less interest to the researchers – and the article's title referred only to the SQ – 'subjects were also given the Empathy Quotient (EQ) to test if previous reports of female superiority would be replicated'.[45] Most of the previous reports cited were led by Baron-Cohen (author or co-author of 15 of the article's 42 references). The result 'as predicted' was that 'normal' – presumably meaning neurotypical – adult males 'scored significantly higher than females on the SQ and significantly lower on the EQ'. The second study reported in the article also fulfilled results 'as predicted'. Here, 47 adults 'with Asperger syndrome' or 'high-functioning autism' (33 males but only 14 females) completed the SQ and EQ questionnaires. As per the hypothesis, the autistic group scored more highly than the 'general population' group on systemizing.[46]

The irony of 'multiple-choice' questionnaires is that they already *restrict* choice (and the UCARC questionnaires ask that respondents complete each statement). This problem is merely a microcosm of a much vaster reality of science and perhaps of *any* search for knowledge. A methodology is a choice made by every researcher. However expertly informed, and however carefully planned, trialled and conducted a methodology may be, its selection excludes other methodologies – thus potentially excluding different results. In a progressive move which should highlight the continuing social and historical subjectivity surrounding both systemizing and autism, the UCARC's 2003 SQ questionnaire was revised in 2006 as the 'SQ-R' to include 'more items that might be relevant to females in the general population'.[47] However, the version of the SQ included in the 2012 edition of Baron-Cohen's *The Essential Difference* is the unrevised original. In an extensive critique of the extreme male brain theory, Jordynn Jack (2014), a professor of English specializing in the gendered rhetoric of scientific narratives, emphasizes that in the 2006 version, the mean SQ score for women rose from 13.2 per cent to 32 per cent.[48] Yet as Jack notices and demonstrates, the SQ-R alterations are primarily gender-*neutral* rather than reflecting 'typically feminine interests' which may also involve systemizing. She adds that 'knitting, sewing and crafting involve spatial reasoning, understanding or designing patterns, and seeing how pieces fit together'.[49] In a hearteningly pioneering gesture of constructive criticism from the humanities to the sciences, Jack suggests how the SQ-R might be further revised towards a more balanced acknowledgement of typically feminine interests. For instance, the statement 'If there were a problem with the electrical wiring in my home, I'd be able to fix it myself' (SQ-R) could be complemented with 'If I lost a button on a shirt, I'd be able to fix it myself'.[50] While these examples invoke very conservative notions of womanhood, there is a crucial distinction here: unlike the UCARC's reports, Jack's narrative is critically *aware* of gender.

Jack notes that Baron-Cohen's 2003 rhetoric, like other popular science texts on gender, tends 'to portray hegemonic masculinity only, and to take that as representative of all males' behaviour'.[51] And, of course, patriarchy oppresses boys and men, as well as girls and women. A further implication of Baron-Cohen's antiquated naming of leadership as an essentially male quality (see earlier) is its reinforcement that in effect, conformity for men means high achievement – and, thus, a life defined by competition. Not all men, whether autistic or neurotypical, assume that being stereotypically male is a good thing. And it can be hard for autistic men, as well as autistic women, to be told that 'autism is an empathy disorder'.[52] Nevertheless, the pressures of hegemonic masculinity on autistic men are minor when compared with how the extreme male brain idea marginalizes autistic girls and women. In the patriarchal terms of *The Essential Difference* – made more conspicuous by remaining implicit rather than acknowledged or questioned – 'hegemonic femininity' would be an oxymoron. Jack critically identifies the counterpart to hegemonic masculinity as 'emphasized femininity' – that is, practices which support patriarchy 'by portraying women as weak, frivolous and emotional'.[53]

In the UCARC's formulations, autistics are in effect people whose condition is so characterized by systemizing that they struggle to respond in the expected ways to what cannot so easily be systemized. But what about excessive empathy? Is that, too, an impairment? And can *autistic* people be excessive empathizers? In Baron-Cohen's work on the extreme male brain theory of autism, no answers – nor even much interest – have been offered in relation to such questions. While interviewing Baron-Cohen, Feinstein, citing work in progress by Carol Gray, pointed out that 'many people with Asperger's syndrome could actually be said to have *too much* empathy'. The leader of the UCARC responded by emphasizing that most autistic people 'are not unkind or uncaring' but 'have difficulty in picking up on other people's cues' and recognizing when 'someone is upset or bored'.[54] But do social cues (and readings of them) too not constitute a process of *systemizing*? Not according to Baron-Cohen, who writes of systemizing and empathizing as if wholly separate realms. He questions whether extreme empathizing even exists; his vague speculations on this indicate more than anything the disinterest in such concerns – associated with femininity – from scientists.[55]

Though the tone of Baron-Cohen's writing on women sometimes appears celebratory, it remains distinctly paternalistic. Praising people's dignity and resilience under inequality risks distracting from, and excusing, the broader systems that sustain their oppression. Frustratingly, the hypotheses of Baron-Cohen and the UCARC are effectively a part of this system. In *The Essential Difference*, women are discussed only in terms of how they may serve (or, at best, compensate for the limitations of) men.

Catherine Faherty, a psycho-educational specialist, formed an adult social group specifically for women with Asperger syndrome because of the struggles they face in being 'a minority within a minority'.[56] Faherty (2006) reports:

> Women with autism have expressed their feeling that more is expected of them than from their male counterparts, simply because of their gender. Members of the group felt that expectations to be sensitive and empathetic – qualities typically attributed to women – are unfair and difficult to meet.[57]

Again, as with Willey's comments quoted earlier, implications abound of how normative ideas of femininity can be repressive even before they intersect with the pressures of conformity to neurotypical expectations.

If empathizing and systemizing are 'wholly different', is it a problem that UCARC seeks to 'measure' empathy only through rigidly *systematic* methodologies (that is, multiple 'choice' questionnaires)? If definitions and diagnoses are to retain consistency, then it is, of course, necessary that medical assessments use systemized methodologies. Unfortunately, the main questionnaires used to decide whether or not an individual reaches the later stages of autism assessment carry what appears to be an implicitly male bias. Again, this should elicit questions over the objectivity and reliability of these questionnaires in their present states.

Like the AQ questionnaire, SQ and EQ tests are only a *part* of diagnostic procedure: assessment also involves face-to-face meetings and, usually, semi-structured observations. But is there no risk that completion of the questionnaires as a first stage of diagnostic assessment might influence perceptions in more extensive psychiatric consultations? And if systemizing really is a male process, as Baron-Cohen tirelessly argues, then one potentially major ramification yielded by his own implicit logic is that women being assessed for autism are being viewed primarily through an implicitly masculine (and, by extension, patriarchal) gaze and frame of reference.

THE EXTREME MALE GAZE: SCIENTIFIC 'EVIDENCE' ON AUTISM AND TESTOSTERONE

The most questionable gap in the logic supporting Baron-Cohen's naming of autism as the extreme male brain is its dodging of the following concern. If male and female brains are as different as the UK's most prominent autism diagnostician theorizes, then is it not likely that autism could therefore *express* itself differently between women and men? Discussing the playing habits of children and the socializing tendencies of adults, Baron-Cohen asserts that females tend to prefer intimate social activity: conversing with other female friends. He then suggests that males are more likely to gravitate together into competitive group activity.[58] But when considering these comments on sex and socializing, it needs to be asked whether male tendencies to socialize in groups – whether that is a generalization, a biological predisposition and/or a cultural expectation – could make male autistics more socially *identifiable*. Autism is made conceivable as a medical and social identity only by comparing a person's presence against that of others. Thus, in group situations – whether mixed, male or female – the differences that constitute autism may become more pronounced (as I quite painfully know from social gatherings). This pattern is also fundamental to most of the autism fiction discussed later in the present chapter: the focus tends to land on a singular autistic figure *in relation* to a group of other, neurotypical characters.

Key publications by the UCARC hypothesize that above-average levels of prenatal testosterone lead to socially male characteristics as located in the brain's right hemisphere. Yet these ostensibly scientific studies are overwhelmingly concerned with testosterone and the right-brain hemisphere, giving barely any scientific acknowledgement to oestrogen, to women or to the left brain. Other hormones besides testosterone might also be relevant to sex differences in the mind, Baron-Cohen (2003) momentarily recognized, but that 'is a topic for another book', which the UCARC does not appear to have yet begun researching.[59] As such, the extreme male brain idea remains limited by an imbalance of scientific attention to the corresponding factors against which the hypothesis may be compared or even defined.

Like many terms in the scientific rhetoric used to conjecture and to (hypothetically) define autism, the extreme male brain is less a theory than a metaphor. *The Essential Difference* details the UCARC's research into hypothesized links between prenatal testosterone levels and autistic traits. The longitudinal research project that periodically studies a sample of children after birth to support this hypothesis warrants brief attention here because the coverage given to these studies in *The Essential Difference* creates what may be a hasty impression of scientific affirmation.[60] (And, in turn, while *The Essential Difference* is a popular science book, it is cited in subsequent UCARC journal articles.)[61]

The Cambridge-based Fetal Steroid Hormones project utilizes samples of amniotic fluid (which had been stored for separate, medical reasons) to measure prenatal exposure to testosterone.[62] Lutchmaya, Baron-Cohen and Raggat (2002) reported that smaller vocabularies in infants (observed at 18 and then 24 months) may correlate with above-average levels of fetal testosterone.[63] In a separate article, also published in 2002, these authors reported that higher than typical levels of fetal testosterone correlated with smaller amounts of eye contact, though this study focused on a different age group to the preceding experiment (12 months).[64] While it is possible to see how these studies found patterns that could parallel certain traits of autism in some people, *none of the children observed in either experiment were in fact autistic.*

In a follow-up 2009 study, many of the same children were the focus of a larger-scale UCARC-dominated study (featuring Baron-Cohen as a co-author) in *British Journal of Psychology*, which attention grabbingly seemed to link autism itself with prenatal testosterone.[65] This experiment was based on responses from mothers (only mothers) to two UCARC-designed questionnaires for screening childhood autistic traits.[66] In a University of Cambridge press release titled 'Research Links Testosterone Levels to Autistic Traits', Baron-Cohen was quoted as remarking on the 'shame' that

> this research was inaccurately reported in some sections of the media that suggested the study demonstrated that elevated foetal testosterone is associated with a clinical diagnosis of autism.[67]

The title of the 2009 *British Journal of Psychology* article was 'Fetal Testosterone and Autistic Traits': the implicit emphasis of Baron-Cohen's earlier
statement concerns *clinical diagnosis* (not just 'traits'). He added: 'We all
have some autistic traits – these are a spectrum or a dimension of individual
differences, like height'.[68] Interviewed by Feinstein for *A History of Autism*
(2010), Baron-Cohen acknowledged that the autistic traits found in his 2009
study were 'not necessarily indicative of autism' because all the children
involved were developing typically – that is, not autistically.[69] Thus, if the
main scientific studies concerning autism and the extreme male brain have
only involved non-autistic subjects, its credibility remains, for the time being,
deeply questionable. What also remains problematic is that the UCARC
publications involved in constructing extreme male brain theory offer very
little consideration to how autistic identity may unhelpfully complicate
self-perception for women through its equation with maleness – *extreme*
maleness, at that. In such ways, the extreme male brain theory marginalizes
women with Asperger syndrome (diagnosed or not) from the very point of
hypothesis.

For as long as autism is researched and narrated as a form of maleness, it
seems inevitable that autistic girls and women will remain under-diagnosed
and under-represented – effectively creating a triad of subordinations around
their identities. In addition to the inequalities of patriarchy, undiagnosed
autistic women face the struggles of this way of being without the possible
self-understanding (or the understanding of others) that diagnosis may potentially help to bring. The issue of concern here extends beyond individual
diagnoses: it also involves the ways in which autism is conceptualized and
researched. How, in the face of the scientific imbalances outlined in this
discussion, can we hope to sketch anything like a meaningful picture of the
relationship between gender and autism? One solution might be for autism
scientists to engage more with perspectives from the humanities, which
would offer a vastly expanded academic framework for discussing gender
(and research methodologies). The most constructive and urgent gesture of
all, though, would surely be for UCARC to consult and represent autistic
women (and their publications) in its research.

FICTIONS OF THE NEW CLASSIC AUTISM

It is poignant and prescient that Les Murray's 1994 poem 'It Allows a Portrait in Line Scan at Fifteen' ends with a teenager 'looking terrified' into the
future and repeating '*I gotta get smart!*'.[70] Within a decade of its publication, cultural interpellations of what it means to be an autistic adult would

make being 'smart' bluntly paramount: smart in the sense of outstanding, yet conventionally measured, intellectual skills and smart in conforming to bourgeois notions of achievement – principally through distinction in professional employment. Essentially, what began to dominate autism portrayals by the 2000s – across novels, films and journalism, and as we have seen, certain areas of science – is an ableist, neurotypical *ideal* of the autistic adult. It is instructive here to group together four of the most commercially enduring autism fictions: Barry Levinson's Hollywood film *Rain Man* (1988), Mark Haddon's young adult novel *The Curious Incident of the Dog in the Night-Time* (2003), the Warner Brothers–distributed American situation comedy *Big Bang Theory* (2007–) and Australian author Graeme Simsion's romantic comedy novel *The Rosie Project* (2013).

The earlier *Rain Man* is actually now becoming an unusual autism portrayal: Raymond Babbitt has spent most of his life living in a psychiatric institution and needs continual support in daily life. In Haddon's novel, Christopher Boone is 15 and attends a special educational needs school. However, the lifestyle of Christopher, who has Asperger syndrome, is notably less limited by autism than that of Raymond. For instance, even at 15, Christopher is able to travel relatively long distances alone. Yet four years after Haddon's novel (and, more to the point, its enormous commercial and media success), *Big Bang Theory* marks another developmental milestone in autism fictions. As chapter 2 pointed out, the signifiers of Asperger syndrome in the main character of Sheldon Cooper are blatant enough to establish this identity – or popular, post-*Curious* ideas of this identity – to enable it to be continually obvious without needing to be named. But the key difference is that, unlike Levinson or Haddon's characters, Sheldon has no need for diagnosis. He is a successful theoretical physicist. While it is probable that he would score 100 per cent on the Cambridge Adult Autism-Spectrum Quotient test, Sheldon's character lacks the decisive diagnostic criteria which is *not* part of that questionnaire: genuine impairment or suffering because of his autistic traits. In 2013, the central character of Graeme Simsion's international bestseller *The Rosie Project* is Don Tillman, who (in the publisher's words) 'is a genetics professor who just might be somewhere on the autism spectrum'.[71] Like Sheldon, and again in contrast with Raymond Babbitt and (to a lesser degree) Christopher Boone, Don Tillman has no need for a formal diagnosis. Across these four fictions from the past 30 years, I see a trajectory in which autistic impairments recede. Meanwhile, what remains is the motif of exceptional ability: in each of these cases, in mathematics or sciences.

Hence, a new kind of classic autism has emerged as a subject of fixation within contemporary culture. It is apparent not only in fiction but also, as chapter 1 and then the previous two parts of this chapter explored, in certain factions of science. Such points of emphasis on (extremely) 'high-functioning' adult autism partly reflect the increased recognition of Asperger syndrome alongside Kanner's autism. But it would be wrong to say that the former has in any simple way superseded the latter in popular culture. What *Big Bang Theory* and *The Rosie Project* 'represent' is not Asperger syndrome, so much as a comforting, inanimately cartoon-like caricature of the condition. In essence, they are merely diluted versions of what had already proven to be the most commercially friendly notions of what it means to be an autistic adult. Thus, if Sheldon and Don can be manufactured to pass as synecdoches for autism by the culture industries, so too can they be made to serve as shorthand for mainstream cultural portrayals of autism in the 21st century.

Fundamentally, the most popular autism depictions are *idealistic* – or at least, idealistic within the bounds of capitalist ideologies. Autism – or the new classic autism – has come to occupy a cultural position that even idealizes disability itself. In the past two decades, it has been the focus of more cultural display than almost any other impairment or condition. And these idealized autism portrayals – within themselves, but also through their uniformity, frequency and commercial success – are distillations of dominant ideologies. In most instances, the lives both real and fictitious used to portray autism in the mainstream have been white. As well as under-representing the ethnic diversity of autism, this means there has been little cultural recognition of how autistic identity can intersect with other forms of marginalization and oppression. While it may be wrong to imagine that in novels and other written narratives in Western culture, most autistic characters are white, there are seldom suggestions of their being part of a racial minority, only a neurological minority.

Although many people with Asperger syndrome experience motor co-ordination difficulties, screen depictions of autism seldom reflect this. Autism has become part of idealized notions of the body. Nor is there much space in mainstream portrayals for the frequent comorbidities of autism, such as epilepsy, relentless anxiety or chronic depression. Bolstered by the 'geek syndrome' synecdoche of Silicon Valley, plus the UCARC's fixation on STEM, the new classic autism tends to utterly disregard the reality that many autistic adults face significant learning impairments. In a disservice to the vast numbers of individual adults actually living with autism or Asperger syndrome, the new classic autism promotes assumptions that most people 'on the spectrum' are fully employed in high-ranking professions which perfectly suit their skills and potential. Of course, the fictional likes of Sheldon and Don are shown to struggle with social and occasionally other aspects of their work as high-flying scientists, but this tends to be presented for comic consumption rather than as anything resembling a genuine attempt to engage with such struggles from an autistic perspective. Meanwhile, in 2016, the National Autistic Society's survey of autistic adults found that under 16 per cent of participants were in full-time employment, and that 51 per cent of those who were employed felt their skills were higher than the job required. The same survey from the National Autistic Society also reported that similar numbers of autistic people wanted to work in the arts (11 per cent) as in information technology (10 per cent).[72]

The new classic autistic adults in fiction and culture are almost invariably able-bodied, heterosexual and middle class. Their supposed disability thus rarely intersects with any other non-normative identity or experience. Chapter 1 critiqued Margaret Atwood's use of autism as a narrative prosthetic in *Oryx and Crake* (2003), but at least narrative prosthesis there enables cultural satire. It may be that my own autism is limiting my appreciation of Sheldon and Don (even their names are similar) – but to me, they seem to have been conceived for comedy value only. Autistic scholar and advocate Laurence Arnold wrote of *Rain Man*:

> Notwithstanding the relationship between Raymond and Charlie, without the savant skills, there would be no plot and his autism and rare skills are presented in such a way as to promote amazement.[73]

Again, the later examples of *Big Bang Theory* and *The Rosie Project* intensify this lack. Without the constant humour brought by their social clumsiness, Sheldon and Don simply would not be characters. They are, to adopt a term used in 1927 by the novelist and critic E. M. Forster, 'flat'. Distinguishing these from 'round' characters in fiction, Forster summarized that flat characters 'are constructed round a single idea or quality'; when there is more than one factor in them, 'we get a curve towards the round'. However, 'the really flat character' can be 'expressed in one sentence'.[74] For instance, 'Don is a genetics professor who just might be somewhere on the autism spectrum'.[75] Flat characters, Forster suggests, 'are easily remembered by the reader afterwards'. Their ability to remain unaltered by experience – admittedly, a prerequisite for a character in a long-running sitcom – gives them 'a comforting quality'.[76] More bleakly, flat characters may be comforting because they reinforce some audiences' own imaginings and prejudices – because they closely resemble other fictional characters.[77] It would be unduly simplistic – or flat criticism – to deny that *Big Bang Theory* and *The Rosie Project* at times convey certain experiences of adult autism in moving, possibly consoling ways. Even I have sometimes admired these, in both texts. But such moments can also distract from the more repressive features of these depictions. Here, a broader critical and cultural view is needed.

In *Dialectic of Enlightenment* (1944), Marxist critical theorists Theodor W. Adorno and Max Horkheimer attack the standardization inherent in mass-produced cultural texts. Under standardization, popular culture – or, in their term, *mass* culture – endlessly repeats the styles, motifs, themes and values already familiar to audiences. Standardized mass cultural texts, they argue, mount a pernicious assault on our very ability to think critically. In doing so, such texts reinforce dominant power structures. Mass culture is, in effect, mass interpellation. According to Adorno and Horkheimer, standardization tells us what to think and how. 'There is nothing left for the consumer to classify. Producers have done it for him'.[78] We can see variants on this within one of the most insidiously standardized patterns in new classic autism, which, for brevity, I will call 'paratextual autism'.

Autism or Asperger syndrome are frequently named in the *paratexts* of films and novels: that is, publishers' blurbs on the backs of books and on websites, and the promotional materials announcing a new film or television series. Using autism to *sell* these products, such paratexts classify key characters before we have the chance to make up our own minds about them. Haddon's novel was a trailblazer in this. The paperback's rear cover declared:

> Christopher is fifteen and has Asperger's Syndrome. He knows a great deal about maths and very little about human beings. He loves lists, patterns and the truth.[79]

Not only has this classified Christopher and the readers' views of him; it also interpellates the audience with a notion of what Asperger syndrome means. Autism itself is not named on the cover, but it certainly was in most contemporary media responses to the novel (acting as further paratexts), in which the then less well-known name of Asperger syndrome was explained as a form of autism via references to Christopher.[80] Parallels with *Rain Man* in the blurb quotation are clear enough via the mention of maths, and the description could also apply to both Sheldon Cooper and Don Tillman. Meanwhile, the UCARC was standardizing the association of autism and STEM subjects through its repeated academic publications and the widespread media coverage of this research.

Adorno and Horkheimer distinguish 'serious' art from the 'mass art' created by the culture industry in the sense that the agenda of the latter's production is (or becomes) overwhelmingly commercial. In addition, they ascribe what they regard as the triviality of mass entertainment to the capitalist conditions under which the majority of audiences consume it:

> Amusement under late capitalism is the prolongation of work. It is sought after as an escape from the mechanized work process, and to recruit strength in order to be able to cope with it again.[81]

In this view, we are all so exhausted by the demands of work (or so drained by the stresses of unemployment) that we seek entertainment to distract us from reality, hence the shallowness of popular fiction and cinema. Again, this principle is applicable to the increasing simplicity and uniformity inherent in the new classic autism as disseminated through popular science as well as film, television and fiction. Audiences – so the culture industry assumes, at least – want to be entertained by texts which demand and prompt minimal critical thinking. Hence, we are being presented with a lengthening parade of fictional adults who exhibit autism in increasingly narrow, shallow and uniform terms. The new classic autism does not glamorize merely adult autistic experience. It also fictionalizes and idealizes the provisions and opportunities for autistic adults in contemporary society. *Is there any way out of this?*

* * *

Adorno's most extensive commentary on standardization and its effects occurs in his 1941 essay on the form he most despised: popular music. Also a composer of and scholar on classical (which he called serious) music, Adorno argued that the standardization of structures, beats and lyrical themes in popular music would always prevent the genre's progression. He viewed any deviations from standardized content as merely superficial details of 'pseudo-individualization', which ultimately distract from the uniform nature of the overall form and content.[82] However, at this point in the chapter – and the present stage in the evolution of autism narratives – a more optimistic viewpoint is not just vital but (as the following sections of this chapter seek to show) justifiable.

Adorno and Horkheimer's 1944 observations can help elucidate wider cultural implications of how autism becomes trivialized in the most commercially successful texts, but it is also worth challenging their passionate yet defeatist stance. Amid standardized forms and structures, the slightest deviations – even while they can simultaneously be dismissed as pseudo-individualization – carry all the more force (including the potential to create something genuinely arresting, for instance in The Who's 'Underture' as a musical contemplation of autism, discussed in chapter 2). Thus, in partial opposition to Adorno and Horkheimer, I do not suggest that in autism narratives – even those aimed at the largest audiences – standardization and progress can ever be true binaries.[83] Like Judith Butler's terms of performativity and performance (to be discussed in chapter 5), the relationship between standardization and progress can be interactive. The latter can *subvert* the former even if it never escapes it.

The 21st-century narratives attacked in this chapter constitute a new classic autism. Yet it is crucial to recognize that in their distance from many realities of adult autistic experience – and even in their distance from *Rain Man* – they expose the malleability of how autism is narrated and of how this is accepted within the culture industry. The next half of this chapter therefore turns to a range of more progressive fictions of adult autism which, while often continuing an emphasis on ability at the expense of recognizing impairment, offer subversive counterparts to the texts discussed earlier. Many of the dominant tropes already identified still remain – but never *all* of them. Despite Adorno and Horkheimer's emphasis that as audiences we are conditioned to want only more of the same, various lesser-known 21st-century autism fictions effectively challenge such contentions that in the culture industry 'imitation becomes absolute'.[84] If imitation becomes absolute, what might then happen is that our familiarity with standardized patterns becomes 'absolute' and that audiences require something more. Each of the next three texts addressed *complicates* the motif of the adult autist as a high-achieving white male. In doing so, these narratives position autism not as a flat motif of amusing social awkwardness but pivotally as a subjectivity and experience which intersects with simultaneous aspects of identity. A cynical view of this could be that such changes to the dominant tropes offer mere pseudo-individualization within standardized patterns. Yet even if that is amid the agendas at work, it does not prevent these portrayals from marking timely progressions in autism fiction.

BRON/BROEN: NEURODIVERSITY, *THE BRIDGE* AND AUTISTIC 'ADHERENCE TO RULES'

In the Swedish-Danish television drama *Bron/Broen* (2011–2016) – broadcast in the UK on BBC Four as *The Bridge* – the significance of adult autism is both central and spectral: central because the series' most long-standing central character, Swedish detective Saga Norén (played by Sofia Helin), convincingly embodies many of the cerebral and social traits of autism; and spectral because although the promotion of *The Bridge* repeatedly stated that Saga has Asperger syndrome, all terminology associated with autism remains absent from the actual script. But despite this unconvincing social avoidance of the name in an era when autism receives so much cultural attention (and despite the ill-judged figure of Saga's refrigerated mother, noted in chapter 2), there are still many progressive elements to how this acclaimed Nordic Noir drama series evokes autistic experience.

As played by Helin, Saga embodies traits of new classic autism as presented on screen through physical glamour and middle-class achievement. A celebrated symbol of the series itself is Saga's green Porsche. However, *The Bridge*'s main point of independence from standard tropes is, of course, the foregrounding of a woman as an autistic adult character. Moreover, each of the three series to date finely illustrates various, complex overlaps of autistic identity with other facets of adult life, including love and sex. Saga's difficulties in adjusting to a relationship once it involves living together are shown throughout the second series. This offers much humour to viewers but not for Saga. However, the main intersections of autistic subjectivity with outward identity in *The Bridge* concern the workplace. Saga is a police detective who, though successful in this role, is soon asked by a new colleague why she has not pursued promotion. She answers that she is 'not cut out for management'.[85] With this detail, the series hints at how senior managerial roles are not designed to accommodate the individualities of autistic adults. The new colleague who is curiously asking Saga about her aspirations is Martin Rohde, a charismatic and kindly Danish detective with whom she is obliged to collaborate on two cases involving both Swedish and Danish residents. The extreme male brain metaphor has received more attention in the UK and US than in Scandinavia, but, nevertheless, there is something tacitly apt in how Saga's peers never seem to entertain the possibility that she is autistic. But Saga's commitment is often exploited; she works longer and harder than any of her (mostly male) colleagues and is never rewarded for this.

While *The Bridge*'s investigative plotline is extensive, throughout the first two series, much of the focus concerns the intense professional (and platonic) relationship between Saga and Martin. Yet, as the frequently stunning shots of the Scandinavian landscape silently articulate, *The Bridge* is a drama that deals with much more than individual personalities. Foremost in the opening shots to most episodes (and the location of key events) is the Øresund Bridge: the five-mile structure linking two nations – Sweden and Denmark – across the water of the Øresund Strait. Correspondingly, an overarching theme across each series of *Bron/Broen*, or *The Bridge*, is hybridity. The original Scandinavian broadcast is scripted in both Swedish and Danish in accordance with the characters' nationalities. Dualities (and their disintegration) are integral to the events and uncertainties played out through the storylines, including sex and gender, life and death, morality and loyalty, innocence and exploitation, sexuality and friendship and power and honour. These themes are noteworthy here because their presence relieves *The Bridge* from being merely an exhibition of autism as a cultural curiosity point. It becomes instead part of a deeper interplay of identities and standpoints. A most obvious meeting of dualities in *The Bridge* is the relationship between the autistic Saga and the socially intuitive Martin. Such pairings of autistic and non-autistic lead characters have been standard in a range of fictions since *Rain Man* and, as Murray observes, this narrative technique 'mediates an idea of the human by a refractive comparison of the two'.[86] However, a further, subtler tension also arises from *The Bridge*: the often subjective relationship between impairment and disability.

In their 2002 reconsideration of the Social Model of disability and whether it had become outdated, Shakespeare and Watson assert the following point in relation to *impairment* as a difference of the body and/or mind, and *disability* as social oppression:

> Impairment and disability are not dichotomous, but describe different places on a continuum, or different aspects of a single experience. It is difficult to determine where impairment ends and disability starts, but such vagueness need not be debilitating.[87]

A basic but useful distinction here is that impairment is located in the experience of the self, while disability is created – albeit often unknowingly – by others. However, autism itself is at the very intersection of impairment and disability because it remains a 'condition' defined according to *social* presence, including language and interaction. Ben Belek's frequently brilliant website *The Autism Anthropologist* praises *The Bridge* as 'a wonderful series' in an otherwise shallow genre of serial killing dramas and comments: 'People always appear to have trouble figuring out what to say to [Saga], how to react to her'.[88] This enables recognition of a deeper implication: conversely to the standard assumptions that autistic people struggle to understand social cues and rules, it is the mostly neurotypical figures surrounding Saga who are confused by *her* behaviour. Through this repeated pattern, *The Bridge* encapsulates one of the greatest contradictions at work in how autism is defined – or, at least, defined from outside. Belek's commentary gives a Social Model reading of *The Bridge*, writing that while having the signs of Asperger syndrome as conceptualized in the West at the present time, Saga is not ultimately autistic because 'autism only exists when there are people around to call it that. And if no one ever does? Then autism simply does not exist'.[89]

Belek does not undermine the neurological distinctiveness of autism but emphasizes the historical subjectivity of its usage as a term to otherize. Nonetheless, despite the fact that autism is never named within the script, Saga's overt Aspergic traits attract much comment (and exclusively shared glances) from her co-workers – and her autistic tendencies are essential not only to her character but also to the plot of each series.

When, in the first episode, her supervisors arrange (while she is elsewhere) for Saga to collaborate with Martin, one colleague asks another (thus interpellating Saga's otherness to the audience), 'Does he know she's a bit – odd?'.[90] Painfully, in Series 2, the audience can see something that Saga cannot: her brusque manner is causing her junior colleague Rasmus to feel taken for granted and even bullied, leading to this confrontation:

> *RASMUS:* It's plain to see something's seriously wrong with you. . . . How the fuck are you allowed to be on the force?
>
> *SAGA:* I'm an excellent detective.
>
> *RASMUS:* Right. Over-analytical robots devoid of any emotions are just what the force needs.[91]

An irony is, of course, that emotional detachment *can* be advantageous (and even essential) in many occupations that involve working with people. Saga is nonetheless distraught after Rasmus's outburst. When Martin tries to comfort her, she reveals, in one of *The Bridge*'s most haunting suggestions of adult autistic experience, that she is upset not because of what he actually said but because Rasmus is 'not the first' to think 'I'm incapable of getting hurt'.[92]

One of *The Bridge*'s most enabling features is the complication it potentially offers to one of the most tedious clichés in how people with Asperger syndrome are perceived from outside. I refer to what Elizabeth Fein – in a 2011 publication titled 'Innocent Machines: Asperger's Syndrome and the Neurostructural Self' – terms our rigid 'adherence to rules'.[93] That last phrase grates with searing irony because the whole definition of autism as an impairment depends on our divergence from 'rules' in the sense of normative uses of communication, routine and even life itself. The notion of overly strict autistic adherence to rules should thus call into question who is 'ruling' the otherness of this identity. In *The Bridge*, Saga's loyalty to the law (and to her identity-defining role as a police detective) supersedes all of her professional and personal affinities with Martin. The increasing tension between them concerns not whether their love will become sexual, but whether Saga will report Martin's transgressions to authorities.

Yet the richest irony of Saga's uncompromisingly literal fulfilment of the law – which she performs as the *only* meaningful set of rules in life – is that so much of *The Bridge* is made entertaining (and heartening) by Saga's transcendence of the pettier rules of social behaviour. It is these unwritten rules that construct the expectations of communication and other interactions against which autism is defined, and Saga flouts them. In doing so, Saga's character not only 'performs' recognizable autism but also offers to highlight the shallowness and even the pointlessness of conventionally acceptable social interaction. A continuing instance of this is Saga's attitude to small talk (or what the UCARC's 2001 Autism-Quotient questionnaire twice asks about as 'social chit-chat').[94] Martin patiently tries to inform (or normalize) Saga with regard to social niceties, but these remain of relatively little interest to her. Yet Saga's transgressions of these frequently imply less an impaired social understanding on her part than a sincere (and vibrantly critical) engagement with whatever the subject may be. This is evident in one of Martin's first conversations with Saga. When he asks if she has any children, Saga surprises Martin with the bluntness of her answer: 'Why would I want to?' And yet surely, in any discussion about having children, what more important question could there be than why we want to?

Such conversational moments are a staple of *The Bridge*, but Saga is similarly anarchic (or merely genuine) with regard to non-verbal gestures. For instance, on more than one occasion in front of others after a long shift at work, she openly sniffs her own armpits and then applies some deodorant. Although, since Saga is fictitious, speculating her intentions quickly risks becoming facile, it is a mark of the neurotypical gaze which the series seems to prioritize that some critics applaud her eccentricities while assuming that she is unaware of how she appears to others. In a lengthy and joyfully enthusiastic commentary on each episode for *The Guardian*, Saga is esteemed as an 'unwitting critic of bourgeois social mores'.[95] But my riposte to this description is that the word 'unwitting' marks a frequently problematic assumption regarding certain manifestations of autistic individuality, which overlooks the existence of autistic *agency*. Thus, a seminal question concerning autistic defiance of superficial social conventions needs to be: is the individual oblivious, or *indifferent*, to the judgements of neurotypical others? Or, more radically, is she *disdainful* of them? Workplaces demand collaboration, but as Saga demonstrates, collaboration does not need conformity. A gift of *The Bridge* is that its lead character inspires deeper contemplation of the meanings of adult autism in everyday life – and not just for neurotypical audiences.

KAY MELLOR'S *THE SYNDICATE* (2015): CLASS, CRIMINALITY, RACE AND ADULT AUTISM

The intersections of autistic identity with racial minority and manual labour have rarely been given exposure in culture or fiction. Yet, with boldness as well as subtlety often lacking in fictional portrayals, these are core themes in the third series of British writer and director Kay Mellor's television drama *The Syndicate* (BBC One, 2015). Through Mellor's writing and direction, as well as performances of Lenny Henry (as Godfrey Watson, a gardener with Asperger syndrome) and Susan McArdle (as Wendy Vickers, his fiancé), *The Syndicate* touches on complexities rarely addressed in psychiatric discourse, let alone mainstream entertainment. Each series of Mellor's *The Syndicate* revolves around a different group of characters who win the National Lottery.

The syndicate of series three is a group of five staff in a country house who share a multi-million pound win but remain on the estate. Precisely while they are learning of their fortune, the glamorous Amy – 17-year-old daughter of a fellow syndicate member – disappears. The mystery of Amy's apparent abduction dominates the storyline, but innumerable sub-plots develop around and between the characters.

In some ways, *The Syndicate*'s 2015 depiction of autism is conventional and therefore questionable. Godfrey's appearances are often peripheral to the rest of 'the syndicate'. Flashback scenes reveal complexities of the other characters' earlier lives, but Godfrey is merely a bystander in these. When, in the last episode, the scene cuts from a dramatic boat chase to Godfrey berating a builder for being 16 hours and 24 minutes late, it feels as though his anxieties are being trivialized for comedy. Godfrey is often laughed at but rarely laughs. Perhaps such details frustrate me not because they are weak spots in the realism but conversely, because they illustrate facets of the 'outsider' status often felt acutely by autistic adults. Nevertheless, such details do little to challenge standard expectations of what an autistic character may provide on a television series; they also exemplify how *The Syndicate* plays to a neurotypical 'gaze'. This is not always problematic, however. As I shall proceed to address, Mellor's directions utilize this neurotypical gaze in provocative but progressive ways.

As if to immediately establish that the audience is viewing an autistic character, Godfrey Watson's first appearances in *The Syndicate* show him agitatedly reciting sequences of numbers and dates. In this preoccupation, he recalls Haddon's Christopher but more pointedly Levinson's Raymond Babbitt (Dustin Hoffman): an autistic savant with seemingly infinite capacities for arithmetic, as well as an eidetic memory. In one of *Rain Man*'s most famous scenes, Raymond's savant abilities help his brother gain a huge casino win. Mellor's opening storyline centres on Godfrey's belief that he has calculated a formula to predict winning lottery numbers. Eager to share his expected fortune, he insists that the whole syndicate use his selection of numbers. However, the member buying the tickets loses Godfrey's list of calculations and chooses her own numbers. The multi-million pound win proves Godfrey's mathematical formula useless. His distress at this outweighs any initial pleasure in now being a millionaire. Godfrey seemingly plays the lottery because he is interested in numbers, not money. After winning, he continues to work in the garden. The failed lottery calculation marks one of several storylines in which *The Syndicate* deflates popular associations regarding autism. Godfrey is not a savant. The allusive wink towards *Rain Man* feels satirical, yet the target seems not to be autism, nor Levinson's actual film, but neurotypical assumptions regarding autistic people. Much of *The Syndicate* proceeds to similarly, sometimes unsettlingly, expose and subvert preconceptions.

Like nearly all fictional adult autistic characters, Godfrey is not just verbal; he is verbose. The script's most valuably realistic portrayal of autistic experience lies in how Godfrey's struggle is not in expressing himself, but in being understood by others. However, a subtle quality of *The Syndicate* is how it points to language as structured interaction in much more subtle ways. Integral to this are Godfrey's most passionate interests: gardening and wildlife. The direction might visually have featured more of the garden's minutiae as a gesture towards his own subjectivity (and hard work). Instead, the lawns, trees and vegetables are primarily represented through his spoken lines, which most other characters ignore. Even so, the garden's importance to Godfrey presents a variant in how autistic subjectivity can be read. Godfrey's seemingly monologue-like style of conversation – mostly about the garden – frequently isolates him from his friends. Yet the garden itself is in a sense his own, highly eloquent, non-verbal form of expression. It is also a form of *response* for him, as he attends to its living organisms in accordance with demands of the seasons and weather.

Although Godfrey and his peers never name autism itself, twice in *The Syndicate*'s script, it is stated that he has a 'condition' (once – and so refreshingly in autism fiction – this is mentioned by the autist himself). That this condition causes him considerable distress is signified by his need for medication to help with his 'darker moods'. However, much of Godfrey's suffering through Asperger syndrome is actually social at root: it implicates the burdens of not simply autistic subjectivity but autistic identity in a neurotypically ordered world. In the only details given of his past throughout the series, the third episode includes this exchange between Godfrey and his boss, Lord Charles Hazelwood:

GODFREY: I went for an interview to work in a bank . . . .

CHARLES: Did you get the job in the bank?

GODFREY: No. They said I was exceptionally skilled but unfortunately not with people. I think it comes with my condition, you know.

CHARLES: Yes, well. I'm sure you're probably right.

GODFREY: That's when I decided to go in for gardening.[96]

More drastically than for *Big Bang Theory*'s Sheldon (physicist) or *The Bridge*'s Saga (police detective), Godfrey's condition – and social attitudes towards it – has limited his employment opportunities. However, the quoted dialogue typifies the depth of subtlety in Mellor's script, capturing the awkward cautiousness which often surrounds – and perhaps fences off – open discussion of autism ('Yes, well. I'm sure you're probably right'). Yet the scene also affirms significant agency on Godfrey's part: although seemingly not his first choice of work, he *decided* to pursue gardening and has been successful.

Living and working among others who accept his condition without pressuring Godfrey to change or conform, his autism seems to affect his life less as disability than *vulnerability*. However, his outward identity is susceptible to gross misunderstanding. Ambiguities surrounding Godfrey's behaviour (perhaps, inevitably, given *The Syndicate*'s format) are dramatized. This enables the series to both play into and subvert problematic assumptions regarding autism. The earlier post-*Rain Man* equation of autism with numeracy played with preconceptions, but subsequent turns in the plot venture deeper, appealing to *prejudice*. When Amy goes missing, the autistic labourer is first to be suspected of her apparent abduction.

Before Amy disappears, Godfrey's affable character has been established as childlike in the sense of being prone to temperamental outbursts, but also in being harmless. However, as Amy's absence lengthens, and the anxieties are heightened, perceptions of Godfrey shift, accentuating a focus on his unpredictable moods, and his great physical strength. While others' fears for Amy intensify, he continues to appear unconcerned. It is Andy – Amy's anguished father – who screams, in Godfrey's presence: 'Well *look* at him, he's such a weirdo!'. Andy is not a regular staff member on the estate; his perception of Godfrey is more an outsider's view. Soon, however, Amy's mother Dawn tearfully tells the police of Godfrey:

> He's a lovely man but you never know with people like him, he can get angry *so* easily.[97]

The wording shifts conspicuously from 'people like him' to Godfrey the individual, but others are more bluntly concerned by his condition. The drama's prominently cast young house manager, Sarah (Cara Theobold), is caring, sensible and highly conscientious. Yet it is Sarah who most questions Godfrey's morality. She gently confronts him, asking, 'You'd never do anything to hurt Amy, would you?'. Godfrey appears puzzled but unperturbed by the question, quietly answering 'No, oh no'. To her own discomfort, Sarah doubts his honesty. She seeks out Sean (Richard Rankin), the estate's gamekeeper (later shown to be recovering from a shameful past) and asks whether Godfrey could be responsible for Amy's disappearance. When Sean emphatically dismisses this suggestion, Sarah is unconvinced, replying that 'we really don't understand his condition'.[98] When the police find photographs of Amy over Godfrey's bed, he is arrested on suspicion of her abduction.

Should I, as an autistic viewer, feel ashamed that as this storyline developed, I too suspected Godfrey? Perhaps. But amid this, I found consolation through what I felt was *The Syndicate*'s resonance of another story.

John Steinbeck's 1937 novella *Of Mice and Men* concerns (among much else) the innocence, dreams and experience of a neurologically impaired labourer, Lennie Small. As a character conceived before autism was medically recognized, Lennie's relationship to the condition is debatable and culturally subjective.

However, like Lennie, Godfrey is a character who combines neurological impairment and physical might, and this troubles those around him.[99] In both texts, the conflation of disability with danger remains troubling. But perhaps most pertinent is the construction of a character who, while appearing accidentally capable of horrific actions, can still inspire compassion.

Godfrey's treatment by the police invokes autism as a disability intensified by the failure of non-autistics to recognize or seek to empathize with its subjectivities. Once Godfrey comes under suspicion, the police interpret his every word and gesture as if enhancing the likelihood of guilt. They scarcely consider how his difficulties in explaining himself may be affected by not just autism but also their own rapid fashion of interrogation. It emerges that Godfrey was keeping these images of Amy because she had asked him to photograph her as part of her modelling portfolio. He is released from police custody without apology. Later, the police bring Godfrey back to the station to help them solve a computer difficulty beyond the capabilities of their specialists. He eagerly complies, but although this confirms his redemption from suspicion, this unpaid deployment of Godfrey exploits his talent and his affable disposition.

The Syndicate achieves something unsettling but important in fictions of autism. It confronts viewers with our own prejudices but then subverts these. Autism is a condition defined by, and against, neurotypicalist notions of normal behaviour. The dominance of the resulting prejudices is such that autistic people themselves may not always be immune to these.

* * *

The Syndicate's acknowledgement of contemporary divides between rich and poor is almost bubblishly lightweight: *all* the main characters are or become rich. Yet Mellor's construction of Godfrey deepens contemporary representations of adult autism by engaging powerfully with more subtle implications of how class and race intersect with disability and in more nuanced ways than many earlier texts. Godfrey is one of few autistic screen characters to be played by a black actor. To date, film and television representations in the West have not adequately recognized Asian and black autism. A major problem incurred by this pattern is that, with rare exceptions – such as Karan Johar's Bollywood film *My Name Is Khan* (2010) – implications of institutional racism (in terms of opportunities, as well as treatment by authorities including police) are mostly absent from screen depictions of adult autism.

People with disabilities often face oppression, but this may also intersect with and be exacerbated by additional marginalization.

Godfrey's paid work, despite his abilities in mathematics and with computers, is predominantly physical labour. He attributes his declined application for bank work to disability, but in a society in which many workplaces are under-populated by black and Asian people in senior roles, it is hard to view this detail without also considering institutional racism. However, *The Syndicate* does not reinforce imaginings of an overwhelmingly white British professional class. Though their appearances are brief, other black and Asian characters include an interior designer, a lawyer and a police constable. Indeed, Godfrey's broadly working-class occupation marks a complex but necessary intervention in autism representation. Some of the most popular fictionalizations of Asperger syndrome misleadingly conflate 'high-functioning' autism with neurotypical notions of high achievement, and thus with the economically comfortable classes. *The Syndicate* offers a valuable counter to this tendency.

Godfrey is not *The Syndicate*'s only character who displays Asperger syndrome. Although the relationship occupies scant screen time (and they are never shown alone), he becomes engaged to Wendy Vickers. To apply Forster's terms, Wendy is a flat character: 'constructed around a single idea or quality'.[100] However, this idea and indeed quality is important. Wendy's every appearance (few though these are) foregrounds her similarity to Godfrey: their shared fascination for tractor technology, but also their apparently shared oblivion – or is it *indifference*? – to conventional social graces. For instance, when Sarah and Sean begin their first date, Godfrey and Wendy decide to join them, ignoring the first couple's apparent wish for privacy. What Wendy tacitly represents is an autistic woman. It is in some ways reflective of the cultural and diagnostic marginalization of women with Asperger syndrome that Wendy's role in *The Syndicate* is so slight. However, other authors – in particular women authors – have, as we shall see, depicted female autism in a series of progressive ways by demonstrating the intersectionality of adult autism with other social factors, not least that of gender itself.

CLARE MORRALL'S *THE LANGUAGE OF OTHERS*: AUTISM, WOMANHOOD AND INTERSECTIONALITY

Novels by women authors with female protagonists are still rarely granted the marks of 'literary' recognition afforded to male equivalents in 21st-century fiction.[101] This pattern is also discernible in novels dealing with autism. Amid the massive expansion of cultural attention to autism following Haddon's

The Curious Incident of the Dog in the Night-Time (2003) and its enduring popularity, English novelist Clare Morrall's third book, *The Language of Others* (2008) – a most innovative narrative of childhood, adolescent and especially *adult* autism – remained unfortunately overlooked. Progressing past a familiar pattern in autism fictions as exemplified in earlier novels by Haddon, Atwood and Coupland in which one (male) individual is singularized as more overtly autistic than his peers, Morrall foregrounds three characters – two parents (Jessica and Andrew) and their son (Joel) – as comparably impaired by undiagnosed autism. Despite this, the family's three autistic personalities are convincingly different. As such, *The Language of Others* recognizes the diversity of autistic identities and experiences in depth, complexity and empathy seldom matched in autism fiction to date. The central character in Morrall's novel is Jessica Fontaine: a divorced single mother and librarian. This discussion will address how *The Language of Others* illustrates autism intersecting with class, sexuality and, most profoundly, gender.

In his frequently incisive but abrasively wry survey of autism novels, Ian Hacking (2009) is firmly unimpressed by *The Language of Others*, noting that it takes until the final chapters for Jessica to see what has been clear to readers all along: she is autistic. Jessica becomes aware of this after the obvious (to readers) autism of her adult son Joel is pointed out to her by his fiancé).[102] In Hacking's summary, when the adult Joel's autism ('which most readers will have guessed at since about page 10') is revealed to his mother,

> she realizes that she herself is genetically tarred with the same brush and comes to understand herself and her problems as the result of Asperger's. . . . We are all kept in the brightly illumined dark, desperately waiting for the heroine finally to realize what is wrong with her.[103]

I interpret (and value) the same effects in Morrall's novel differently. Jessica's present-tense narratives cover the months before, during and following what *for her* is the revelation of autism (which occurs in the novel's 25th of 27 chapters). The sequences recalling Jessica's early life invoke much of the difficult introspection brought by identification with autism in adulthood.

'It's a joke, I thought. I should laugh, but I couldn't'.[104] 'Miranda grasped my arm . . . I felt the need to reciprocate, but didn't know how'.[105] 'How did people read expression in eyes? They were just physical objects.'.[106] Unlike Hacking, I do not read these as merely unsubtle signals to readers that Jessica is autistic. The second-by-second need to concentrate on multiple details when in company and the eventual exhaustion (or worse) that this can bring if not relieved are constant features of autistic subjectivity, and Morrall's prose captures them convincingly.

The Language of Others loosely follows the Bildüngsroman tradition as a narrative of growth from childhood to adulthood. Major events in Jessica's life – including university, marriage, motherhood and divorce – are narrated through the prism of autistic subjectivity. Her epiphany is the sudden realization of how undiagnosed Asperger syndrome has shaped both her inner and her social life, converging in her often frustrated need for private space and 'stillness'.[107] Deviating from the Bildüngsroman tradition, the protagonist's journey is neither spiritual nor spatial. Valuing consistency and routine, Jessica attends a local university and lives in the same area throughout her life (travelling abroad only once, for her honeymoon). The identities that intersect in Morrall's novel – including an individual's life before and after self-identification with autism – are intensified by the shifting perspectives across the book. In between Jessica's first-person narratives of her past and present, other chapters omnisciently depict her childhood and reveal (to readers at least) how others perceived her. These interventions relate concerns expressed by her mother and aunt that Jessica may be autistic (despite the dismissal of this suggestion by a male doctor in the 1970s).[108]

The novel's childhood sequences establish Jessica's exceptional abilities in music, especially at the piano. Through this thematic strand, Morrall quietly diverges from contemporary autism narratives in two refreshing ways. Jessica is autistic and talented, yet neither idiot nor savant. As an adult, she becomes an accomplished (though infrequent) concert pianist, but what the novel elevates over measurable achievement is Jessica's *love* of playing the piano and the ability it brings her to express herself. Her most fulfilling communication with her closest friend, Mary, occurs not through conversation but music, and their performance of a piano duet is rapturously evoked:

we are masters – mistresses – of the universe. Nothing compares with this. Nothing.[109]

High aptitude for music in some autistic people was first noticed by Kanner (1943).[110] Under the new classic autism, however, associations of musical talent have been somewhat obscured. *The Language of Others* compensates for this intriguingly. Jessica is musically talented and so is Andrew, her (still more overtly) autistic husband. As if directly subverting the STEM trope in autism fiction, Morrall's novel has Andrew explicitly stating his dislike for and ineptitude at mathematics.[111] Although Jessica and Andrew's son Joel *does* conform to the millennial STEM intersection with autism, this bears its own critical significance, as will later be shown.

The suggestive title *The Language of Others* is apt for many reasons, principal among which is Jessica's constant attention to the social demeanours of those around her, from which she seeks to learn. But what truly renders this a progressive and necessary novel is its stark illustration of how undiagnosed adult autism may be made doubly impairing through its convergence and conflict with gendered roles and expectations. The key feature of the novel in this respect is Jessica's changing relationship with Andrew as a girlfriend, fiancé, wife and divorcee – and, consequentially, her roles as a housewife, and mother.

Jessica and Andrew meet when both are studying music at university. From the outset of the novel, when they are shown meeting again decades later, Andrew's autistic traits are conveyed in all but name. The opening scenes foreground his favouring of comfortable clothes even if they are dishevelled; his repetitive stimming movements 'from foot to foot'; and his unpredictable conversation, alternating between silence and apparent harshness to Jessica and others. More subtly telling is Jessica's perception that Andrew always 'cultivated' a 'neglected' appearance.[112] She had first realized that she loved him when (while they were courting) she found him crying.[113] Such details establish how, while both adult characters daily face social and sensory distress through different autistic traits, their relationship is founded partly on Jessica's feelings of wanting to protect and help Andrew. Although eager to receive such attention, only rarely does he recognize or respond to how Jessica similarly needs him. Whether this imbalance comes because Andrew is autistic, or because he is a chauvinist (or because he is, alongside these things, generally selfish) is not a question that the novel seeks to answer. What *The Language of Others* does instead is to show that these subjectivities can converge. A consequence of this is that for Jessica, autistic experience intersects with patriarchal ideologies in deeply repressive ways.

* * *

While Jessica's musical ability (indeed musical *language*) is inextricable from her many and sometimes impairing autistic traits, *The Language of Others* illustrates how the flourishing of talent depends on social and economic factors. For most of her adult life, Jessica is prevented from pursuing her passion for music by the simultaneous demands of marriage and motherhood.

Andrew, an exceptionally gifted violinist, abandons his music degree before completion, thereafter ceasing any involvement with music for decades. This marks an act of agency: he sees that he is not obliged to 'perform' a certain version of himself for others.[114] However, while Andrew is oppressed by the high expectations of his parents – and by conventional notions of achievement itself – he in turn behaves oppressively to Jessica. Whereas Andrew *chooses* to give up the violin, the bleakest way in which gendered expectations bear down on Jessica's life is that the chauvinistic attitudes of those around her – and her internalization of these – all but force her to forsake the professional pursuit of music. Unlike the male protagonists of the more well-known autism fictions mentioned earlier, Jessica is prevented from utilizing or fulfilling her main strengths.

When Jessica marries Andrew at the end of her second year of university, he immediately starts behaving abusively and threateningly towards her.[115] Owing to her being 'distracted' by Andrew's constant domestic and emotional demands, as well as by learning that she is pregnant, Jessica achieves a lower degree than expected.[116] After her graduation (in 1983), Andrew insists that Jessica's role be that of a housewife while he works in a series of different, mostly menial occupations. Notions of social status are implicitly at work here: a mark of middle-class households in post-war Britain was the ability to manage on a husband's income alone.[117] However, Andrew's primary concern is his personal satisfaction, which depends on Jessica's obedience towards him. Even while she is pregnant, he insists that she not only prepare his breakfast but also sit with him while he eats it, despite her swaying with physical discomfort and frequently having to rush to the bathroom because of morning sickness.[118]

As well as forsaking music, Andrew opts to quit a series of quite different jobs. In chapters set in the 1980s, the brevity and variety of his occupations hint at struggles to be accepted or understood in work environments unsympathetic to the effects of his undiagnosed autism. In turn, Andrew's attitudes and behaviour towards Jessica are become grimly abusive. He remains indifferent to her struggles with the roles of housewife and mother, and, amid these, her frustrated needs for space and solitude (or even just a rest).

After resigning from an insurance agency, Andrew insists that Jessica find a job while he contemplates a different career. When she asks if this would mean her having to quit such a job once *he* found a new one, Andrew replies that it 'would only be right' that he should earn the income, because that is what men are 'supposed to do'.[119] Given her social anxieties, Jessica is hesitant about finding employment. She is also aware that, in effect, she already has one (unpaid) and unrelieved job, as a wife and mother, and sees that she would be expected to maintain these duties on top of paid work.[120]

Of course, such immediate manifestations of patriarchy permeated millions of households in the era of Jessica and Andrew's marriage.[121] Yet this is part of what makes Morrall's novel so critically substantial. Its central character frequently and starkly expresses and demonstrates autistic subjectivity, but her character is never reduced to being *merely* an autistic person.

A demonstration of Andrew's growth as a person across the novel is that when Jessica follows his insistence that she find work by enrolling on a part-time librarian's course, Andrew surprises her by honouring his promise to look after Joel. Nonetheless, an imbalance persists. Whereas Jessica oversees all practical aspects of the boy's upbringing, including emotional labour and, increasingly, discipline, the time Andrew spends with Joel is leisurely.

A consequence is the creation of a bond between father and son, which is partly defined by the exclusion of Jessica. Nonetheless, she recalls how it elicited both pride and relief for her to see 'a connection' after all between Andrew and Joel.[122] Much to Jessica's shock however, Andrew soon after decides to move out of their home and, for years, their lives, never saying goodbye to his son.[123]

The Language of Others continually positions its protagonist at the convergence of social interpellations. Jessica is undermined, ordered around and, on occasions, physically intimidated by her husband. Her wealthier friend Mary sides with Andrew in pressurizing Jessica to find a job.[124] Her support for Joel in his homework is doubted by his teacher, who seems to blame the boy's mother for what the school sees as Joel's problematic disinclination to socialize (and indifference to football).[125] Yet the most complex facet of Jessica's roundedness as a character is her own tendency to internalize patriarchal (as well as unknowingly ableist) assumptions – and eventually, these yield the most ambiguous implications of her self-identification as autistic.

Jessica fears for her son, Joel, because with the unemployed Andrew as a role model, 'how would he know what men were supposed to do?'.[126] Like Andrew, the adult Joel expects Jessica to act as an unpaid domestic servant. He continually ignores or forgets her requests that he perform small domestic chores, or just clear up after himself while she is at work. This exacerbates Jessica's main frustration in the present-day chapters: her continually unfulfilled need for some personal time and space when she returns from work at the library. However, Jessica's annoyance at her 23-year-old son and the disorganization of his life as an undiagnosed autistic also brings some of her own, oppressively conventional attitudes to the fore. Although she has no romantic relationships before or after Andrew, Jessica expects Joel to find a partner – a female partner – but is astonished when he actually does so, and feels sorry for his fiancé, Alice.[127] While she is genuinely caring towards other characters, the reader can see the limits of Jessica's empathy in ways that she herself cannot. Her love for Joel is never in question, yet he remains a pitiable irritant to her for most of the novel.[128] His mother's view and expectations of him, showing Jessica's own internalization of neurotypical values, are harshly negative, until, that is, Alice tactfully informs Jessica that Joel 'has Asperger's . . . a form of autism'.[129] At this point, *The Language of Others* again transcends the standard limitations of autism fiction in two ways. First, Morrall critically refers via Jessica to the cultural fascination of which this novel is a part. When Alice asks Joel's initially confounded mother if she has heard of Asperger syndrome, Jessica replies affirmatively that:

'The whole world talks about it nowadays'. . . . My mind is racing through volumes of half-remembered information, newspaper articles, radio documentaries, televisions [*sic*] chat shows.[130]

Second, in a variant on a type of exchange familiar to many autistic adults, Jessica proceeds to ask:

> 'Isn't there a danger you start thinking that everyone who's a bit different has something wrong with them?'
> [Alice:] It's not to do with having something wrong. You have to see it as a condition, rather than an illness.[131]

Interviewed in 2008, Morrall (who is also a music teacher) states that she had read Haddon's *The Curious Incident of the Dog in the Night-Time* (2003) and wished to write about 'milder' forms of Asperger syndrome because

> 'I just worried that children who are less extreme might be labelled as being dangerous or very peculiar, when what they really want to do is fit in with everyone'. She adds: 'The side of Asperger's I wanted to write about was the milder form, where it is arguable how abnormal you are. . . . What is "normality?" I would argue that everybody has an element (of autism) in them'.[132]

For many autistic readers, Morrall's comment that 'everybody has an element' of autism is likely to be grating. That sentiment – and sentimentality – is apparent in *The Language of Others* through the regular but fleeting attention directed to quite innocuous micro-traits of autism in the novel's more incidental characters.[133] In an era when UCARC continues to popularize the idea that autism can be indicatively measured in terms of a 'quotient' or 'score', it is easy to notice that almost everyone has some traits or other that, when more overt or impairing, can be associated with autism. However, for people actually diagnosed – and diagnosis only happens if such tendencies are deemed to be negatively impacting on a person's wellbeing – it is not usually helpful to be told that 'we're all a little bit autistic'. The interpellation has a tendency to sound reactionary and to trivialize the distressing circumstances of a minority of people by implying that all others share their struggles. The effect of this can actually be to reinforce a sense of isolation.

While Morrall's conjectural remark that 'everybody has an element' of autism is problematic, it corresponds in *The Language of Others* with something more subversive, in the sense of its critical stance on medical authority (also conveyed in the novelist's expressed concerns regarding children and diagnosis). The doctor who laughed at Jessica's mother over concerns that her child was autistic (in the 1970s) is dismissed by the girl's aunt as outdated in his knowledge and 'too old to be practising'.[134] It remains ambiguous as to whether Joel (who keeps much of his life private from his mother) has actually been assessed for autism, though Alice 'recognised it' immediately because her brother has been formally diagnosed.[135] Most intriguingly, both despite and because of the utter certainty of her epiphanic self-identification as autistic weeks after the conversation with Alice, Jessica – in contrast with her mother's attempts on her behalf – at no point contemplates being tested for autism herself. Nor does she divulge her revelation to any other character. And why should she? Although the vast absence of diagnostic experiences from representation in autism fiction is in some ways disabling to autistic communities, Jessica's decision demonstrates autistic agency and self-knowledge. It is as if she no more requires a psychiatrist to confirm that she is autistic than she needs a chiropodist in order to ascertain that she has two feet.

Yet paradoxically, it is the *undiagnosed* status of her autism that creates, for Jessica, a 'disability'.[136] A most empowering effect of realizing that she has Asperger syndrome is that it enables her to stop feeling guilty or inadequate about her overwhelming need for periods of solitude. Through this motif, the novel portrays what is in effect a neurological intersectionality, between the different experiences of autistic subjectivity. Staying with Andrew at the home of her parents and sister while they are engaged, Jessica becomes exhausted by the constant expectations of interaction, intimidated by the impending changes that marriage will bring, leading to an ostensible spell of undiagnosed depression:

> There was a heaviness inside my head . . . every action seemed to require enormous effort. Recently I had been waking too early in the morning. I'd be fresh and clear for a few seconds, then a desolate, sinking sensation would creep into my mind.[137]

Contrastingly, when Joel leaves home and Jessica has accepted (and embraced) the reality of Asperger syndrome, she finds a hitherto elusive peace in being able to love others without needing them; 'I thrive on the emptiness of my house'.[138]

Not all autistic adults are fortunate enough to afford a house of their own, to themselves. Nor is Jessica, for long. Shortly after her expressions of thriving in an empty house, another major change occurs when she becomes a grandmother. Sensing that her newfound emotional and domestic space is being encroached, she envisages being frequently expected to babysit. Although, holding her grandson, Jessica declares 'I fall in love all over again', this 'fall' and this 'again' imply a return to the self-sacrifice that has been so much a part of her womanhood.[139] What is different now is Jessica's awareness of her *own* needs. Nonetheless, for all the empowerment found by her awareness of autism, there are subtle ways in which Jessica's internalization of this identity is significantly defined by men.

Although it is Alice who educates her about Asperger syndrome by referring to Joel, the moment at which Jessica suddenly sees herself as autistic is directly linked with one of the novel's most misogynistic figures: her cousin

Philip. His treatment of Jessica during childhood (she realizes on her wedding day) is paralleled in her subsequent relationship with Andrew.[140] When they were teenagers, Philip sexually attacked Jessica and sadistically broke the talented pianist's finger while bizarrely accusing her of having teased him.[141] When she reluctantly faces him again near the novel's end, Philip denies any memories of mistreating Jessica and tells her that she was an 'unassailable fortress', seemingly beyond intimacy with anyone.[142] Almost instantly, Philip's Bettelheim-like metaphor of a 'fortress' prompts the novel's turning point:

> It's me, I realise with sudden clarity. It wasn't Andrew who passed it on [to Joel], it was me.[143]

The exchange shows how Philip retains a power to profoundly influence Jessica, now shaping her own self-perception much as he did her expectations of men. Thus, while her self-recognition of her own autism becomes liberating, Jessica's internalization of ableist values – and therefore her view of her own inferiority – is such that she never seems to recognize (unlike the reader) that Andrew, too, had a 'disability'.[144] While Morrall's novel necessitates consideration of the highly complex (and incalculably diverse) matter of whether and how autistic people might be differently vulnerable to interpellations, far less ambiguous is the sometimes brutishly oppressive verbal and physical treatment which Jessica endures from men. And with this, Morrall's novel carries a variant on this chapter's opening concern: autism remains defined – or *ill*-defined – by the forces of archaically patriarchal standards.

The Language of Others plays to various motifs of new classic autism, yet it also impels criticism of them. Key to this are the younger characters in the novel, and how their paths into adult careers (and identities) differ from those of their parents' and grandparents' generations. Joel's maternal grandfather, Roland – who quietly demonstrates various autistic ways, and in whom Jessica sees many similarities with her son – ran a briefly lucrative confectionary company.[145] Joel, too, has an entrepreneurial flair. And, like his parents, Joel also has a high (though not savant) talent in a specific area, despite struggling with social aspects of daily life. Joel's greatest interest is computers and, still in his early twenties, he is running a very successful games design company. Through this, *The Language of Others* points towards an important social pattern. The emergence, expression and fostering of autistic talent remain historically variable. Roland was a businessman and Jess and Andrew were musicians, but Joel, born in the 1980s, is far more interested in computers. The autistic brother of Joel's fiancé Alice, meanwhile, is studying engineering at Cambridge University. While this range of talents in Morrall's Aspergic characters recognizes autistic diversity, the generational distinction appears as something of a warning. Joel and his future brother-in-law reached adulthood in the early 2000s – the point when influential commentators such as Silberman (2001) and Baron-Cohen (2003) began to emphasize associations of autism with talents in STEM areas. *The Language of Others* features a wild and glorious range of liminally autistic characters, yet all of the younger ones – also including Luke, a talented teenage mathematician whom Jessica encounters at work – express themselves through STEM subjects. A cultural streamlining of autistic abilities and, indeed, identities is tacitly apparent.

FAMILY AND PHENOTYPE: READING AUTISM IN MEG WOLITZER'S *THE INTERESTINGS* (2013)

Autism is understood to be a congenital condition, there at birth, even if not detectable until later. But still in other, as-yet scientifically unfathomed ways, autism also appears to be somehow present even before conception: somewhere in the galactically vast possible combinations of individual human genomes. At present, while there is no biological test, clinicians use what is effectively a *narrative* form of autism genetics. The orthodox scientific consensus that autism is something we inherit biologically means that many diagnosticians and researchers are eager to hear about past family members who expressed traits which may now, posthumously, be read in terms of the autism spectrum. This also means that any discernible autistic tendencies in parents of children (or adults) who are being assessed for autism are likely to be noted by clinicians. In 2014, a study led by Kristen Lyall and John Constantino attracted widespread media attention by reporting that mild or 'sub-clinical' autism traits in parents, combined with 'preferential mating', appeared to raise the likelihood of autism in their offspring.[146] As with almost any study on autism and genetics, this provides yet more evidence against the 'refrigerator parent' myth, but it remains worrying to consider how an emphasis on sub-clinical autism in parents could potentially become implicated in eugenic agendas. But, then, concerns about eugenics should already be paramount in any culture or period that so fixatedly otherizes and sensationalizes both the impairments and the abilities that constitute autism.

In an era of autism science and history when the genotype (genetic cause) remains unknown but the phenotype (demonstration of observable traits) is believed to be reliably identifiable, it becomes possible for living relatives – including childless family members – to passively (or even unknowingly) influence another individual's autism diagnosis. The said influence may remain slight, but still creates a delicate situation when, as it usually is, the other person being assessed is younger or (as for many families) is one's child. Crucially, the unknown autism genotype is biological, but the accepted phenotype is a *narrative* phenomenon. As such, it is rife with subjectivity and complexity, and can entail various emotions. Some years before I was diagnosed autistic, a cousin was assessed for Asperger syndrome. I thought a lot about how she would feel about the diagnosis (or identity) that might result from the assessment. Since it had already been suggested to me by mental health professionals that I might look into being assessed for Asperger syndrome myself, I privately wondered whether other relatives' narratives of my own self-presentation might influence this person's diagnosis, even if only fractionally. I even came close to wishing I had made more effort to suppress my own autistic tendencies – before realizing how little control I actually had over those. Only later would I see that within such reactions, I was internalizing wider social interpellations that autism is an inherently negative 'impairment'. I wanted to escape that mindset for my relatives' sake, as well as my own. Altogether, these concerns and considerations regarding the autism phenotype seem worthy of more open, more critical discussion than they have so far received in either scientific or cultural narratives. However, there is one recent text in which the autism phenotype is not just extensively portrayed but is made a point of varied, often stark emotional and critical consideration, and this narrative will be the focus of the present discussion.

*   *   *

American author Meg Wolitzer's tenth novel *The Interestings* (published in 2013) is a state-of-the-nation scale epic, set from the mid-1970s to the late 2000s and addressing themes and events including the Vietnam War; the Watergate scandal; religion; drugs; the emergence and spread of AIDS; the influence of the Internet; child exploitation; the 9/11 attacks in New York; and, through the 2000s, the rise in autism diagnoses. 'The Interestings' are a group of bohemian friends who meet as teenagers at an arts-based summer camp in 1974, and Wolitzer's novel – a television adaptation of which was piloted in 2016 – weaves their lives and relationships into contexts of these modern historical events.[147] Autism is named and discussed by Wolitzer's characters in *The Interestings*. However, in a development that may signify the decline of paratextual autism as critiqued earlier in this chapter, autism and related terms were not referenced in the promotional materials surrounding this novel. Nor are they mentioned in the publisher's quotations of praise in the paperback edition, including numerous commendations from high-profile literary review pages.[148] Reading the novel's opening chapter however, I strongly identified with the unusual sensory and social experiences of two key characters: Jules Jacobson and her close, ultimately platonic friend, Ethan Figman.

In Wolitzer's 2013 novel, readers of chapters set in the past are able to recognize the nature of certain situations ahead of the characters. It is apparent to the audience before Jonah that he has unknowingly consumed hallucinatory drugs and also that the Christian commune his mother has joined is slowly turning into a dubious cult. It is also chillingly obvious to us, but not to Robert, that the symptoms of his sudden illness in the early 1980s are those of the AIDS virus. And throughout the novel, a similar trick of narrative perspective enables readers to see that both Jules and Ethan show many defining features of Asperger syndrome. I read *The Interestings* keenly waiting to see not *if* these two characters would be diagnosed autistic but how they would feel when this seemingly inevitable revelation occurred. In fact, neither Jules nor Ethan is assessed or named as autistic in the novel (though Wolitzer's prose skillfully alludes to autistic identity in multiple other ways). And, when Ethan's infant son Mo is diagnosed with autism in the early 2000s, the father begins to see – with much unease and even some resentment – how his autistic child closely resembles his own needs and struggles.

* * *

Even in the opening paragraph of *The Interestings*, autistic tendencies are made recognizable in the character of 15-year-old Julie (soon to become Jules) Jacobson, through immediate references to stimming. In a captivating example of how the written word may reveal physical experience more precisely and intimately than screen portrayals, Jules's compulsions towards repetitive movements are not presented merely as signifiers of autistic identity: they are narrated to articulate sensory delight. Sitting for the first time with fellow attendees of the summer camp at night, Jules longs

> to unfold a leg or do the side-to-side motion with her jaw that sometimes set off a gratifying series of tiny percussive sounds inside her skull.[149]

In another form of physical stimming as an aural experience, Jules also enjoys splitting individual hairs on her head and hearing them 'crackle'.[150] While it is by no means the case that everyone who so engages and delights in repetitive movements is autistic, the quoted detail is only the most eloquent of various, otherwise more obvious signifiers on the novel's first page that Jules may be autistic. She is introduced as an 'outsider' who detrimentally considers herself a 'freak'. As she carefully observes the interactions around her, we are told that 'irony' is new to Jules. Yet here, Wolitzer deftly defies expectations of a post-*Curious*, Sheldon Cooper–like spectacle of a character whose 'literal' understanding of language can make an audience feel superior because we can see more of their social ineptitude than they can. While Jules learns to imitate (and quickly surpasses) the ironic wit of her friends, throughout the novel, her conversational manner is apt to being misunderstood by even those closest to her. She is interpellated by others as being prone to 'weird' comments and considered 'funny' in 'a good way'.[151] In one scene, with poetic surrealism reminiscent of Asperger's 1944 quotations of remarks from autistic children, Jules asks her fellow Interestings whether they had noticed how Ronald Reagan's head is 'shaped like a bottle of that brown kind of glue'.[152] Then – 'semi-relatedly' – she asks if her friends have noticed how pencils look like collie dogs (none of them have).[153] Such communication gaps yield some of the novel's most poignant depictions of neurodiverse communication, for Jules is highly receptive to others' feelings and expressions. She eventually becomes a therapist, a job she finds fulfilling, and is much valued by her clients. Prior to this, Jules sought a career in acting and was hurt when her drama tutor advised her to quit.[154] Yet, in a sense, Jules is acting throughout most of the novel: trying to be accepted despite her social unease. The main sign that Jules truly loves (and is loved by) her husband Dennis is that she seems not to feel obliged to hide or pretend anything in his presence.

The character whose life most complexly intertwines with that of Jules is Ethan Figman. Not unlike Jessica and Andrew in Morrall's *The Language of Others*, Wolitzer's Jules and Ethan present two central adult characters who consistently demonstrate a range of autistic tendencies. However, as in many friendships and relationships between autistic (or liminally autistic) people, the ways in which these characters differ, *combined* with what they seem to share, serve to enhance their bond, even if these various points of connection remain unspoken.

Five chapters into the novel, Jules and Ethan's most outward autistic traits are quietly yet clearly juxtaposed when the Interestings reunite shortly after their first summer together. Jules, thrilled to be back among the group of friends with whom she has become almost obsessed, makes comments 'to no one in particular' and is ignored; she also improvises pun-based jokes to which Ash replies affectionately (though without laughing): 'Yes, you are definitely still you'. Meanwhile, Ethan stands 'rocking a little bit, slightly nervous'.[155] In this scene, expressions and traits often deemed autistic are evident, but what is most incisive is how the novel shows that these can be enhanced by both excitement and anxiety – a fact of autistic life which deserves greater recognition and understanding (for it can impact considerably on how a person presents while being assessed for diagnosis or, for that matter, how s/he performs in job interviews).

Ethan is a talented animator who rapidly distinguishes himself through a career in television production by his late teens. By his mid-twenties however, he has quit this job because he feels the popular adult cartoon on which he was recruited to work is becoming mean-spirited and juvenile in its humour.[156] He contrasts the demands of his career against what he recalls as the carefree atmosphere of Spirit-in-the-Woods, the arty summer camp where he met his fellow Interestings a decade earlier. Talking with Gil, his father-in-law, Ethan confesses that he was probably 'spoiled' by the camp because it allowed him to be 'expressive and imaginative' – while in the corporate media world, he is obliged to 'adhere' to a 'vision' that isn't his own.[157] Although his artistic gifts truly flourish once he is able (with his in-laws' financial support) to pursue his own independent projects, Ethan – like many autistic people – is viewed by those around him as prioritizing not the expressive and imaginative but the closed and systematic.

Not unlike the figure of Saga Norén in *The Bridge* as discussed earlier, Wolitzer's Ethan sometimes frustrates those around him with what they view as his inflexible adherence to rules. Yet crucially, these are Ethan's *own* rules. Ash says of her husband to their friends while he is absent:

> Ethan has all these views of life that no one can control. . . . All these ideas about what's ethical and what's not.'[158]

Temple Grandin (after citing Kanner's 1943 paper) expansively discusses 'rigidity of thinking' as a core characteristic of autism.[159] However, it is vital to recognize and appreciate that while 'rigid' or inflexible thinking may be a commonality of autistic people, this does not make us some kind of homogenous population. Rigid thinking is still subjective thinking: it can, therefore, lead naturally to profound *diversities* throughout the autism spectrum. Resistance (or resilience) to the examples and interpellations of other people creates difference from fellow autistics, as well as from neurotypicals. Thus, to quote Stuart Murray: 'One possibility that always seems to provide unease is that the spectrum of autistic subjectivity might be as wide as the spectrum of non-autistic subjectivity'.[160] Here, Murray is challenging how autism is prevalently narrated from outside – that is, by an ableist culture. But this suggestion of 'unease' is also powerful in a bleaker way. To emphasize how rigid autistic thinking spawns independence of mind is liberating in its defiance of stereotypes. Yet, the same emphasis is also liberating in the sense that to voice this very thought is to acknowledge the *aloneness* that can sometimes be a part of autistic thought and feeling.

Through the character of Ethan, Wolitzer's novel brilliantly illuminates how 'rigidity' of autistic thinking can be enlightening not just for the autist but for art (or academia) when a thought is followed through until a new conclusion is reached or, indeed, discovered. Disparaging of orthodox values and mainstream culture, Ethan attempts to tell Jules of his frustration with what he can only call the 'circumscribed world' of dominant – and rigid – social values.[161] His means of dealing with this is to create an imaginary alternative.

Thus, *The Interestings* valuably complicates the tropes of new classic autism by endowing Ethan with an outstanding capacity for the human attribute denied to autistic people in prevailing psychiatric generalizations: creative imagination. As a child, he frequently lay in bed 'dreaming up an animated planet'.[162] This monotropic reverie becomes the basis of an entire career for Ethan Figman. Abandoning his corporate media job, he successfully pitches a new television series, *Figland*, based on the interplanetary adventures of 'a nerdy and lonely kid', named Wally Figman.[163] Figland, as a fantasy planet, is Ethan's means of satirizing the society, culture and politics of contemporary America. The series becomes internationally successful, making Ethan and his wife, Ash, enormously wealthy. This development continues standard cultural tropes of the adult autist as someone to whom spectacular achievement not only comes but comes easily. As such, Ethan as a literary character is at times close to being caught up in a 'circumscribed world' of autism narratives. However, like Mellor's *The Syndicate* and Morrall's *The Language of Others*, Wolitzer's *The Interestings* invokes standard tropes of new classic autism before proceeding to subvert them.

Although chapter 1 of *Naming Adult Autism* considered cultural and political problems posed by shallow denials of autistic imagination, Wolitzer's characters Jules and Ethan illustrate something of the logic behind these prevailing assumptions. Ethan has an extraordinary ability to imagine fictional scenarios and how audiences might respond to them. However, like Jules, he continually struggles to imagine – or, rather, to *reliably* imagine – implications of how his own manner is interpreted. Ethan is more apt to wrongly imagine what others may be trying to convey through unspoken language: including Jules. On more than one occasion, he mistakes her physical ease around him for an invitation to sexual contact and is surprised when she continually resists his gestures.[164] Despite the awkwardness this causes, their bond continues.

What Jules and Ethan share is more than merely a group of neurological traits. In contrast with their other friends among The Interestings, Jules and Ethan came from financially unprivileged families. Ethan identifies with and admires Jules because

> she hadn't been coddled. Ethan hadn't been coddled either; they had this in common, along with a certain skewed sensibility. Jules didn't care if she seemed dignified or not.[165]

Unlike in fictions such as *The Bridge* or *Doc Martin* as criticized in chapter 2, the lack or absence of 'coddling' experienced by Wolitzer's two seemingly autistic characters is no regurgitation of the refrigerator parent trope. Jules's father died when she was a teenager, and her mother was not affluent.

Although Ethan grew up amid his parents' 'bad marriage', any simplistic suggestions that this explains his autistic ways are notably countered later in the novel.[166] Marvelling at his originality of mind while lamenting his personal insecurities, Ethan's wife Ash asks him whether these were caused by his mother, his father, or both. 'Neither', he replies, adding: 'I was born like this'.[167] What *The Interestings* then daringly proceeds to invoke, more starkly than Morrall's novel, is the presence of the autism phenotype in the parent of an autistic child.

Much of *The Interestings* concerns the tension between inner subjectivity and outward identity. Wolitzer's narrative often prioritizes the unwanted, unspoken thoughts of the key characters – primarily Jules and Ethan. In Ethan, what brings out the most contradictory, sometimes unpleasant (but always convincingly human) feelings is his reluctant acceptance that Mo – his infant son with Ash – is autistic. One of Ethan's most revealing remarks about Mo actually arrives within a lie. It occurs in the (often socially divisive) form of the Christmas family newsletter. Distributed to Ethan and Ash's hundreds of friends around the world, the Ethan-authored section prioritizes their daughter, and how she is thriving at Yale University while studying theater and art history. Ethan adds:

> We would have loved her even if she were a math geek, which she certainly is not. However, as many of you also know, her younger brother Mo is, and we love him no less for it.[168]

Ethan's lie, which becomes clear only later in the novel, is that his autistic son is 'a math geek'. Mo scarcely even shows an *interest* in maths. In this Christmas newsletter for 2003 – the year of Haddon's novel and Baron-Cohen's *The Essential Difference* – Ethan untruthfully plays to a popular cliché as if to make his child's autism seem more acceptable, or, at least, more acceptable to himself as a father.

Wolitzer's novel is unusual in that the procedure of autism diagnosis (albeit from a parent's perspective) is given some degree of narrative within the plot. Despite much anguish, the diagnosis means for Mo's mother, Ash, that the family can 'move forward', knowing now that he is not 'generically emotionally fragile', but that he has a distinct diagnosis, named as pervasive developmental disorder, not otherwise specified (PDD-NOS). The narrative elucidates: 'He was on the autism spectrum, the doctors had explained, and now he could get some real help.'[169]

PDD-NOS (pervasive developmental disorder, not otherwise specified) is a subcategory of autism diagnosis. As 'NOS' acknowledges, the term has an imprecise relationship to both classic autism and Asperger syndrome. Walker et al. (2004) suggested that what should distinguish PDD-NOS within the autism spectrum is the presence of fewer repetitive behaviours.[170] In using this lesser-known name, Wolitzer's novel provides more detailed terms of reference than most autism fictions. There is, however, a significant gap in how the assessment procedure is presented in *The Interestings*. From Kanner (1943) and Asperger (1944) onwards, most clinicians have given considerable attention to how parents may demonstrate the autism phenotype; and Ethan is determined not to attend his son's assessment. Planning an elaborate lie in advance to excuse himself from the two-day observation at the clinic, he persuades Jules to accompany Ash and Mo instead.[171]

Mo is the most 'interesting' (i.e., prominently featured) of the children born to the group of friends in Wolitzer's novel. Nonetheless, the narrative never seeks to venture into Mo's mind. Although verbal, he is presented as greatly more disadvantaged than Ethan or Jules. Mo's character remains resolutely a portrayal of autism from outside. The sequences narrating his infancy portray a restless child who is easily distressed in his 'heightened sensitivity and irritability'.[172] Ethan and Mo do not share the same approach to verbal language nor body language, and the father considers his son non-reciprocal. A main theme in the novel's last chapters is Ethan's 'sorrow' and 'suffering' at 'all the possibilities' that were 'now blocked off' for Mo. At times, Ethan also feels 'anger and indifference' towards his son.[173] Ethan roundedly epitomizes not just the autism phenotype but the misguided disappointment (and suffering) of autism parents so memorably challenged in Jim Sinclair's polemic 'Don't Mourn for Us' (1993). Ethan begins to devote his time to campaigning against the plight of child labourers in Jakarta. He experiences deep and politically radical compassion for hundreds of children whom he has never met, but is unable to accept the autism – the person – of his son.

Essential to the (very) gradual enlightenment of Ethan's feelings towards Mo is his acceptance of *why* he feels so conflicted. In Ethan's case, this involves the recognition that he, the father, is himself autistic. The epiphany is delivered silently – not through any expression ever given on Ethan's part but through the omniscient narrative:

> Mo's problems made Ethan feel as if the world would now see his own distorted nature, revealed through his son. Ethan had imagined his life was nearly perfect except for the flawed son; but the flaw was in the father.[174]

To the end, Ethan – with his rigid thinking – is unable to escape his view, or the cultural interpellation, that autism is a 'flaw'. Sinclair's words to parents are pertinent again:

> Push for the things your expectations tell you are normal, and you'll find frustration, disappointment, resentment, maybe even rage and hatred. Approach respectfully, without preconceptions . . . and you'll find a world you could never have imagined.[175]

On a visit to Ethan and his family, Jules observes how, at 19, Mo has an adult's body 'but a restless, awkward demeanor'.[176] He requires assistants (whom his parents are able to pay for) to help him with various tasks. Mo's social graces, as empathically noticed by Jules, seem to be the result of continual effort rather than free intuition:

'I'm home for a break', he said. Then added, as if he'd rehearsed it, 'I don't like school, but what else am I going to do'.[177]

The absence of a question mark neatly conveys Mo's tone of voice. It is through Mo, ahead of Ethan or Jules, that Wolitzer's novel offers a sense of how, in autism, social customs are a burden because, alongside everything else that might be going on, these constantly need to be *remembered*. Somehow, even in adulthood, the unspoken rules of polite interaction often seem beyond instinct; honouring these never quite becomes automatic in the way it seems to do for non-autistics. This is shown when, during Jules's visit, Mo's helper arrives to take him elsewhere and Ethan has to prompt Mo to say goodbye to Jules and himself before leaving.[178]

What eventually yields a moment of intimate connection between the dying Ethan and his adult autistic son is not a change in Mo, but one in his father. Until this point, their relationship has been one sided: Ethan seeks to teach and in effect normalize Mo, but seldom attempts to engage on Mo's terms. When this finally happens, the novel quietly implies how Ethan's internalization of rigid, neurotypically based notions of language have in effect separated the father and son, rather than connecting them. What brings out of Ethan an unprecedentedly open expression of emotion before Mo – through tears – is the son's simple, stalling expression through another kind of language: he slowly plays an instrumental song for his father on a banjo.[179]

Although, to autistic readers, the sensory and social experiences of Jules in Wolitzer's *The Interestings* might be just as resonant as those of Ethan, Jules's own moments of identification with autism are more oblique than those of her closest friend. However, their last meeting is most telling, skirting as it does around the naming of autism in a manner that has become something of a code between the two friends. Ethan tells the self-abasing Jules that her greatest quality is being 'wry' – to which, Jules adds 'And awkward':

[ETHAN:] 'Okay, fine, wry and awkward. Awkward and wry. A combination I happen to have a soft spot for. But maybe it's an easier combination for a boy'.
'Yes', she said. 'It definitely is. Awkward and wry does not usually work for a girl. It makes everything hard'.[180]

Awkward and wry: exchanging this phrase is the closest Jules and Ethan get to naming autism in themselves. These words invite attention through their close and conspicuous – even autistic – repetition. The four namings of 'awkward' almost stutter towards 'autistic'. 'Wry' then deflects from this. The combination carries yin and yang-like properties. Awkward is a feeling. Wry can be the expression a feeling, and its transference to another. To be awkward is to be passive. Wryness is often deliberate. Awkward is conspicuous. Wry is more distinctive. Wryness can be an ability, but awkwardness is always impairing. 'Awkward' is how Jules sees the autistic Mo.[181] Awkward and wry can both be perceptions and interpellations of the person from outside – not unlike autism, which often similarly combines distinctive ability with conspicuous impairment. And, as Ethan and Jules agree, awkward and wry can be a more difficult combination for a girl than a boy: 'It makes everything hard'. Such is the way in an era when science and culture remain jointly under-attentive to the needs, or even just the *identities*, of autistic women.

CONCLUSION: CULTURAL DISABILITY

The last four autism fictions explored in this chapter are progressive in distinct, divergent ways. As such, they differently indicate – and may enhance – the decline of the culturally disabling imposition that is the new classic adult autism. *The Bridge*, *The Syndicate*, *The Language of Others* and *The Interestings* all recognize that autism is not reducible to a single entity or identity; it is always in interplay with simultaneous social processes. *The Bridge* is the most commercially successful of the four main fictions discussed and has been remade by a range of international television companies. Even so, no version of this series has attracted anything like the media excitement given to the main emblems of the new classic adult autism: *Curious Incident*, *Big Bang Theory* and *The Rosie Project*.

It is to the credit of Morrall's and Wolitzer's novels (and their publishers) that the names of Asperger syndrome or autism were not used in paratextual blurbs to promote these books. Perhaps this marks a broader distinction between the promotional tactics of literary fiction and television drama respectively. The BBC's promotion of *The Syndicate* named the character of Godfrey as having Asperger syndrome even before filming was completed. For the intended audience then, there was, to paraphrase Adorno and Horkheimer, little left for the consumer to classify in Godfrey's person. Yet, despite the script's contrasting and thus conspicuous restraint from naming Asperger syndrome or autism within the actual series, Godfrey's 'condition' is still talked about by the characters: most important by himself. In this willingness to address aspects of autistic identity, even if evasively, *The Syndicate* carries a progressive feature more extensively realized in Morrall's *The Language of Others*. So far, little such discussion – or *expression* – has been offered in *The Bridge* regarding Saga's otherness. In a candid exchange at Nordicana 2014 (the UK's festival of Nordic fiction and film), an audience member valiantly asked Sofia Helin (who plays Saga):

> *Question:* [Saga] is clearly flawed, on the spectrum of autism. . . . Why is that not addressed? It's obviously deliberately not addressed.
>
> *Helin:* I said early in the process . . . [autism is] not something we should tell everybody . . . keeping the audience really curious about . . . what is it with her [we all agreed] about that being a good idea. . . . I think Saga . . . doesn't see herself as someone with Asperger's. She has probably read – she knows, probably, that she would have it if she'd ask [for] some expertise. But in some ways, during her logic and smart thinking, she's managed to step away from these experts during school and so on.[182]

Helin, who is Swedish, is here speaking English as a second language, and perhaps the resonance is coincidental – but the suggestion of keeping the audience 'curious' is still telling. Helin's comments establish what she views, and plays, as Saga's agency in regard to her neurological identity. However, the limitation of *The Bridge* here is also that of nearly all autism fictions since *Rain Man*. The verbal adult autist is a recurrent presence in fiction, yet with the powerful exception of Morrall, authors do not grant these imagined characters the agency *to speak of their own autism*. It is always named for them (or even against them) via paratext, or at best – as in Wolitzer's *The Interestings* – it is given to readers to identify and contemplate the person's neurological state.

* * *

In one sense, paratext is the ultimate metaphor for diagnosis: medically, autism and Asperger syndrome remain names conferred (or denied) by powerful agencies *outside* of the individual. Yet paratextual autism fiction – where the condition is named only on the outside of the actual text – incurs and promotes a series of repressive cultural limitations. The relegation of the name 'autism' to the paratext severely restricts the possibilities of how a narrative or script might critically acknowledge this condition as an experience, an impairment, a disability, a diagnosis, and a social label. In the most frustrating gap, the absent *name* of autism within the text of (for instance) *The Bridge* tends to undermine the reality that autistic adults may need to talk about this subjectivity and identity. Moreover, the textual absence of the name means that processes of formal assessment for adult autism – and the often massive emotional ramifications of their aftermath – are left unrepresented. Paratextual namings of fictional characters as autistic usually evade addressing the condition as a disability, because the health and lifestyles of these characters are seldom significantly *impaired* by autistic tendencies. When authors or publishers declare a lightly unconventional character as autistic, the popular theory that autism and Asperger syndrome are too easily diagnosed (confronted in chapter 5) acquires false, but influential, illustration.

The new classic adult autism is a *culturally* disabling phenomenon, and not just to autistic people. The neurotypical gaze becomes exploited into being the neurotypical stare. The popularity of fictions such as *Big Bang Theory* suggests that undiagnosed adult autism is a more compelling (but also more comfortable) spectacle for audiences than the experience of living with both impairment and diagnosis might be. In a most blatantly commercial use of paratextual Asperger syndrome, potential readers of Graeme Simsion's *The Rosie Project* (2013) were promised that the protagonist, Don Tillman, might be 'somewhere on the autism spectrum'; the novel's humour depended heavily on the fact that everyone can see that but him.[183] More progressively, autism is discussed directly (albeit with dubious allusions to refrigerator parentage) in Simsion's more sensitive, often more convincing sequel, *The Rosie Effect* (2014).[184] Maybe that could prove a sign that the nadir of new classic autism and the simplifications it entails has now passed. But it is too early to say.

Asperger syndrome is sometimes named as a 'hidden' disability, but that is potentially misleading. UCARC's reliance on the most ultimately innocuous autistic 'traits' to support much of its research promotes the (usually unhelpful) idea that we are all to some degree autistic. However, it also encourages the sense that autism itself can easily be observed and detected in, and by, anyone. A problematic effect of this is the undue otherizing of certain behaviours (such as enthusiasm for specific topics, or a preference for intellectually curious conversation over small talk). In turn, such constructions of otherness reflect and enhance the social currency of 'normalcy' itself. A related and under-explored consequence is to intensify, if not create, the isolation of those children and adults who are, in effect, *liminally* autistic.

The liminally (or sub-clinically) autistic are people who cannot quite, or cannot quite consistently, pass as neurotypical, and whose autistic tendencies or phenotype occasionally become noticed by others in ways that may be difficult for the person. All autistic people diagnosed in adulthood have endured this liminal stage in some way. Sometimes, as the subtext of chapter 5 will show, those who are liminally autistic, unprotected by the use of the name or known reason of autism, can find themselves gazed at, even goaded or prodded, not unlike the 18th-century 'madmen' in the asylums, discussed in chapter 2 via Foucault.

To be neurodivergent but not diagnosed can lead to many painful, sometimes injurious social (and professional) experiences. People diagnosed with autism in adulthood will know that all too well. It presents a very different set of circumstances to those central to, say, *Big Bang Theory*, in which Cooper is endearingly oblivious to the occasional jibes of others (not to mention how these are loudly rewarded via Pavlovian shrieks of laughter from the audience). Eight decades on from the first medical recognitions of autism, what still remains to be represented, expressed and debated in autism fictions is how it *feels* to be formally, or even informally, given this name.

That adult diagnostic procedures (or outcomes) are so seldom even *mentioned* in autism fiction might indicate the distance of most authors and producers from this experience and identity. That is a shame because as well as endowing literary and screen fictions with a more appropriately daring social realism for the present era, the recognition of such procedures and their meaning could be culturally informative. Such developments might deepen public recognition that, usually, people are diagnosed autistic only when the ways by which this condition is defined converge to cause actual impairment for the individual.

For some adults, autism diagnosis itself has an unexpectedly paratextual element. Usually, the person is told of the outcome in person, at the end of the assessment. However, in some clinics, it is still standard practice to confirm the diagnosis on paper by presenting the patient not with a letter, but a *copy* of a letter, addressed only to his or her general practitioner. And I am not the only person to receive the following well-intentioned and widespread advice to the newly diagnosed from specialists: *If you decide to tell friends or colleagues that you have autism, they will probably reply that they have known all along.* So the question remains then: how does it feel?

NOTES

1 Kanner, 'Autistic Disturbances'. Cf. Murray, *Representing Autism*, 30, 204n.
2 See Wing, 'The Definition and Prevalence of Autism'.
3 National Autistic Society, 'Gender and Autism'.
4 Gould and Ashton-Smith, 'Missed Diagnosis or Misdiagnosis?'.
5 Yaull-Smith, 'Girls on the Spectrum', 30, 31.
6 See Willey, *Pretending to Be Normal*, 9–12. Susan Dunne similarly suggests in her 2015 memoir how autism diagnosis in women often comes 'late' (*A Pony in the Bedroom*, 95).
7 Willey, *Pretending to Be Normal*, 63–64.
8 Cf. Baron-Cohen, *The Essential Difference*, 129.
9 Baron-Cohen, *The Essential Difference*, 9.
10 For further discussion, see Jack, *Autism and Gender*, 124.
11 See Baron-Cohen, *The Essential Difference*, 155–69.
12 Baron-Cohen, *The Essential Difference*, 2–3.
13 Baron-Cohen, *The Essential Difference*, 1. Original emphasis.

14 Baron-Cohen, *The Essential Difference*, 1.

15 Asperger, 'Autistic Psychopathy', 84–85; cf Baron-Cohen, *The Essential Difference*, 149.

16 Frith in Asperger, 'Autistic Psychopathy', 84n, 85n.

17 Constant translated and summarized in Ribas, *Autism*, 9. See also Feinstein, *A History of Autism*, Kindle location 895.

18 Asperger, 'Autistic Psychopathy', 85.

19 Asperger, 'Autistic Psychopathy', 87–90.

20 Asperger, 'Autistic Psychopathy', 85.

21 Asperger, 'Autistic Psychopathy', 84.

22 See Beauvoir, *The Second Sex*, 35–69.

23 Beauvoir, *The Second Sex*, 35.

24 For a more poetic juxtaposition of Beauvoir and Baron-Cohen's emphases, see McGrath, 'Ventriloquy Soliloquy'.

25 See Baron-Cohen, *Mindblindness*, for the fullest exposition of this theory.

26 Baron-Cohen, *The Essential Difference*, 105–15.

27 Baron-Cohen, *The Essential Difference*, 8.

28 'The Extreme Male Brain Theory of Autism' was the title of a 2002 article by Baron-Cohen in the journal *Trends in Cognitive Science* 6, 248–54.

29 Baron-Cohen, *The Essential Difference*, 2–3.

30 Baron-Cohen, *The Essential Difference*, 5.

31 Baron-Cohen, *The Essential Difference*, 96–111.

32 Nielsen et al., 'An Evaluation of the Left-Brain vs. Right-Brain Hypothesis', 1.

33 Aberg et al., 'The "Creative Right Brain" Revisited'.

34 For various responses to Sperry's theories on brain lateralization, see Hamilton, 'Paths in the Brain'. See also Bradshaw and Nettleton, 'The Nature of Hemispheric Specialization in Man'.

35 See Baron-Cohen, *The Essential Difference*, 118–26.

36 See Baron-Cohen, *The Essential Difference*, 126–30.

37 Baron-Cohen, *The Essential Difference*, 94.

38 Baron-Cohen, *The Essential Difference*, 130.

39 De la Cuesta and Mason, *Asperger's Syndrome for Dummies*, 82.

40 De la Cuesta and Mason, *Asperger's Syndrome for Dummies*, 82.

41 Baron-Cohen, *The Essential Difference*, 216.

42 These two questionnaires are reproduced in Baron-Cohen, *The Essential Difference*, 200–11.

43 Baron-Cohen et al., 'The Systemizing Quotient'.

44 Baron-Cohen et al., 'The Systemizing Quotient', 361. The group of 278 adults comprised 114 males against 164 females.

45 Baron-Cohen et al., 'The Systemizing Quotient', 361.

46 Baron-Cohen et al., 'The Systemizing Quotient', 361.

47 Wheelwright et al., 'Predicting Autism Spectrum Quotient', 49.

48 Jack, *Autism and Gender*, 128. See also Wheelwright et al., 'Predicting Autism Spectrum Quotient', 49.

49 Jack, *Autism and Gender*, 128. See also Gould and Ashton-Smith, 'Missed Diagnosis or Misdiagnosis?'.

50   Jack, *Autism and Gender*, 129.

51   Jack, *Autism and Gender*, 124.

52   Baron-Cohen, *Essential Difference*, 137.

53   Jack, *Autism and Gender*, 124. Jack adopts the term 'emphasized femininity' from Raewyn W. Connell.

54   Feinstein, *A History of Autism*, Kindle location 4999.

55   Baron-Cohen, *The Essential Difference*, 7.

56   Faherty, 'Asperger's Syndrome in Women', 10.

57   Faherty, 'Asperger's Syndrome in Women', 13.

58   Baron-Cohen, *The Essential Difference*, 47.

59   Baron-Cohen, *The Essential Difference*, 110–11. For a list of research outputs from the UCARC's Fetal Steroid Hormones study, see https://www.autismresearch centre.com/project_15_foetaltst.

60   Baron-Cohen's theories on gender also bear an influence on the most directly interpellative forms aimed at autistic adults, the self-help book. Ruth Searle's *Asperger Syndrome in Adults: A Guide to Realizing Your Potential* (2010) reiterates UCARC's gendered theory as if to explain autism itself to both men and women. See Searle, *Asperger Syndrome*, 45–60. Similarly, in *What Men with Asperger Syndrome Want to Know about Women, Dating and Relationships* (2012), psychologist and Asperger Syndrome specialist Maxine Aston provides a series of interesting reflections via her experience as a therapist, but the overall implication is that it is primarily autistic *men* who enter into relationships (and heterosexual relationships at that). Again, this directly reinforces Baron-Cohen's assumptions to an autistic audience. See Aston, *What Men with Asperger Syndrome Want to Know*, 125–26.

61   See, for instance, Auyeung et al., 'Fetal Testosterone and Autistic Traits', 4, 19.

62   See Cambridge Autism Research Centre, 'Fetal Steroid Hormones: A Longitudinal Study'.

63   See Lutchmaya et al., 'Foetal Testosterone and Vocabulary', 418, 423.

64   Lutchmaya et al., 'Foetal Testosterone and Eye Contact'.

65   Auyeung et al., 'Fetal Testosterone and Autistic Traits'.

66   The two questionnaires were the Childhood Asperger Syndrome Test and the Childhood Autism Spectrum Quotient questionnaire.

67   University of Cambridge, 'Research Links Testosterone Levels to Autistic Traits'.

68   University of Cambridge, 'Research Links Testosterone Levels to Autistic Traits'.

69   See Feinstein, *A History of Autism*, Kindle location 4986.

70   Murray, *New Collected Poems*, 414.

71   Penguin Books, 'The Rosie Project' (summary).

72   For a comprehensive breakdown of the survey, see the National Autistic Society, '11 Shocking Statistics about Autism and Employment'. https://www.the guardian.com/tmi/2016/oct/27/11-shocking-statistics-about-autism-and-employment

73   Arnold, 'The Social Construction of the Savant', 1.

74   Forster, *Aspects of the Novel*, 73.

75   Penguin Books, 'The Rosie Project' (summary).

76 Forster, *Aspects of the Novel*, 74.

77 Cf Murray, *Representing Autism*, 91–92.

78 Adorno and Horkheimer, *The Dialectic of Enlightenment*, 125.

79 Haddon, *Curious Incident* (publisher's blurb).

80 For examples of how Asperger Syndrome was explained as a form of autism with reference to Haddon's Christopher, see Fowler, 'Books', and Hall, 'Innocents and Their Experiences'.

81 Adorno and Horkheimer, *The Dialectic of Enlightenment*, 137.

82 Adorno, 'On Popular Music', 442, 444–46.

83 For expansion on this tension between standardization and progress, see McGrath, 'Ideas of Belonging', 144–55.

84 Adorno and Horkheimer, *The Dialectic of Enlightenment*, 131.

85 *The Bridge*, Episode 2.

86 Murray, *Representing Autism*, 13. See also Hacking, 'How We Have Been Learning', 501–2.

87 Shakespeare and Watson, 'The Social Model of Disability', 24.

88 Belek, 'Bron/Broen'.

89 Belek, 'Bron/Broen'.

90 *The Bridge*. Episode 1.

91 *The Bridge*. Episode 15.

92 *The Bridge*. Episode 15.

93 Fein, 'Innocent Machines', 30.

94 Cambridge Autism Research Centre, 'The Adult Autism Spectrum Quotient', statements 17, 38.

95 Jefferies, 'The Bridge Recap'.

96 *The Syndicate*, episode 3.

97 *The Syndicate*, episode 2.

98 *The Syndicate*, episode 2.

99 For a superb discussion of Lennie Small as an 'autistic victim', see Loftis, *Imagining Autism*, chapter 3, Kindle edition.

100 Forster, *Aspects of the Novel*, 73.

101 For a critical delineation of how literary prizes have favoured male novelists, as well as novels with male protagonists, see Watkins, 'Women's Post-Apocalyptic Fiction'.

102 Hacking, 'How We Have Been Learning', 512–13.

103 Hacking, 'How We Have Been Learning', 512–13.

104 Morrall, *The Language of Others*, 19.

105 Morrall, *The Language of Others*, 121.

106 Morrall, *The Language of Others*, 127.

107 Morrall, *The Language of Others*, 364.

108 Morrall, *The Language of Others*, 36–37.

109 Morrall, *The Language of Others*, 155.

110 See Kanner, 'Autistic Disturbances', 124, 144. Cf. Morrall, *The Language of Others*, 119.

111 Morrall, *The Language of Others*, 235.

112 Morrall, *The Language of Others*, 5.

113 Morrall, *The Language of Others*, 82.

114 See Morrall, *The Language of Others*, 71–81.

115 Morrall, *The Language of Others*, 127, 149–51, 187–88, 266–70, 279.

116 Morrall, *The Language of Others*, 175.

117 See Gunn and Bell, *Middle Classes*, 194.

118 Morrall, *The Language of Others*, 174.

119 Morrall, *The Language of Others*, 238.

120 Morrall, *The Language of Others*, 238–39.

121 For a quantitative and critical study of this, see Oakley, *The Sociology of Housework*.

122 Morrall, *The Language of Others*, 243.

123 Morrall, *The Language of Others*, 267–71.

124 Morrall, *The Language of Others*, 240.

125 Morrall, *The Language of Others*, 227–30.

126 Morrall, *The Language of Others*, 176.

127 Morrall, *The Language of Others*, 48, 53, 171.

128 Morrall, *The Language of Others*, 178.

129 Morrall, *The Language of Others*, 333.

130 Morrall, *The Language of Others*, 334.

131 Morrall, *The Language of Others*, 335.

132 Kean, 'Clare Morrall'.

133 Morrall, *The Language of Others*, 84, 92–94, 103–4, 156.

134 Morrall, *The Language of Others*, 37.

135 Morrall, *The Language of Others*, 334.

136 Morrall, *The Language of Others*, 345.

137 Morrall, *The Language of Others*, 113.

138 Morrall, *The Language of Others*, 368.

139 Morrall, *The Language of Others*, 376.

140 Morrall, *The Language of Others*, 127.

141 Morrall, *The Language of Others*, 209–11.

142 Morrall, *The Language of Others*, 345.

143 Morrall, *The Language of Others*, 345.

144 Morrall, *The Language of Others*, 345.

145 Morrall, *The Language of Others*, 163.

146 Lyall et al., 'Parental Social Responsiveness'.

147 Newell, Mike. Director. 2016. *The Interestings*. Amazon Video.

148 Wolitzer, *The Interestings*.

149 Wolitzer, *The Interestings*, 3.

150 Wolitzer, *The Interestings*, 9.

151 Wolitzer, *The Interestings*, 22.

152 Wolitzer, *The Interestings*, 58. Asperger reported how, when asking 'Fritz V.' to describe the similarities between a fly and a butterfly, the child's (supposedly) 'nonsensical' reply was: 'Because he has a different name' and that 'the butterfly is snowed, snowed with snow'. Asperger, 'Autistic Psychopathy', 45; see also 53–54, 62.

153 Wolitzer, *The Interestings*, 58.

154 Wolitzer, *The Interestings*, 200.

155 Wolitzer, *The Interestings*, 96.

156 Wolitzer, *The Interestings*, 197.

157 Wolitzer, *The Interestings*, 210.

158 Wolitzer, *The Interestings*, 188.

159 Grandin, 'How People with Autism Think', 138, passim.

160 Murray, *Representing Autism*, 3.

161 Wolitzer, *The Interestings*, 124.

162 Wolitzer, *The Interestings*, 97.

163 Wolitzer, *The Interestings*, 223.

164 Wolitzer, *The Interestings*, 19, 30, 206–7.

165 Wolitzer, *The Interestings*, 199.

166 Wolitzer, *The Interestings*, 97.

167 Wolitzer, *The Interestings*, 221–22.

168 Wolitzer, *The Interestings*, 48; cf. 318.

169 Wolitzer, *The Interestings*, 52.

170 Walker et al., 'Specifying PDD-NOS'.

171 Wolitzer, *The Interestings*, 330.

172 Wolitzer, *The Interestings*, 446.

173 Wolitzer, *The Interestings*, 318–19.

174 Wolitzer, *The Interestings*, 333.

175 Sinclair, 'Don't Mourn for Us'.

176 Wolitzer, *The Interestings*, 446.

177 Wolitzer, *The Interestings*, 447.

178 Wolitzer, *The Interestings*, 447.

179 Wolitzer, *The Interestings*, 462.

180 Wolitzer, *The Interestings*, 452.

181 Wolitzer, *The Interestings*, 446.

182 Nordicana, 'The Bridge Q + A'.

183 Penguin Books, 'The Rosie Project' (summary).

184 Simsion, *The Rosie Effect*, 76–80.

Chapter 4

'Title'

All the little laws
you thought were yours
are now Asperger's.

Chapter 5

Performing the names of autism

'To be injured by speech', writes Judith Butler, 'is to suffer a loss of context, that is, to not know who you are'.[1] In the most professional and thus sensitive clinical practices (and practises) – which I was fortunate to receive locally, and via the National Health Service – autism diagnosis is intended to enable and support people. Despite this, the name of autism remains injurious, because it continues to be medically defined in terms of deficiency.[2] The interpellation of diagnosis as felt in chapter 4 can be injurious in just that way that Butler's words suggest: a loss of context. If even science does not yet understand what autism actually *is*, how does that impact on the subjectivities of people so named? Am I feeling, remembering or fearing in this way because I am autistic – or just because I'm human? Such confusion can be compounded by neurotypical psychiatric tendencies to view autism as a condition in which empathy and imagination are lacking.[3] Therefore, a most profound question is: how, in a neurodiverse world, are any of us to know our own 'autistic' inner experiences from those that are actually shared, to some degree, by most of those people around us (whether they are autistic or not)?* This chapter cannot answer

---

* *'World Is Sudden'*

For many autistic people, inescapable changes to daily routine can create extremely heightened states of mental and sensory disorientation. Moving house, completing a course, changing jobs – the pure fear these might inflict upon autistic sensibilities is not easily understood by non-autistics, since it tends to be accepted that *everyone* finds these changes challenging. But there is a difference between the neurotypical adult enduring temporary upheaval and the autistic adult left in utter emotional, sensory and practical displacement for long periods. For autistic adults on low incomes, being forced to move from one rented room to another can feel like an assault on her or his entire consciousness.

Major changes in autistic lives, as in other lives, are not limited to practical situations. A life and consciousness can also be changed by shifts in identity. Sometimes, even eventually positive developments of this kind occur unexpectedly, without choice. And, as so many autistic people find change itself terrifying, the ramifications for self-perception involved with adult autism diagnosis can, for some, be massive. 'World Is Sudden': paraphrased from Louis MacNeice, 'Snow' (1935).

185

such questions. However, in exploring certain possibilities of 'autistic criticism', I reflect on how narratives which seem to *accidentally* (or just naturally)
articulate autistic experience might also resonate with more diversely shared
human subjectivities, and what might be learned from this. The texts used are
E. M. Forster's novel *Howards End* (1910) and Roland Orzabel's song 'Mad
World' (1982), with particular attention to its 2001 interpretation by Michael
Andrews and Gary Jules. First though, I address the changing – and contestable –
properties of autism as a name and, via theory from Butler, a *performance*.

NAMING THE SELF AUTISTIC

The reference to 'Asperger's' in chapter 4 is a metaphor: my medical diagnosis is actually that of autism. However, both names have always tended to
fluctuate. Therefore, from the subjective and momentary adoption of a medical model in the previous, brief chapter, I now turn to the more subversive
properties of autism and Asperger syndrome as contestable names, for these,
like any names, are continually renewable and redefinable by the ways in
which any individual (including fictional characters) *performs* this identity.
By performance, I mean the capacity to reinforce – but also transform – the
established associations and expectations concerning autism. In effect, it has
been, to a crucial degree, the people observed and written about by Kanner,
Asperger and others, ahead of the scientists themselves, who have established
the meanings of what we now call 'autism'.

To be named autistic is to be assumed subordinate. To name oneself
autistic – to name oneself anything – is an expression of agency. However,
the legacy of Kanner's formative research on autism persists: one reason for
Wing's 1981 formulation of 'Asperger syndrome' as a clinical category was
to counter the presiding assumption that to be autistic was to be incapable of
speech. Thus, to *name* oneself autistic, even now, is doubly subversive. First,
there is the speech act itself: once considered by definition to be incompatible with autism. Then there is the *acceptance* of the name – which can call
into question the past negativity of its connotations. Yet there is also a further
way in which to name the self autistic disturbs the current power structures: it
resists the cultural and conceptual *confinement* discussed in chapter 2.

In dominant medical models, adult autism continues to be named and
conceptualized primarily from outside the individual, by others. As chapter 3
observed, this process is compounded in the cultural phenomena of new classic autism. In both scientific and literary discourses, adults 'on the spectrum'
are usually positioned as *other* to the audience, as well as to most figures
or characters surrounding them. It is here worth reiterating that the name
'autism' is conjectural and somewhat metaphorical in essence. Its nominal
properties are reduced to 'self', via the Greek *autos*. Yet embedded in the

word are tensions which, though seemingly incidental to the name as used since the 1940s, still permeate the wider outside discourse surrounding this identity. First, 'autism' as a name pertaining to 'self' is granted medical, legal and even social acceptance only when conferred by influential *others*. In a second paradox, this name connoting a subjectivity limited to the self is applied to vast numbers of individuals, who often differ drastically from one another. Such inherent contradictions within prevailing notions of autism undermine the sheer diversity of those of us so named. Speaking anecdotally, this effect is often most pronounced in social conversation, where discrepancies in equality towards disabled people may be deemed more permissible than in published forms, and where the recipient is often the sole target of the interpellation. I am not alone in having received comments like 'Autistic? My wife works with autistic five year olds, and you're nothing like them' (said as if you should resemble a five-year-old and as if the children in question are a group of identical clones). This, in turn, highlights the deeper, rarely mentioned social complexity of adult autism: the contestable liminality of how it is named and by whom.

Despite the evident cultural fascination with (or fixation on) autism as addressed through this book, there is conspicuously less public interest – or, at least, less readiness from the culture industries to *honour* such a public interest – in the perspectives of autistic adults themselves. The observation in 2008 from autistic scholar and advocate Gyasi Burks-Abbott remains pertinent: fiction by non-autistics takes socio-cultural precedence over non-fiction by autistics. Thus, non-autistic authors can become misleadingly revered as 'the necessary medium between autistic and non-autistic reality'.[4] Against this trend, however, the poetry of Les Murray is continually empowering.

ANGER, FAITH AND THE REALIZATION OF ASPERGER SYNDROME: LES MURRAY'S 'THE TUNE ON YOUR MIND' (2006)

A key focal point of the exploration of autism and otherness in chapter 2 was Murray's 1994 poem 'It Allows a Portrait in Line Scan at Fifteen', which reflects on the poet's relationship with his adolescent son. Twelve years later, Murray names his own autism in a shorter, even more abstract poem, 'The Tune on Your Mind' (2006).[5] Although sonnet-like in structure, the 14 lines are relatively short on syllables, presenting independence from the form's conventional iambic pentameter. The shorter lines also enhance the sense of a song or 'tune' on the mind: something recurrent, and haunting.

In Murray's 2006 poem, published in his 68th year, the revelation of identifying the self as autistic intersects with spiritual – specifically Roman

Catholic – sensibilities. Like most of Murray's volumes, the collection carrying 'The Tune on Your Mind' (*The Biplane Houses*, 2006) is dedicated 'To
the Glory of God'.[6] Yet this 'Glory' as addressed in much of Murray's work
entails mystery, complexity and frustration. His poems are thus more in tune
with psalms than songs of praise. Progressing through a range of puns crafted
off the name 'Asperger', psalm-like tones are accentuated via the ecclesiastically redolent language of the opening lines:

> *Asperges me Hyssopo*
> the snatch of plainsong went
> *Thou sprinklest me with hyssop.*[7]

The third line is a (King James) English translation of the Latin *Asperges me
Hyssop*, sung in the Catholic Solemn Mass. It derives from Psalm 51 line 7:
'Purge me with hyssop, and I shall be clean'. But amid the evocation of Mass
and what the poem calls the 'clerical intent' of the opening line, there is, as
the title implies, a different tune on the mind here. The Latin opening echoes
throughout Murray's poem (*Asparagus with hiccups* in the fifth line), before
marking the brink of epiphany in the seventh: *Asperger, mais. Asperg is me*.[8]
The puns endow this line with surrealism and, in doing so, transcend linguistic boundaries. The earlier 'hiccups' evolve into the stutter-like '*Asperger,
mais*' ('Asperger, but' in French) and '*Asperg is me*' (Asperg is a town in
Ludwigsburg, Germany). Read aloud, these phrases resound as 'Asperger's,
me. Asperger's me' yet, within the poem on the page, there is still something
somehow unsayable about this – and 'The coin took years to drop'.[9]

A coin in a cliché can still be a coin, and in Murray's eclectically (even
evasively) allusive 'Tune on Your Mind', the 'coin' lands as a late, unexpected gift. What the poem's second half suggests is that the gift is not autism
itself but the agency and ability to coin a quiet name for one's own way of
being. In the subsequent lines, this extends to naming, if not accepting, certain tendencies and compulsions within the self:

> Lectures instead of chat. The want
> of people skills. The need for Rules.[10]

'The Tune on Your Mind' thus embodies the greatest contradiction of agencies inherent in naming the self autistic (whether the identification comes
from the individual or from others). This contradiction concerns the question of agency not just in accepting the name of autism (which Murray's
poem never unambiguously does) but in exploring the contestable space of
what this name might or could mean. The three statements in the two lines
quoted earlier are complicit with the medical rhetoric of autism as deficiency
('want', 'need'). For those of us with a 'need for Rules', the name of autism
might be appealing and empowering as an explanation. And while it is an

explanation derived from medical orthodoxy, it is once again imperative to consider how, from Kanner and Asperger onwards, the name of autism has essentially been a response, from outside, to the idiosyncrasies – as well as numerous diversities – of a group of individuals whose way of being *preceded* such medical recognition. Therefore, with what and whom do we then identify? With the suppositions of medical authority or the lives of other autistic people? Can (and should) we even try both?

Murray's 'The Tune on Your Mind' starts and ends by allusively petitioning a different notion of authority: that of the Christian God. The poem names strengths of autism, as well as certain vulnerabilities, asserting a position less marooned than *independent* from conformist society as the true 'Ship of Fools'.[11] Continuing a motif from Murray's 1994 'Portrait in Line Scan' of his son's autism, 'The Tune on Your Mind' also declares the speaker's 'great memory'.[12] However, at a 2007 poetry reading, Murray also commented on how the vividness of autistic recall can be painful, yielding unwanted memories of past events or regrets.[13] 'The Tune on Your Mind' concludes that hyssop – which in Psalm 51 and in the Catholic Solemn Mass is invoked to cleanse and redeem but which in Murray's poem is punned into synonymity with autism – 'can be a bitter herb'.[14] Psalm 51 is a petition for mercy and forgiveness from God, and a confession of sin. By allusively juxtaposing the naming of the self as autistic with redemption, Murray's poem enables manifold readings. Among these is a tacit sense of anger at God – *Thou sprinklest me with hyssop* – but this same line alludes to forgiveness. Perhaps, as with all the texts addressed in this book, the earlier commentary speaks more of what is on *my* mind than on the author's (or yours). And this might point towards something else: Murray's poems on autism can be enabling towards the articulation and recognition of autistic perspectives – including other autistic people's perspectives. 'The Tune on Your Mind' remains richly, often playfully, allusive, but 'hyssop can be a bitter herb' and – not unlike the name of autism in Murray's earlier 'Portrait in Line Scan' – the name of Asperger syndrome itself is set at a distance, as if still hard to accept. Most valuable of all however is the poem's effect as a whole: to name and narrate autism in the person's own individual way.

THE POLITICS OF A NAME: ASPIES, *DSM-5* AND THE PSYCHIATRIC RETRACTION OF ASPERGER SYNDROME

In an assertion which has proven relevant to Disability Rights movements, the author, film critic and Civil Rights campaigner James Baldwin wrote:

That victim who is able to articulate the situation of the victim has ceased to be a victim: he, or she, has become a threat.[15]

There is, of course, another semantic property of the name 'autism', alongside 'self'. The suffix – 'ism' can connote prejudice but can also signify an ideology, and a political movement. *Autism* can thus connote the emergence of self-advocacy from those who identify with this name. One of the major developments here is the familiarity of the word 'Aspie' as an adjective but more potently a noun, by those who identify with Asperger syndrome. The name appears to have been claimed by online communities of people so diagnosed in the mid-1990s.[16] An Internet search for 'Aspie' on 5 January 2017 yielded 1.8 million results.

It is demonstrably easy for some people to scoff that what became named 'Asperger syndrome' was just called being 'odd' or 'peculiar' in previous decades – but it shouldn't be forgotten that those, too, were socially imposed labels. The difference, by the 1990s, was that Aspies, much more easily than people just interpellated as odd or peculiar people, could form a *community*. 'Aspie' was first included in *The Oxford English Dictionary* in December 2013. The timing is intriguing, for June of that year had brought the fifth edition of the American Psychiatric Association's *Diagnostic and Statistical Manual of Mental Disorders* (*DSM-5*).[17] In *DSM-5*, the name 'Asperger syndrome' (first included in *DSM*'s fourth edition in 1994) is no longer recognized: instead, the condition's main traits are absorbed into an expanded definition of 'Autism Spectrum Disorder'.[18] This controversial move is also an obvious illustration of the historical and geographical subjectivity of what autism can mean. In UK clinics, which mostly favour the World Health Organization's *International Classification of Diseases* (*ICD*) over *DSM*, Asperger syndrome has continued to be diagnosed in accordance with *ICD*, which first included the term (ahead of the American Psychiatric Association) in 1992.[19] However, the 11th edition of *ICD*, due in 2018, is expected to follow *DSM-5* in expanding the classification of 'Autism Spectrum Disorder' to encompass what is now called Asperger syndrome while discontinuing the latter name as a distinct category.[20]

Momentously – though not in a wholly progressive sense – the American Psychiatric Association's removal of Asperger syndrome from *DSM-5* was largely a reaction to how masses of individuals (epitomized by self-identifying Aspies) were informally adopting this medical name on their own terms. By the early 2010s, one of the most scathing medical critics of Asperger syndrome as a medical term was American psychiatrist Allen Frances – who, two decades earlier, had been one of the main advocates for the inclusion of this and other categories in *DSM-IV* (1994). In *Saving Normal* (2013), whose lengthy subtitle declares 'An Insider's Revolt against Out-of-Control Psychiatric Diagnosis', Frances laments how *DSM-IV*, intended as 'a careful and conservative manual', began to be used in unforeseen, ostensibly more liberal ways.[21]

In a 2011 opinion piece called 'The Autism Generation', Frances railed against what he viewed as the condition's 'overdiagnosis', stating that this

> has been fuelled by widespread publicity, Internet support and advocacy groups, and the fact that expensive school services are provided only for those who receive the diagnosis.[22]

Frances estimates that 'about half' the cases contributing to the rise in autism diagnoses in the US are 'probably service driven' – that is, children are apparently being given the diagnosis 'incorrectly' because it provides a 'ticket to more attention in the school system' and more extensive 'mental health treatment'.[23] As a 21st-century variant on the parent-blaming that has shadowed autism since Kanner's era, the implication that families are pressuring doctors to diagnose a child in order to access extra services is a cliché which should be treated with far greater caution. Like most proponents of the judgement, Frances provides no evidence to support it. However, if those who support the discontinuation of Asperger syndrome as a medical category are primarily equating it with the provision of extra (or different) services for individuals in schools and beyond, a right-wing economic agenda becomes transparent.

The main targets of Frances's wrath are the clinicians and pharmaceutical firms who may benefit financially from the rise in autism diagnoses. Unfortunately, the civilian casualties of his crusade to 'save normal' include autistic people and their families. Frances points out that Asperger syndrome refers to individuals 'who are strange in some ways' but 'not nearly so gravely impaired' as those with 'classic autism'.[24] It has seldom been suggested otherwise. But Frances's cynicism is clear when he points out that many 'normally eccentric' adults have discovered and embraced their 'inner autistic self'.[25] However, Frances's V-turn from supporting the inclusion of Asperger syndrome in *DSM-IV* to becoming one of the term's most derisory critics remains – however authoritative – subjective.

Lorna Wing – who established Asperger syndrome as a clinical category in 1981 – titled a 2005 article 'Reflections on Opening Pandora's Box'. Wing maintained that 'describing and naming the syndrome has had mainly positive effects' and reiterated her belief in the importance of Asperger syndrome as a specific diagnosis within the autism spectrum. Wing comments in 2005 that adult psychiatrists are becoming more alert that 'high-functioning autistic disorders' can underlie other psychiatric conditions. She also noted 'the growth of specialist services', but added: 'many more are needed'.[26] How the removal of Asperger syndrome from *DSM-5* might affect the availability or even existence of specialist services remains to be seen. Wing concluded the 2005 article by stating: 'Nothing exists until it has a name'.[27]

In *The Book of Woe: The DSM and the Unmaking of Psychiatry* (2013), psychotherapist and investigative journalist Gary Greenberg illuminates the debates, processes and controversies behind the finalizing of *DSM-5*. He reflects:

> Psychiatry's appeal is not just about the possibility of cure. . . . It's in the naming . . . Give a name to suffering . . . and suddenly it bears the trace of the human.[28]

Greenberg interviews Dr Catherine Lord, an advisor on *DSM-5*, who emphasizes that the aim of removing Asperger syndrome as a medical category was 'not to change prevalence' of autism diagnoses.[29] Greenberg paraphrases Lord as follows:

> 'People use "Asperger's" and "autism" colloquially', Lord told me. Tightening the criteria would give the masses 'who don't know much about autism less of a feeling that everyone who's socially awkward has autism'. . . .
>
> If people want to call themselves Aspies, that's fine by Lord. 'We're not trying to take away that identity. . . . It's very helpful to some people. It's just not a medical diagnosis'.[30]

But Lord's medical conception of autism appears somewhat restricted by earlier equations of this condition with childhood: she co-designed *ADOS2*™, the bundle of assessment tools – mostly young children's books, dolls and toys – sold to clinics around the world to assess autism in adults, as well as infants, as critiqued in chapter 2. Nonetheless, her comments critically hit on major developments in the evolution of autism as a name. For as well as hinting that the *DSM-5* change was a reaction to the influence of Aspies, Lord's comment on people using the names of Asperger's and autism 'colloquially' also implicates – and should indict – the role of popular culture and especially paratextual namings of autism as criticized in chapter 3. As Frances admits, the lesson of responses to *DSM-IV* since 1994 is that it is not just the American Psychiatric Association, but doctors, advocacy groups, media and culture who 'get to vote on how the written word will be used and misused'.[31]

With *DSM-5*, the American Psychiatric Association clearly attempts to quell this democratic (but potentially repressive) malleability of how autism is named. Therefore, here is the key thought: if literary and screen cultures can influence psychiatry into repressive gestures by how they name and 'represent' autism, then such narratives also have the potential to shift medical orthodoxies in more enlightening ways. The name of Asperger syndrome remains contestable. Its medical transience will not necessarily be paralleled by social or cultural obsolescence – because, importantly, the diagnosis will continue to be medically and legally recognized for the many people who were diagnosed with Asperger syndrome prior to the recent changes. Furthermore, where, why and how people choose to use this name can have some bearing, however small, on its continuing, declining or developing cultural and political meanings.

The effective denial of Asperger syndrome in *DSM-5* reduces the nuance of diversity in what autism can mean. As such, it further complicates the already-delicate notion of attempting to identify with people whose language and opportunities may be more drastically limited by autism (and society). At the same time, however, the wider name of 'Autism Spectrum Disorder' enables a potentially subversive *unity*. 'Autism' is a historically and medically subjective term, but the ways of being, or set of 'traits' to which it refers – even if themselves historically and medically subjective – are often deeply distressing for individuals. To have a name for these can enable expression, and promote understanding, of the person's situation. That is why I value the names of both autism and Asperger syndrome, in all the diversities of each. It is also why, once the shock and confusion manifest in chapter 4 began subsiding, I am glad to have the formal diagnosis of autism. However, this book has sought to identify and critique two major problems in *how* autism is named. First, it continues to be narrated and 'represented' almost overwhelmingly from outside: by psychiatric researchers and by the authors and producers of cultural texts. Second, *because* these are outside narratives, they reinforce a series of frequently drastic assumptions, simplifications and stereotypes – and these are bound up in the dominant, almost pervasively oppressive social and political values of our time, namely capitalism and patriarchy. Therefore, in order to begin considering how these problematic tendencies in the naming of adult autism might be confronted (and even transcended), I will now turn towards a wider theoretical framework.

AUTISM, PERFORMATIVITY AND PERFORMANCE

Here, it becomes incisive to contemplate autism diagnosis as 'performativity' and the self as 'performance' via these theoretical terms as adapted from Judith Butler. Although Butler's uses of these terms refer primarily to gender, the agencies and processes to which they refer are empoweringly applicable to the possible meanings of autism as a historically subjective and contestable name.

Influenced by Derrida, Butler's starting point for defining performativity concerns how a socio-political expectation of a gendered identity 'ends up producing the very phenomenon that it anticipates'.[32] Thus, in Butler's critical rhetoric, dominant social conventions create a framework of expected behaviours. This framework is performativity. Her work develops this term from the linguistic sense of performative speech acts, which affect reality by their very utterance (e.g., when a judge issues a prison sentence or a registrar pronounces that a couple are now married).[33] Another performative speech act is the formal diagnosis of a person as autistic (or 'with autism'). Performativity signifies authority and thus convention. Yet these conventions include unspoken rules, which come to function as such through their very repetition. Butler states:

> Performativity is not a singular act, but a repetition and a ritual, which achieves its effects through its naturalization in the context of a body, understood, in part, as a culturally sustained temporal duration.[34]

Through these concerns with gender, as well as 'repetition', 'ritual' and the body, Butler's theory of performativity – and, more subversively, that of performance – is richly pertinent to critical considerations of autism.

As Hans Asperger's 1944 suppositions regarding 'male' intelligence (see chapter 3) illustrate, performative or dominant assumptions surrounding gender are historically subjective. Yet, to use Butler's most evocative metaphor, repeated acts and expectations *congeal*: something fluid becomes solid, hence the 'naturalization' of gender which emerges through the illusion that certain conventions (and expectations) are natural, inevitable and static. To quote one of Butler's most influential assertions then, gender – but, more significantly here, convention itself – is created by

> a set of repeated acts within a highly rigid regulatory frame that congeal over time to produce the appearance of substance, of a natural sort of being.[35]

In one sense, such a process of repetition creating the sense of permanence is what leads to an autism diagnosis. This is not to deny that autism is a life-long condition; I am simply referring to how it comes to be named. For what makes autism socially subversive is that a different 'rigid regulatory frame' is constructed, *by the autist* herself or himself rather than by the more collective 'repeated acts' that create and sustain ideas of normalcy.

Butler emphasizes how, while the regulatory socio-political 'frame' of what is expected (and accepted) of gendered identities becomes 'rigid', the essence of gender – and identity itself – can remain fluid, even if not truly free from convention. What limits such freedom is that under performativity, the dominant framework remains a cultural reference point. We can perform both towards and away from dominant social expectations, but either way, our identities *refer* to the performative structure. Such is the interplay between autism and neurotypicality. Crucially, however, Butler goes on to assert:

> Just as bodily surfaces are enacted *as* the natural, so these surfaces can become the site of a dissonant and denaturalized performance that reveals the performative status of the natural[36]

When the 'performative status' of the seemingly natural is uncovered, so is its essence as a social construct – and, thus, as something which may be subverted or rejected. To quote Davies (2012) in her astutely nuanced application of Butler's (sometimes ambiguous) terms of performativity and performance, there is

> a distinction to be made between the 'performative' as the compulsory, restrictive script of gender that all subjects must recite and 'performance' as the expression of the subject's agency to alter these repetitions, to produce a subversive transformation.[37]

Therefore, while performance may be culturally bound to *refer* to performativity (whether by compliance or opposition), it is precisely this bind that enables performance to expose the dominant performative framework as a *choice* – which does not have to be obeyed.

The naming of autism – most profoundly in psychiatric diagnosis – is a performative speech act. In emphasizing this, I am not suggesting that autism is *merely* a name (even though that may be so in the fictions of paratextual autism critiqued earlier). One of the great complexities inherent in the historical recognition of autism is the sense that this way of being long preceded autism as a nominal, medical category. This is most substantially evidenced by the 'case' of Hugh Blair (1708–ca. 1760) as investigated by Houston and Frith.[38] But it is also paramount to remember that the children observed in the 1940s by the seminal researchers on autism were in one sense the true authors of what autism 'means': in effect, Kanner (1943) and Asperger (1944) merely *interpreted* their impairments and abilities in accordance with (and against) a wider performativity of statistically shaped ideas about child development.

* * *

Butler's *Excitable Speech* (1997) is a polemic on the process of naming and how interpellation can become subverted into a two-way process. 'One is not simply fixed by the name that one is called', Butler emphasizes;

> the injurious address may appear to fix or paralyze the one it hails, but it may also produce an unexpected and enabling response. If to be addressed is to be interpellated, then the offensive call runs the risk of inaugurating a subject in speech who comes to use language to counter the offensive call.[39]

This process of redefining a name on the subject's own terms is best illus-trated by the emergence of the name 'Aspie' as a source of pride. And its continued usage, regardless of the American Psychiatric Association, will render it newly subversive. Of Aspies, Catherine Lord stated that the associa-tion is 'not trying to take away that identity' – which is just as well because it is unlikely that it ever *could* do so. Lord's caveat that Aspie is 'just not a medical diagnosis' may undermine the term's validity for *some* who adopt the name.[40] Yet Butler's emphasis that performativity and performance are not binaries remains instructive. To name oneself autistic, or an Aspie, is still to carry (and reinforce) the legacy of a term conferred by others and still interpellated in frequently negative terms. But it is not only autistics nor any mental health patients who are both caught between and free between the performativity of a diagnosis and the performance of a self. The same is true of orthodox psychiatry itself. In conferring or withholding diagnosis, practitioners are conforming to the rules of its criteria, as also is the person diagnosed (or not). Obviously, there are authorities who have the power to alter the boundaries of performativity, as the American Psychiatric Asso-ciation's tightening of the diagnostic category 'Autism Spectrum Disorder' demonstrates. But again, performativity and performance are interactive, and a synonym for limitations can be *scope*.

Butler (1997) points out that the reclamation of names such as 'queer' show how speech might be 'returned' with a new, empowered meaning; it can be used

> against its originary purposes, and perform a reversal of effects. . . . the change-able power of such terms marks a kind of discursive performativity . . . [and] a ritual chain of resignifications whose origin and end remain unfixed[41]

Yet the 'chain' of resignifications can still remain restrictive. The name 'queer' is now more frequently used 'against its originary purposes' of oppres-sion but retains another original element in its usage to *distinguish*. The latter effect will always be true of both 'autistic' and Aspie. However, this does not rule out the possibility of the first effect: the naming of autism against its originary purposes.

In her introduction to the 1999 edition of *Gender Trouble*, Butler links her 1990 book with *Excitable Speech* to state that

> speech itself is a bodily act with specific linguistic consequences. Thus speech belongs exclusively neither to corporeal presentation nor to language, and its status as word and deed is necessarily ambiguous.[42]

The physical body – so fundamental to what defines autism for the individual through sensory particularities – is often (though by no means always) what distinguishes some autistic people within social environments. This can happen in countless and variable ways, but some of those that are most otherized in society include differences in eye contact; motor coordination struggles; the extent, tone or volume of speech; and repetitive movements (stimming). Often, these harmless features are extremely difficult – and draining – to even attempt to control. Yet there is another dimension of physical presence which often is, or can be, within the agency of the autistic mind. I refer here to 'repetitive movements' on a grander scale, in the form of social routines.

Since one of the most distinctive signifiers (or performances) of autism is the creation and following of repetitive routines, it is widely assumed that autistic people lack spontaneity.[43] But that is a classic instance of how autism is often misunderstood when viewed from rigidly neurotypical perspectives. I am writing this in the small, quiet café which I happen to visit almost every evening, and where I sit and either write or read. This may sound, and look like, stereotypically autistic behaviour in its solitary and routine nature. However I am here tonight not because I was here last night, nor the months of nights before it. I have come here because on every one of those different nights, *being* in this café is what I have felt like doing and have chosen to do. To conceptualize or label such behaviours as merely a routine would be to risk confusing autist for automaton. To assume that autism is somehow incompatible with spontaneity is to misperceive the role of choice and thus the presence of *agency* in an autistic life – and the potency of autistic ways within the interplay of performativity and performance. Somewhere near the centre of this tension is a blistering issue of who is assumed to have the right and reason to name autism – and how, and whether, they are heard.†

---

† *X, Y, Z and I*

Years before being diagnosed autistic, I found myself temporarily but indefinitely working in the offices of a data-collecting service. Surprisingly, and much to my relief – for this job came after a long spell of unemployment – I was kept on following a three-month trial. Yet one year later, to my increasing (and surely not invisible) distress, I was still failing almost daily at some aspect or other of office multi-tasking, thereby 'slowing down the whole team'. Working with me, I was informed in one disciplinary meeting, was 'like working with a new employee on their first day, every day'. It was pointed out to me that X had been in the job for only two weeks and was already outperforming me. Y, I was told, was 'too nice to say anything' (to me) but had expressed to our supervisor that she found me 'painfully slow' and 'frustrating' as a colleague. And then there was Z, with whom I worked most directly. A fan of *The Office*, Z would refer to me as 'the special needs child' in my presence. He sometimes mimicked my facial twitching and often mocked my 'special' interest in The Beatles. I still feel unlikely to forget the occasion when he did all of these things at the same time – after which he patted me on the shoulder and quietly told me 'That was just a bit of fun'. But then when Z became our new 'team leader', his humour, and its peculiar dependence on me, did not alter. 'James, have you ever seen *Rain Man*?' Z once asked in front of X and Y. I said I hadn't (though I had). Z slyly added that the actor Dustin Hoffman looked a lot like me. Z appeared to assume that – like some fictional character named autistic by an author or director, but never by his peers (let alone himself) – I had never heard of Asperger syndrome. He was not to know that two counsellors had separately suggested I 'find out about it' or 'maybe speak to a specialist'. One morning, X came into the office and laughed 'Hey James, I've been reading your

The capacity for subversion of performative expectations lies inherent in their very properties of convention and expectation: 'not a singular act, but a repetition and a ritual, which achieves its effects through its naturalization in the context of a body'.[44] However, the tension between the performativity and the performance of autism must not be trivialized. In the face of cultural assumptions based on Kanner's 'classic' autism as fundamentally a form of impairment, *Rain Man* (1988) offered a performance of autism which, through its corresponding emphasis on mathematical talent, expanded the popular cultural framework of how autism could be imagined. But the film's critical, commercial and cultural success – which itself suggested how the naming of autism, previously absent from mainstream cinema, could present a novelty – was so intense that Dustin Hoffman's *performance* (in every sense of the term) became, in effect, absorbed into the regulatory performative framework. In doing so, *Rain Man* – or, rather, its success – created an established set of expectations to which later autism portrayals could play: the most obvious example being Haddon's *Curious Incident* novel. One of the most hazardous responses a commentator can give to any narrative of disability is to overestimate its representativeness. Doing so risks implying that a single representation – or a singular reading of the text – can be, however faintly, instructive in understanding the personalities, abilities, lifestyles and wishes of every individual diagnosed (or even undiagnosed) with a certain condition. Transgressions become absorbed and deradicalized, and this is one of the fundamental reasons why the term (and assumption) of autistic *representation* needs to remain problematized.

Of the various narratives addressed in this book, a distinction is evident between performative interpellations of what autism is or should be and *performances* of autistic agency. The most culturally favoured narratives – coincidentally or not – conform to and reinforce the performativity of autism as (to paraphrase Butler) 'a highly rigid regulatory frame' of expectations. These expectations include maleness; high achievement (or neurotypical notions

---

life story'. He then held up a copy of Haddon's *Curious Incident of the Dog* – to the loud amusement of Z, the charismatic team leader whom X clearly admired very much. And since I was so inept at much of the multi-tasking office work itself, complaining about these moments – or simply expressing how they felt – seemed utterly impossible: because I partly felt that I deserved all this, for being such a painfully slow and frustrating office colleague. But the main revelation came one afternoon when, while I should have been working, I sat reading Lorna Wing's *The Autistic Spectrum* at my desk. I made no effort to hide the fact that I was reading and not 'inputting data' in the usual way; this was a performance, of sorts. When Z approached me, I closed the book so that he would see its title. His response did not wholly surprise me, though I had not ruled out the hope that it might have been different. Z said: 'For God's sake, you're not now thinking you're autistic are you? Is that going to be your excuse for every mistake?'. I said nothing but thereafter, X, Y and Z dropped the jokes about autism. It was as if, on seeing that I *got* the joke, it lost its appeal for them. But there were, I sense, other patterns of power at play (and at risk) in Z's reaction. This exchange between us was my first and most personal witnessing of some of the politics involved in naming adult autism.

of this); a predisposition towards the most academically and economically lucrative professions (science, technology, engineering, mathematics); and a disinterest, if not an impairment, in engaging with the arts and humanities, and thus with critical theory – including critical responses to autism itself. The most regulatory narratives of autism – in both their cultural popularity *and* their ultimately conventional, uncritical namings of this way of being – include the questionnaires and related research projects of the Cambridge Autism Research Centre; Hollywood film (*The Accountant*); television comedy (*Big Bang Theory*); and – throughout autism history, from Kanner's refrigerator parents to the American Psychiatric Association's insinuations that families are manipulating diagnoses of their children in order to access additional educational services – the blaming of parents. As such, a strikingly conformist, performative framework of what it means to be autistic continues to be interpellated to audiences across a range of forms and genres. Again, it seems ironic that a highly rigid, repetitive outlook continues to be projected onto autistic subjectivity – for it is also there in the dominant narratives from outside: the normative, performative social structures against which autism is named.

Each chapter of *Naming Adult Autism* has ultimately prioritized more progressive and yet less culturally rewarded narratives. And what is key to their value is not just their independence from the rigid, commercially mainstream depictions named earlier; the more innovative and also more convincing narratives of autism also differ from *each other*. Les Murray's 'It Allows a Portrait in Line Scan at Fifteen' (1994) is not merely a depiction but a sublime performance of empathy from a neurodivergent father to his more overtly autistic teenage son. Still transcending both social and literary conventions over two decades later, Murray's 'Portrait in Line Scan' does not flinch from articulating the anxieties presented by autism both in the self and others, yet elucidates the roles of oppressive social structures that render autism as *other*. Murray's equally idiosyncratic 2006 poem 'The Tune on Your Mind' conveys tacit self-acceptance of Asperger syndrome, but firmly in the speaker's own terms – to which spiritual reverence, but also a degree of anger, are essential. Douglas Coupland has obliquely but publically identified with Asperger syndrome, and while the liminally autistic adults of his *Microserfs* (1995) as well as the later *JPod* (2006) may not transcend the stereotypes of the new classic autism, Coupland's characters voice prescient, if difficult, questions regarding the naming and meanings of autism. Tito Rajarshi Mukhopadhyay's poetic narratives in *How Can I Talk If My Lips Don't Move* (2008) powerfully contradict psychiatric assumptions that what autistic children see in mirrors is merely their own reflection. Joanne Limburg's *The Autistic Alice* (2017) illustrates the nonsensical within the supposedly normal and scintillatingly exposes how social expectations of independence ultimately function as demands for conformity.

It is also heartening that authors who have not publically identified as neurodivergent have composed some of the most exquisitely sensitive and progressive autism novels. Clare Morrall's *The Language of Others* (2008) is perhaps the least famous autism novel discussed in this study. However, its portrayals of how autistic identity can intersect with parenthood, work and, most of all, gender remain indispensable. Meg Wolitzer's *The Interestings* (2013) also deals compellingly with autism and gender. In its sustained but unobtrusive attention to both sensory and social experiences of adult autism – and the ways in which these two realms meet – Wolitzer's might potentially prove to be one of the most autism-friendly novels yet written. It is with consideration of how autistic and neurotypical subjectivities may themselves intersect – for they have never been binaries – that I shall conclude *Naming Adult Autism*.

The final two sections of this book will explore further ways of performing autistic agency through the creation of autistic criticism. 'Critical Autism Studies' is a term established in 2010 by Michael Orsini and Joyce Davidson, though similar stances from autistic authors began emerging in 1993 with Jim Sinclair's essay 'Don't Mourn for Us'.[45] Poet and academic Kate Fox's wryly incisive reflections on autism, class and gender inform a range of her projects, including the stage show *Portrait of the Autist as a Young Woman* (2011).[46] In 2012, Laurence Arnold launched *Autonomy, the Critical Journal of Interdisciplinary Autism Studies*.[47] Monique Craine is a neurodiversity coach and advocate; her blogs frequently address the intersectionality of autism with dyspraxia and dyslexia.[48] Gillian Quinn Loomes's self-reflective 2009 article on the value of advocacy for adults seeking autism assessment remains an essential contribution to critical research. Loomes's most recent article, titled 'It's Only Words' (2017), addresses the impact of autism diagnosis on social identity from an inside perspective.[49] Artist, athlete and academic Penny Andrews is a regular and dynamic speaker on autism rights, and has helped to pioneer a series of 'best practice' guides for universities concerning autistic students.[50] Along with many more individuals than can be mentioned here, the diverse and expanding scenes of critical autism studies also include numerous authors and advocates cited in the previous chapters, including Damian Milton, Sonya Freeman Loftis, Dinah Murray and Wen Lawson.

Unlike many others in the autism community, I am not an especially frequent or forthcoming figure in the related social media or conference networks, for much the same reasons that I tend to drift outside of most other social realms (and there is also the fact that I have been too busy writing this book; but perhaps it might now change). Meanwhile, the last two sections of this chapter seek to further demonstrate autistic criticism as literary and cultural praxis.

AUTISTIC CRITICISM 1: REVISITING E. M. FORSTER'S *HOWARDS END* (1910)

To return to a concern of chapter 1: the very act of critical autistic engagement with literary texts is essential to the evolution of autism as a medical and cultural phenomenon. There are two fundamental reasons for this. First, autism continues to be extensively yet often misleadingly depicted in both literary and screen fictions. Second, autistic people are assumed by many diagnosticians – as well as producers of cultural texts – to be somehow indifferent to fiction itself. This means that as well as being exploited by many cultural narratives, autistic people are implicitly discouraged from critically responding to these narratives.

So far, this book has prioritized texts within which, or around which, autism has been either directly named or tellingly signified. In this last contemplation (for now), I explore a different approach, presenting a consciously autistic critique of two narratives which are *not* directly nor obviously associated with autism. My wish in this is to demonstrate how works of art (or certain details therein) might enable a textual (or imaginative) meeting space across neurodiverse subjectivities, including those of non-autistic people.

I will begin by revisiting and partially revising (from a post-diagnosis perspective) certain assertions in my first publication on autism.[51] The personal and micro-political context of my writing a piece titled 'Reading Autism' (2007) relate to the events outlined in the earlier footnote titled 'X, Y, Z and I'. Working in a minor administrative role while suffering with undiagnosed autism, I was made acutely aware that my apparent social clumsiness and general 'slowness' were incurring much frustration from clients, colleagues and supervisors. Earlier, gentle but very memorable suggestions to me from counsellors that I consider speaking to my doctor about being assessed for Asperger syndrome became oddly difficult to contemplate following up when peers began to draw attention to my liminally visible 'special needs'.

After one particularly humiliating reprimand following an error traced back to me, I awoke the next morning and, for the first and only time, phoned in to the office where I worked to report myself absent due to sickness. I then spent the day writing a proposal for an extended review essay on Asperger syndrome from a literary critical perspective and emailed this to the editorial board of an American journal. The proposal was accepted and the essay was published. It contained two main parts. The first questioningly reviewed two books by Professor Michael Fitzgerald, in which the psychiatrist author posthumously 'diagnosed' Asperger syndrome in various dead, white (and nearly all male) authors and artists ranging from Jonathan Swift (1667–1745) to Andy Warhol (1928–1987).[52] Since Fitzgerald obviously never met these subjects in person, his evidence for their autism was based on (selective) readings of biographies in which their contemporaries commented on how odd and erratic the behaviour of these individuals seemed. Given the situation of 'X, Y, Z and I', it disturbed me to read how unquestioningly an eminent psychiatrist (and authority on autism) could conclude that these people's lives and legacies were reducible to a diagnosis framed in mostly negative terms. At times, it too closely resembled mere name-calling: part of the psychiatrist's evidence for Swift's autism was the biographical detail that unfriendly others in London's elite coffee houses nicknamed him 'the mad parson'.[53] Thus, 'Reading Autism' concerned how narrative alone could create the basis of a psychiatric disorder. I decided to apply Fitzgerald's methodologies to two characters in fictional texts, to see how readily, if not randomly, autism could be named. Here, an admission of small regret is due. The publication stated that two adjacent books 'were randomly pulled off a shelf'.[54] This was true, but I ought to have recognized and reflected on the methodological bias involved: it was a shelf in my room, of my favourite books. The under-thought implication of books being 'randomly' selected was that autism can be seen almost anywhere once we know its traits. It is probably more likely that the two books used were important to me because I so identified with certain characters. One of these was the eponymous (and single) character in Samuel Beckett's 1958 play *Krapp's Last Tape*: a solitary man obsessed with the concept of time, who converses with his younger self by listening to and talking back over tape-recorded monologues he made years earlier.[55] The other book is the one to which I now return, with different emphases: E. M. Forster's novel *Howards End* (1910).

In 'Reading Autism', the main (though not sole) observations concerning *Howards End* revolved around how the diagnostic criteria for autism might tell us more about the seemingly inscrutable presence of Mrs Ruth Wilcox, a core figure in Forster's novel. I will now invert that focus to think about how the same character in this 1910 work of fiction might enable us to think more deeply about some of the ways of being that are, in the present day, named autistic. As a point of contrast against dominant trends in current fiction, *Howards End* offers examples of autism as performance prior to the conceptualizing of the condition as a diagnosis (and thus as a performative structure of meanings in Butler's sense).

Forster's omniscient narrative states that Mrs Wilcox 'was not intellectual, nor even alert'.[56] Her ongoing relevance, however, involves how, from an earlier time, her often awkward behaviour highlights the social (and historical) subjectivities involved in what causes autistic ways to become impairing. For instance, Mrs Wilcox appears depressed when obliged to stay at the family's London flat. In the first scene to show her there, Mrs Wilcox is spending one of her recurrent days in bed because 'there is nothing to get up for in

London' – unlike at Howards End: the small country house she owns (and where she was born).[57] Mrs Wilcox can illustrate how agency and impairment often coexist in flux within autistic experience. Sensory particularities can be bothersome in environments which accommodate limited diversity, and shopping is an ordeal for Mrs Wilcox; the 'din is so confusing'.[58] Yet sensory rituals also yield delights for her. At Howards End – puzzlingly to her guest, Helen Schlegel – Mrs Wilcox loves to 'trail' through her meadow, repeatedly sniffing handfuls of hay.[59] This discussion will focus mainly on Mrs Wilcox's social experiences – for while it can be demonstrated that she faces social impairment, it must be added that this is often caused by the inability or occasional unwillingness of others to better understand her.

In the 1944 critical study that established Forster's reputation as one of the great novelists of his generation, Lionel Trilling opines that Mrs Wilcox 'is not, in the usual meaning of the word, a "sensitive" woman', and adds that 'her distinction [comes] from her lack of distinguishing traits'.[60] From a different historical (and perhaps neurological) perspective to Trilling, I disagree with both of his assertions. The plot of *Howards End* largely concerns the changing relationships between the English Wilcox family and their London neighbours, the German sisters Margaret and Helen Schlegel. As seen by the younger Helen, Mrs Wilcox is inexplicably 'different'; to the more bohemian Margaret, who becomes as close as anyone to the older English woman, Mrs Wilcox – 'a woman of undefinable rarity' – is intriguing but sometimes exasperating, distant and rude.[61] Significantly, however, it is the scene in which she faces a most rigidly structured social occasion – a lunch party given in her honour by Margaret – that Mrs Wilcox's apparent impairment becomes most acute. Yet crucially, the social intuition and the empathy of those around her are also questionable. Only when the lunch was nearly over did the other (younger) guests realize that she had not participated in their conversation:

> There was no common topic. Mrs Wilcox, whose life had been spent in the service of husband and sons, had little to say to strangers who had never shared it[62]

Collisions of class, age and gender contribute to Mrs Wilcox's unease here.[63] Nonetheless, throughout my research on autism, I have come across no description of the conversational isolations it can entail that matches the following in its consoling resonance:

> Twice [Mrs Wilcox] deplored the weather, twice criticized the train service on the Great Northern Railway. They vigorously assented and rushed on, and when she inquired whether there was any news of Helen her hostess was too much occupied . . . to answer.[64]

There are two conversational struggles here. First, for Mrs Wilcox, there 'aren't such things' as 'plain questions' from others – they always seem complex and in turn, as she comments elsewhere in the novel: 'I always sound uncertain over things. It is my way of speaking'.[65] Second, I recognize here a more subtle, rarely mentioned difficulty in autistic conversation, in which the sensory directly affects the social. As well as sometimes being uncertain when it is appropriate to speak in a conversation, I find it very difficult to guess – and even control – the volume of my voice. Sometimes, it is loud enough to stun other people in a room; more often, like Mrs Wilcox's, it is so quiet as to go unnoticed. A similar tendency is discernible in Meg Wolitzer's character of the 'awkward' Jules Jacobson in *The Interestings*: she is sometimes ignored in group conversations – partly because she makes comments 'to no one in particular'.[66]

At this point, I can freely acknowledge that my identification of and with Mrs Wilcox through the performative structure of my own autism diagnosis is possibly mere projection. And this brings to me deeper and broader concerns of the autistic literary criticism I am seeking to perform. The signs of autism in Mrs Wilcox, as a fictional character created in 1910, may have been entirely fortuitous on Forster's part – or, three decades before autism as we now know it was conceptualized, he may have based her character on a person or persons he had encountered (perhaps even himself). Even so, regardless of how coincidental the autistic ways of Mrs Wilcox might be, they are prescient in demonstrating how compelling these can be in a fictional character. Most vitally, Mrs Wilcox's character and social experiences empower me to not just identify but *articulate* some of the subtler nuances of autistic experience. Projection or not, there is empathy at work in this criticism – and, in contrast to the performative structure of the autistic mind as conjectured by the UCARC, autists do experience empathy, and reading fiction can often provide an immersive experience of it.

*   *   *

Mrs Wilcox leaves the social gathering early – a habit familiar to many autistic adults. Afterwards, the other guests dismiss her as 'uninteresting'.[67] Margaret, too, is sometimes silently 'bored' by Mrs Wilcox, who is apt to give 'too minute an account' of situations.[68] The older woman's voice is characterized by 'even, unemotional tones' with 'little range of expression'; it quickens only when she talks of Howards End.[69] Margaret discerns that 'though a loving wife and mother', her older friend 'had only one passion in life – her house'. Mrs Wilcox seems never to realize that Margaret (whom she only sees in London) has 'heard more than enough' about Howards End and that 'the nine windows, the vine and the wych-elm' meant nothing to her.[70]

Neurotypical commentators, particularly autism psychiatrists, often cast autistic people as bombarding and boring all whom they meet with 'information' about their 'special interests'.[71] In various fictions, the prominence of this trait is a hammer-heavy means of establishing that a character may be on the spectrum. But there is a great distinction between a cultural text bombarding its audience with pointers that a character is autistic and the ways in which many autistic people actually express themselves. For what tends to get lost is recognition that in presenting highly detailed speech or writing, the autist might not be *indifferent* to the recipient but, sincerely, indeed generously trying to connect with this person through a gesture of *sharing*. And if such speech centres on an autistic person's most passionate enthusiasms – such as Mrs Wilcox's fascination with the garden and history of Howards End – she or he might be offering to share what is most deeply precious to her or him. It is thus sadly ironic that many professionals seem to hear autistic speech 'literally' and fail to empathize with the multiple possible reasons *why* an autistic person may be telling them about something.[72]

* * *

Prior to the medical and social emergence of autism as performative structure, some of the characteristics that now constitute the name were (in part at least) performances that subverted social convention by revealing so much of it to be a *choice*. This is shown through Mrs Wilcox's oscillations between silence and unexpected bluntness at the lunch party at which she is the main guest. Speaking only when spoken to, Mrs Wilcox, for whom there are no such things as 'plain' or simple questions, answers briefly and evasively when asked for her opinions on art and politics at the lunch, causing a 'chill' to fall on the conversation.[73] She then surprises guests of the socially progressive Margaret by commenting: 'I sometimes think that it is wiser to leave action and discussion to men', adding 'I am only too thankful not to have a vote myself'.[74] However, Mrs Wilcox's comments at other points are quite radical, especially when speaking to Henry, her conservative husband, whom she would ask 'why do people who have enough money try to get more money?', and to whom she would also assert: 'if the mothers of various nations could meet, there would be no more wars'.[75]

Compared against her comments on the suffrage debate, it is as if Mrs Wilcox is deliberately being provocative. Narrated almost entirely from the outside, Mrs Wilcox's ability to confound others through her unpredictable expressions points to one of the most profound ambiguities concerning autistic ways: is she oblivious to social etiquette or indifferent to it? This question is critically essential in contemplating the (many) meanings of autism.

Foremost, it highlights the neurotypical assumption that social eccentricities are a matter of accident rather than expression: a perspective which undermines the agency of autistic subjectivity and the often-subversive (or even enlightening) value of autism as performance.

Apologetically told by Margaret that it was clear she had 'loathed' the lunch party experience, Mrs Wilcox – not inclined towards politeness for its own sake – responds:

> I enjoyed my lunch very much, Miss Schlegel, dear, and am not pretending, and only wish I could have joined in more. For one thing, I'm not particularly well just today.[76]

Those remarks to Margaret contain the only direct mention from Mrs Wilcox of the unspecified illness that leads to her unexpected death aged 51. She tells her husband that she is dying only in her final days, though she had known this for some time; he considers this the only instance of her ever having 'deceived' him.[77] Yet Mrs Wilcox's final illness is, as she states, only 'one thing'; it complicates, rather than diminishes, her autistic ways – for 'she and daily life' were always 'out of focus: one or the other must show blurred'.[78] After her death, Mr Wilcox reflects on his wife's 'unvarying virtue' and the 'wonderful innocence that was hers by the gift of God'.[79] However, Henry Wilcox's view of his late wife's 'unvarying' steadiness (or predictability) swiftly turns when, after her funeral, an abruptly written note to him by his wife reveals that she wishes for Margaret to inherit Howards End.

Trilling writes that Mrs Wilcox 'represents England's past' in Forster's 1910 novel.[80] This is apt, given her emphatic preference for the country over the city amid the novel's extended motifs of urbanization, and her death (which occurs just a third of the way through the narrative). Yet Mrs Wilcox is compelling to 21st-century readings for a further reason: most autistic characters in fiction of our present era are heterosexual. To date, it has attracted surprisingly little attention from critics, but there are numerous, consistent suggestions in *Howards End* that Mrs Wilcox's affection for Margaret is amorous.

Forster's next novel after *Howards End* was *Maurice*. First drafted in 1913–1914 but not completed until 1960 (and only published in 1971, after his death), *Maurice* is a novel openly dealing with male homosexuality.[81] Forster (1879–1970) was a gay author who privately wrote, aged 85: 'how *annoyed* I am with Society for wasting my time by making homosexuality criminal. The subterfuges, the self-consciousness that might have been avoided'.[82] Subterfuge is discernible around Mrs Wilcox's feelings for Margaret; self-consciousness, perhaps, less so. When the older Mrs Wilcox, remarks to the 29-year-old, 'I almost think you forget you're a girl', Margaret interprets this as a criticism that she is immature. 'Inexperienced', the two of them gradually clarify, is what Mrs Wilcox meant.[83] Musing over her friend's mercurial shifts between intimacy and distance, Margaret silently reflects:

> When physical passion is involved, there is a definite name for such behaviour – flirting – and if carried far enough is punishable by law. But no law – not public opinion even – punishes those who coquette with friendship.[84]

While they are later Christmas shopping together in London, Mrs Wilcox invites Margaret to see Howards End while the rest of the Wilcox family are away.[85] Margaret initially refuses but, seeing Mrs Wilcox's 'lonely figure' walk away after they exchange 'due civilities', the younger friend begins to change her mind. 'There was question of imprisonment and escape' in her friend's offer, Margaret reflects – seemingly alluding to legal transgression, rather than anything more ominous – but, convinced that the invitation must be important, she dashes to catch up with Mrs Wilcox at Kings Cross Station.[86] Mrs Wilcox then insists that Margaret must stay at Howards End for the night because 'It is in the morning that my house is most beautiful.'[87] However, almost immediately, Mrs Wilcox's husband and daughter accost the two women in London, having unexpectedly returned early. 'Miss Schlegel, our little outing must be for another day', Mrs Wilcox suddenly declares, leaving Margaret alone at the station without saying goodbye.[88]

Prominent autistic authors have written of same-sex relationships (Daniel Tammet), of celibacy (Temple Grandin) and of gender dysphoria (Wen Lawson).[89] Yet autism fiction remains a rigidly heteronormative realm. Most fictional autistic characters in literature and on screen are heterosexual, just as most of them tend to be normative in every other identity except for autism. This is the very tendency that renders autism itself a *flat* construction in the majority of fictional narratives. It is telling that it takes a novel from 1910 to queer this convention.

Given the subterfuge at work in how Mrs Wilcox makes her ostensible propositions to Margaret, and the sudden end to their relationship with the older woman's death, autism and sexuality never fully intersect in *Howards End* in the sense of a relationship being fully realized. However, Mrs Wilcox cherishes Howards End profoundly, and it is far more in the novel than a place where she might be alone with Margaret for the night. She stuns her family by bequeathing the house to Margaret – thus favouring her new female friend over her husband – but Forster's narrative continually exudes how Howards End, with its gardens and meadows, is of the deepest importance to Mrs Wilcox. To the rest of her family,

> Howards End was a house: they could not know that to her it had been a spirit, for which she sought a spiritual heir.[90]

Howards End is, alongside many other things, a novel of love for a *place*. Mrs Wilcox's wish for Margaret to sleep there conveys more than just a covert sexual proposition. In Forster's novel of motor cars, railways and the expansion of the suburbs out of London and into the Home Counties, the small, rural property of Howards End clearly signifies a (now slightly twee) notion of England's past. But Mrs Wilcox was born there; it represents *her* past, too.

Hans Asperger wrote that the phenomenon of serious homesickness testifies to how autistic people are 'capable of strong feelings'.[91] Often, the past has an unusually intense persistence in autistic subjectivity, as the capacity for vivid recall intersects with the anxiety caused by change. This is suggested in Morrall's Jessica Fontaine, whose childhood home, Audlands – the grandness of which seems to symbolize her love for this place rather than material wealth – is a continual source of solace in her memory and imagination. It distresses her to see its decline. Intense yearning for the past is also felt by Wolitzer's Jules, who quickly becomes preoccupied with memories of her first visit to the arts-based summer camp, when she first met the Interestings. But most intensely, it is Mrs Wilcox who 'worshipped the past' – and she wishes to share that with Margaret, via Howards End.[92] However, like Mrs Wilcox's husband and children, Margaret is never able to fully empathize with this 'woman of undefinable rarity'. In an era when autism had yet to be given a name, Mrs Wilcox's greatest struggle is to be understood.

AUTISTIC CRITICISM 2: NEURODIVERSE MEETING POINTS IN 'MAD WORLD'

Autistic critiques of art and culture could prove valuable in promoting awareness of neurodiverse subjectivities. Equally important, however, is the gesture of autistic criticism as an expression of agency. In the present era of reductive cultural (and diagnostic) stereotypes that to be autistic is to be talented at STEM subjects (or else nothing), critical autistic engagement with art and culture may open up new spaces within the performative framework of what the name 'autism' can mean.

The possibilities of autistic criticism as a textual practice are quite probably limitless, but here, the focus of my 'obsessive interest' – or monotropism – will be on a popular song which has prompted strikingly impassioned responses (and feelings of identification) from autistics and non-autistics alike. This song is Roland Orzabel's 'Mad World' (1983): a successful hit single for his band Tears for Fears that year.[93] Now better known however is composer Michael Andrews and singer Gary Jules's 2001 interpretation, specially recorded for Richard Kelly's film *Donnie Darko* (2001).[94] Since Tears for Fears' original was abrasively up-tempo and synthesizer-heavy, Andrews and Jules's much slower, instrumentally minimal interpretation arrestingly defamiliarized a well-known song to newly accentuate its mood of isolation. 'Mad World' is also among many well-known songs covered by Scottish singer Susan Boyle (2011), whose sometimes eccentric behaviour (for a popular musician, at least) had been frequently and sensationally reported by the media as signifying apparent mental illness.[95] In 2013, Boyle revealed that the previous year, she had been diagnosed with Asperger syndrome aged 51, commenting that she hoped her disclosure of this would give others 'a much greater understanding of who I am and why I do the things I do'.[96]

In a public Wrong Planet.net thread titled 'Asperger's Syndrome in Popular Music', various contributors praise 'Mad World' (particularly Andrews and Jules's *Donnie Darko* version) as a song evoking feelings known to many autistic adults.[97] On a 2006 forum discussing autism and songs, both the 1983 and the 2001 versions of 'Mad World' are celebrated, with one contributor suggesting that the latter be used by the UK National Autistic Society.[98] In a 2016 'Asperger's Soundtrack' of songs curated on the blog The Silent Wave, Andrews and Jules' interpretation of 'Mad World' is the first of 23 tracks appraised.[99] Numerous similar responses to 'Mad World' in relation to autism have appeared online internationally in blogs and forums.[100] I became aware of these commentaries only *after* deciding to mention the song in this book and looked online to see if it had caught many other autistic people in the way it had me. Apparent deficiencies in reciprocation and empathy, so often cited in constructions of autism, are implicitly challenged by such expressions of identification via art forms.

There are of course countless thousands of songs, films, novels and other texts that inspire identification both from autistic and non-autistic people.[101] And it should not be forgotten that intense feelings of identification or consolation in relation to a song may be a form of obedience not just to a creative agenda on their authors' parts but to the commercial intentions of lucrative culture industries too. Adorno would not have approved of academic celebrations of popular music. But in the case of 'Mad World', what I find interesting and heartening is not just how a song so nakedly expressing isolation and vulnerability (as well as humour) resonates with autistic experience but crucially, how a much-vaster audience presumably recognize these feelings too. In case this seems like a reinforcement or justification of the (often-trivializing) non-autistic assumption that 'we're all a bit autistic', let me immediately clarify my central points in this discussion, for which Orzabel's composition is merely an illustrative example. 'Mad World', in all its versions, offers a distillation of certain aspects of autistic subjectivity and experience with effect far surpassing many novels, films and even scientific texts which name, or purport to represent, autism. However, what I want to do in this (inevitably subjective) critique is not to textually 'diagnose' the song's content as autistic as part of some reductive or psychiatric style of analysis. Instead, I want to use 'Mad World' in order to reflect more deeply on some of the *meanings* of isolation, expression and anxiety themselves from within the context of autism.

*   *   *

Invoking a sight and scene reminiscent of William Blake's 'London' (1794), 'Mad World' has the singer observing the faces of others and witnessing the exhaustion in each.[102] It is a mad 'world', and suffering is what all people in Orzabel's lyric share. Yet this does not unify them: it divides them. There is both conformity and *competition*: these people are all out in the morning on their 'daily races' that ultimately lead 'nowhere'. Listening in 2017, this imagery of a frantic, constant race makes me think not just of the more obvious pressures to succeed (or to not be left behind) but of how capitalism has enforced disabled people into a different kind of competition or hierarchy.[103] In January 2017, the UK's *Independent* newspaper reported that the number of young people arriving on accident and emergency wards with psychiatric problems had doubled since 2009, yet mental health state services were facing annual cuts in government funding of approximately £538 million.[104] With less and less support made available in the UK for disabled individuals – not just financial aid but access to state health services – only those deemed by professional others to be most urgently in need are 'entitled' to support.‡

In 'Mad World', people's 'glasses' – glasses to drink from and/or spectacles to see through – are filling with tears. Yet this is followed by 'no expression'. In one sense, this seems to contradict the preceding lines describing weary faces, thus disrupting the logic and conformity of the context – much as autistic identity itself often eludes and defies expectations. 'Reading' the faces of others remains a complex topic within and around autism, incurring

---

‡ The 'Marks of weakness, marks of woe' on the faces in Blake's poem also resonate now in a terrifying new way, in which suffering is interpreted as something to be quantified: more as marks *for* weakness, marks *for* woe. For if a person does not score high enough on the imposed rankings of suffering, then her or his situation is compounded by being unable to access support. As further funding cuts are inflicted, the levels of urgency required for receiving state support are intensifying. And we can also see, feel and witness this on an almost daily social level. As mental health crises are escalating, a most oppressive and divisive consequence of the current political climate is the fear that our individual struggles will be viewed as trivial, or worse, as a reflection of our character – because *everyone*, it often seems, is under stress. In this sense, the resonance of songs as bleak as 'Mad World' might partly be an indictment of the historical period in which we are living.

much confusion. Many autistic people are seen from outside as somehow lacking expression; we are also believed to be impaired at recognizing the body language of others. Research indicates that autistic people respond more slowly and less reciprocally to facial gestures.[105] Yet, it is bleakly ironic that autism itself should be so often interpellated to the world as a 'disorder' in which people apparently show a deficiency in self-expression. How much space for expression is actually provided for autistic people in society, culture, art, media and politics? Something which has both driven and freed my anger towards certain authors and authorities across the preceding chapters is the awareness that they are unlikely to read this book. That I know because, first, their work so rarely acknowledges perspectives from the diverse body of writings from within autistic communities and, second, the dominant authors' rhetoric of negativity betrays an assumption that autistic people are unlikely to read the texts that supposedly represent us in the first place.

'No expression', repeats Gary Jules as Michael Andrews' piano alternates between B-flat and F-minor.[106] A painful inference for many people is that the absence of expected expressions from individuals – especially those whose autistic subjectivity is not known or recognized – marks some kind of rejection of those around them. Long into adulthood, I have regrettably damaged some precious relationships by accidentally appearing non-expressive when others have told me of feeling upset about something or have even been tearful. I can only say that while I was listening, and genuinely trying to help the person, what I was not imagining was how she or he might be interpreting my outward manner – or the apparent lack of one. Yet this can also be painful for autistic people. To recall occasions of my own non-reciprocation to others hurts more than almost any memories of explicit rejection from others.§

* * *

---

§ **Two Units**

Until around the age of 12, I experienced an inexplicably heavy and somehow insurmountable self-consciousness over talking to others in the presence of my family. If I was being met at the school gates by a family member and another child spoke to me (in however friendly a way), I would behave as if she or he was not there. The same would happen when I was with others in a public space and I saw children – friends, even – from school: they would say 'Hi James' and I simply could not answer. I sense this had something to do with autism in a different way, of inhabiting just one aspect of my identity (or even self) at a time. Even now, it can sometimes take a lot of effort to overcome the feelings of chaos involved when introducing one of my friends to another for the first time.

My saddest memory of non-reciprocation persists from when I was eight years old, and features a girl, slightly older than me, who attended the same primary school and was in the 'Special Unit' for children with learning difficulties. Like me, she always seemed to be away from other children in the playground. We would often see each other wandering around, but never spoke. One long lunchtime break, when a strikingly old-fashioned car appeared opposite the gates, the girl and

Adorno wrote that mass culture, especially popular music, reinforces political oppression by distracting listeners from the misery of regulated routine and a conformist society.[107] Yet there are ways in which 'Mad World' does something more akin to the opposite, confronting this state directly. Unusually (and disturbingly) for such a popular song, suicidal impulses are suggested. Following the repetition of 'no expression', the singer's *inner* feeling is stated. While hiding, and wishing for the alcohol-redolent drowning of sorrows, dreams of death bring consolation. As one autistic response to 'Mad World' online anonymously asserted, this song seems to articulate both autism and self-destructive thoughts, before emphasizing that suicidal *feelings* are not necessarily the same as suicidal intentions nor desires.[108] Sometimes, contemplating mortality can be a means of coping. In my case, that is a privilege elicited by my not yet having faced serious physical illness nor immediate threats of famine, war or environmental catastrophe. But suicide rates among autistic people are alarmingly high. A Swedish study in 2016 reported that the risk of suicide in autistic individuals could be as much as nine times higher than that of the non-autistic population.[109] It is also paramount to acknowledge that in the present decade, suicide is becoming an increasingly common cause of death among adults of all abilities and ages. Isolation, rejection, the sense of being ignored: these themes in 'Mad World' and countless other texts are also pertinent, of course, to the non-autistic population. What defines autism as 'impairment' in this sense is the question of *scale*.

'Mad World' evokes feelings known to many people, yet does so with rare intensity. Some of the lyric's most unusual and yet most universally reverberating expressions articulate childhood experiences. The later verses endow these with a melancholy complexity more often sounded in poems or novels than popular songs. The lyric recognizes how, as children, we wait for 'happy' birthdays to bring futures in which we finally feel truly satisfied and yet they somehow do not. But the moments with which some autistic individuals most intensely (if expansively) empathize in the song arrive in its fragmentary narrative of a first day at school, and the utter trauma at which it hints. As the adult autism blog The Silent Wave suggests:

I stood together. It was the closest she and I would ever be. Again we did not speak. We simply gazed at this black and red vintage car for several minutes, until its elderly owner appeared and drove away. The girl and I then separately sauntered off. In the following summer holidays, waiting for a bus with my grandad, I saw the girl from school approaching, accompanied by her family. I cannot see or say quite who she was with because the moment I saw her, I looked right away. When I didn't see them pass, I looked up: the girl was waiting with her family to cross the busy road. As they did so, she turned back to me and waved. It was a clear but somehow shy kind of wave – the holding up of a still, small hand. Even as an adult now diagnosed autistic, it remains a matter of deep pain to remember that although the girl from school maintained this wave, looking back at me as she was led across the road, I somehow could not – and did not – wave back.

This song accurately illustrates how I felt as a child, especially in kindergarten and the first few grades. . . . That was the beginning of my observation of the 'Mad World' around me that still holds true for me to the present day.[110]

In school, 'no one knew' the 'very nervous' singer of 'Mad World'. To my seemingly inescapable autistic sensibilities, this speaks of not just loneliness but the marginalization of an identity. Although no one knew I was autistic, others did see I was different, and they called me different names (I am not just referring to other children). The teacher's 'lesson' in 'Mad World' is to look *right through* the singer, as if denying the child's agency or even existence. But though no one in the lyric 'knew' the singer, perhaps *we* do, as listeners. Billions of individuals recall feeling nervous on starting school. And this again brings us to autism and the question of scale. For some autistic people, the sheer social confusion (and fear) as experienced in the first days of school is an almost constant state.

* * *

This book has frequently been doubtful of how autism is named in contemporary literature, science and culture. Often, the commentaries have concerned the ways in which autism is otherized yet also homogenized in many of the most popular narratives. In the preceding response to 'Mad World', I have attempted to illustrate how autistic criticism need not (and should not) be concerned only with texts which nominally or intentionally pertain to autistic identity. It is rarely helpful to say that 'we're all a bit autistic': doing so threatens to falsely diminish or even deny the struggles involved with the realities of autistic identity in contemporary society. But nevertheless, art and culture can create imaginative meeting points for people of diverse subjectivities and identities. Art and culture can empower people to empathize with other lives, in deeper ways. Humanities, indeed.

Experiment. Interpretation. Narrative. Representation. Subjectivity. Theory. The search for truth and understanding. These elements are integral to the sciences; they are also at the core of the arts and humanities. It could be collectively insightful for these spheres of learning to begin studying autism more collaboratively – along with women and men who embody the experience, the knowledge, and the name of adult autism.

NOTES

1 Butler, *Excitable Speech*, 4.

2 For an extended critical discussion of this, see Duffy and Dorner's article 'The Pathos of "Mindblindness"'. See also Murray, *Autism*, 19–23.

3 Baron-Cohen's *Mindblindness* (1995) is the most sustained exposition of this assumption.

4 Burks-Abbott, 'Mark Haddon's Popularity', 295.

5 Murray, *The Biplane Houses*, 25.

6 Murray, *The Biplane Houses*, 5.

7 Murray, *The Biplane Houses*, 25.

8 Murray, *The Biplane Houses*, 25.

9 Murray, *The Biplane Houses*, 25.

10 Murray, *The Biplane Houses*, 25.

11 Murray, *The Biplane Houses*, 25.

12 Murray, *The Biplane Houses*, 25.

13 Les Murray, poetry reading, the Tai Chi Village Hall, Didsbury, Manchester, 13 October 2007.

14 Murray, *The Biplane Houses*, 25.

15 Baldwin, *The Devil Finds Work*, 115. This quotation was central to an inspiring history of Disability Rights Movements by David Hevey, during the lecture 'An Evening with David Hevey', Leeds Beckett University, 7 December 2015.

16 OED Online, 'Aspie, n. and adj.'

17 OED Online, 'Aspie, n. and adj.'

18 American Psychiatric Association, *Diagnostic and Statistical Manual*, 50–59.

19 For further details on how the *ICD* and *DSM* came to first include Asperger Syndrome, see Greenberg, *The Book of Woe*, 189–90.

20 National Autistic Society, 'Autism Profiles and Diagnostic Criteria'.

21 Frances, *Saving Normal*, 139.

22 Frances, 'The Autism Generation'.

23 Frances, *Saving Normal*, 147. See also Greenberg, *The Book of Woe*, 200–1.

24 Frances, *Saving Normal*, 148.

25 Frances, 'The Autism Generation'.

26 Wing, 'Reflections on Opening', 197.

27 Wing, 'Reflections on Opening', 202.

28 Greenberg, *The Book of* Woe, 13–14.

29 Greenberg, *The Book of Woe*, 204.

30 Greenberg, *The Book of Woe*, 204.

31 Frances, *Saving Normal*, 139.

32 Butler, *Gender Trouble*, Kindle location 183.

33 See Butler, *Excitable Speech*, 2–3.

34 Butler, *Gender Trouble*, Kindle location 183.

35 Butler, *Gender Trouble*, Kindle location 1237.

36 Butler, *Gender Trouble*, Kindle location 3707.

37 Davies, *Gender and Ventriloquism*, 10.

38 See Houston and Frith, *Autism in History*, in particular 149–60.

39 Butler, *Excitable Speech*, 2.

40 Greenberg, *The Book of Woe*, 204.

41 Butler, *Excitable Speech*, 14.

42 Butler, *Gender Trouble*, Kindle location 369.

43   These assumptions are, for influential example, encoded in statements 2, 25, 34 and 43 of the Cambridge AQ questionnaire. See Baron-Cohen et al., 'The Autism-Spectrum Quotient'.

44   Butler, *Gender Trouble*, Kindle location 183.

45   Orsini and Davidson, 'Critical Autism Studies'. See also O'Dell et al., 'Critical Autism Studies'.

46   Fox, *Portrait of the Autist*. See 'Kate Fox', https://katefoxwriter.wordpress.com/2010/08/14/portrait-of-the-autist/.

47   *Autonomy, the Critical Journal of Interdisciplinary Autism Studies*. http://www.larry-arnold.net/Autonomy/index.php/autonomy/index.

48   See MCCAS: Monique Craine's Coaching and Advocacy Service. http://www.mccas.co.uk/index.html.

49   Quinn, 'An Evaluation of the use of Advocacy'; Loomes, 'It's Only Words'.

50   Fabri, Andrews and Pukki, *A Guide to Best Practice*.

51   McGrath, 'Reading Autism', 106–11.

52   Fitzgerald, *Autism and Creativity*; *The Genesis of Artistic Creativity*.

53   Fitzgerald, *The Genesis of Artistic Creativity*, 33. Cf. Glendinning, *Jonathan Swift*, 77, but also 78.

54   McGrath, 'Reading Autism', 106.

55   See McGrath, 'Reading Autism', 108–11.

56   Forster, *Howards End*, 86.

57   See Forster, *Howards End*, 80–81.

58   Forster, *Howards End*, 90.

59   Forster, *Howards End*, 20, 36.

60   Trilling, *E. M. Forster*, 104.

61   Forster, *Howards End*, 38, 95.

62   Forster, *Howards End*, 84.

63   For more extensive discussion of Mrs Wilcox's class liminality, see McGrath, 'Reading Autism', 108.

64   Forster, *Howards End*, 84.

65   Forster, *Howards End*, 36, 80.

66   Wolitzer, *The Interestings*, 96.

67   Forster, *Howards End*, 88.

68   Forster, *Howards End*, 82.

69   Forster, *Howards End*, 80, 81.

70   Forster, *Howards End*, 95.

71   See Baron-Cohen, *The Essential Difference*, 133. See Baron-Cohen et al., 'The Autism-Spectrum Quotient', 31, 39, 41; see Attwood, *Complete Guide to Asperger's Syndrome*, 220.

72   The further irony here is that feeling overwhelmed by communication with others in conversations dictated by neurotypicalist conventions is one of the most draining experiences faced by autistic people.

73   Forster, *Howards End*, 36, 86.

74   Forster, *Howards End*, 87.

75   Forster, *Howards End*, 99.

76 Forster, *Howards End*, 88.

77 Forster, *Howards End*, 99.

78 Forster, *Howards End*, 86.

79 Forster, *Howards End*, 99.

80 Trilling, *E. M. Forster*, 105.

81 Forster, 1971. *Maurice* (London: Penguin, 1992).

82 Quotation from Forster's 'Sex Diary', ca. 1965 in Moffat, *E. M. Forster*, 319.

83 Forster, *Howards End*, 85.

84 Forster, *Howards End*, 89.

85 Forster, *Howards End*, 93.

86 Forster, *Howards End*, 94–95.

87 Forster, *Howards End*, 96.

88 Forster, *Howards End*, 96.

89 See Goodman, 'Temple Grandin'; Tammet, *Born on a Blue Day*, 155–63; Lawson, 'Gender Dysphoria and Autism'.

90 Forster, *Howards End*, 107.

91 Asperger, 'Autistic Psychopathy', 83.

92 Forster, *Howards End*, 36.

93 Tears for Fears, 'Mad World'.

94 Andrews and Jules, 'Mad World'.

95 Boyle, 'Mad World'.

96 Deveney, 'Susan Boyle'.

97 Wrong Planet.net, 'Asperger Syndrome and Popular Music'.

98 Aspergers and ASD UK Online Forum, 'Aspie's Song'.

99 Silent Wave, 'One Aspie's Asperger Soundtrack Explained'.

100 See, for instance, Kurstilbud, 'Mad World. Gary Jules' (a Norwegian blog).

101 See Silberman, *Neurotribes*, on science fiction, 233–40.

102 'And mark in every face I meet/Marks of weakness, marks of woe'. Blake, 'London'.

103 A detailed, polemic and vital study of this is Stronach's *A Very Capitalist Condition*.

104 See Broomfield, '2 Charts'

105 See, for instance, Dawson, Webb and McPartland, 'Understanding the Nature of Face Processing'. See also Kiln et al., 'The Enactive Mind', 139–40.

106 For an excellent musicological (and cultural) commentary on 'Mad World', see Pacheco, 'Mad World Deconstructed'.

107 See Adorno, 'On Popular Music', 442–46.

108 Here, I shall prioritize the author's privacy over academic referencing conventions because of the personal nature of the post in question and the possibility that she might not want her details made public (hence my rephrasing of her basic point). I am nonetheless indebted to the anonymous author for writing a post which enabled me to articulate that important point.

109 Hirvikoski et al., 'Premature Mortality in Autism Spectrum Disorder', 235–37. For a concise breakdown and commentary on these findings, see Bazian, 'People with Autism are Dying Younger'.

110 Silent Wave, 'One Aspie's Asperger Soundtrack Explained'.

Bibliography

Aberg, C. A., Doell, K. C., and Schwartz, S. 'The "Creative Right Brain" Revisited: Individual Creativity and Associative Priming in the Right Hemisphere Relate to Hemispheric Asymmetries in Reward Brain Function'. *Cerebral Cortex* (20 September 2016). Accessed 5 December 2016. https://www.ncbi.nlm.nih.gov/pubmed/27655932.

Adorno, Theodor W. 'On Popular Music'. In Adorno, T. W. and Leppert, R. D., eds. *Essays on Music*. London: University of California Press, 2002. 437–69. Originally published 1941.

Adorno, Theodor W. and Horkheimer, Max. Translated by Cumming, John. *The Dialectic of Enlightenment*. London: Verso, 1997. Originally published 1944.

Alderson, Jonathan. *Challenging the Myths of Autism*. London: HarperCollins e-books, 2011. Kindle edition.

Alderson, Jonathan. 'Why Aren't We Trying to Cure Autism?' *Huffington Post* (Canada). 10 June 2015. Accessed 8 August 2016. http://www.huffingtonpost.ca/jonathan-alderson/autism-research-cure-asd_b_7497998.html.

Alexi, Dani. 'Autistic Academic'. Accessed 15 May 2017. http://neurodiversitymatters.com/autisticacademic/about/.

Althusser, Louis. 'Ideology and Ideological State Apparatuses'. In Althusser, Louis, ed. *Lenin and Philosophy and Other Essays*. New York: Monthly Review Press, 2001. 85–131.

Ambitious about Autism. 'Ambitious about Autism'. Accessed 18 October 2016. https://www.ambitiousaboutautism.org.uk/.

American Psychiatric Association. *Diagnostic and Statistical Manual of Mental Disorders*. Fifth Edition. Washington: American Psychiatric Publishing, 2013.

Andrews, Michael and Jules, Gary. 'Mad World'. Sanctuary, single. 2003. CD.

Armitage, Simon. 'Rock of Ages'. In Corcoran, Neil, ed. *'Do You, Mr Jones': Bob Dylan with the Poets and Professors*. London: Chatto & Windus, 2002. 105–26.

Armitage, Simon. 'The Stone Beach'. *The Guardian*. 3 August 2002. Accessed 7 January 2017. https://www.theguardian.com/books/2002/aug/03/poetry.simonarmitage.

Arnold, Laurence. 'The Social Construction of the Savant'. *Autonomy* 1:2 (2013): 1. Accessed 8 January 2017. http://www.larry-arnold.net/Autonomy/index.php/autonomy/article/view/AR2/pdf.

Ashton, Elizabeth. 'Extending the Scope of Metaphor: An Examination of Definitions Old and New and Their Significance for Education'. *Educational Studies* 23:2 (1997): 195–208.

Asperger, Hans. '"Autistic Psychopathy" in Childhood'. Translated by Frith, Uta. *Autism and Asperger Syndrome*. New York: Cambridge University Press, 1991.

Asperger, Hans. 'Problems of Infantile Autism'. *Communication* (magazine of the UK National Autistic Society) 13 (1979): 45–52.

Aspergers and ASD UK Online Forum. 'Aspie's Song'. Accessed 19 December 2016. http://www.asd-forum.org.uk/forum/index.php?/topic/7820-aspies-song/.

Aston, Maxine. *What Men with Asperger Syndrome Want to Know about Women, Dating and Relationships*. London: Jessica Kingsley, 2012.

Attwood, Tony. *The Complete Guide to Asperger's Syndrome*. London: Jessica Kingsley, 2006.

Attwood, Tony and Grandin, Temple. *Asperger's and Girls*. Arlington, Texas: Future Horizons, 2006.

Atwood, Margaret. *In Other Worlds: SF and the Human Imagination*. London: Hachette Digital, 2011. Kindle edition.

Atwood, Margaret. *MaddAddam*. London: Virago, 2013.

Atwood, Margaret. *Oryx and Crake*. London: Virago, 2013. Originally published 2003.

Atwood, Margaret. *Writing with Intent*. New York: Avalon, 2005.

Atwood, Margaret. *Year of the Flood*. London: Virago, 2013. Originally published 2009.

Autism Independent UK. 'Autism Independent UK'. Accessed 18 October 2016. http://www.autismuk.com/.

Autism Research Centre. 'Fetal Steroid Hormones: A Longitudinal Study'. Accessed 15 August 2016. https://www.autismresearchcentre.com/project_15_foetaltst.

Autism Research Centre. 'Systemizing in Autism Spectrum Conditions'. Accessed 12 August 2016. http://www.autismresearchcentre.com/project_2_systemize.

Autism Self Advocacy Network. 'Statement on Autism Speaks Board Appointments'. Accessed 3 August 2016. http://autisticadvocacy.org/2015/12/statement-on-autism-speaks-board-appointments/.

Autism Speaks. 'About Us'. Accessed 3 June 2016. https://www.autismspeaks.org/about-us.

Autism Speaks. 'Autism Speaks Welcomes Three New Board Members'. Accessed 3 August 2016. https://www.autismspeaks.org/news/news-item/autism-speaks-welcomes-three-new-board-members.

Autism Speaks. 'Mission'. Accessed 3 August 2016. https://www.autismspeaks.org/about-us/mission.

Autism Teaching Tools. '*Tuesday*: A Wordless Book by David Wiesner'. Accessed 2 November 2016. http://www.autismteachingtools.com/page/bbbbqj/bbbbgf.

Autist's Corner. 'Metaphor at the Expense of Characterization: Autism in Margaret Atwood's "Oryx and Crake"'. 28 August 2008. Accessed 23 January 2015. http://autistscorner.blogspot.co.uk/2008/08/metaphor-at-expense-of-characterization.html.

Auyeung, B., Baron-Cohen, S., Ashwin, E., Knickmeyer, R., Taylor, K., and Hackett, G. 'Fetal Testosterone and Autistic Traits'. *British Journal of Psychology* 100 (2009): 1–22.

Auyeung, B., Baron-Cohen, S., Wheelwright, S., and Allison, C. 'The Autism Spectrum Quotient: Children's Version (AQ-Child)'. *Journal of Autism and Developmental Disorders* 38 (2008): 1230–40.

Baldwin, James. *The Devil Finds Work*. New York: Vintage, 2011. Originally published 1976.

Barnbaum, Deborah R. *The Ethics of Autism*. Bloomington: Indiana University Press, 2008.

Barnes, Richard. 2013. *Tommy: The Who*. In The Who. 2013. *Tommy: Super Deluxe Edition*. London: Polydor. Liner notes.

Barnes, Richard and Townshend, Pete. *The Story of Tommy*. London: Eel Pie, 1977.

Baron-Cohen, Simon. 'Autism and Minds Wired For Science'. Paper presented at *Wired 2012*. Available as a video clip in Steadman, Ian. 'Watch Simon Baron-Cohen's Full *Wired 2012* Talk about Autism', *Wired*. 18 January 2013. Accessed 25 June 2016. http://www.wired.co.uk/article/simon-baron-cohen.

Baron-Cohen, Simon. *The Essential Difference*. London: Penguin, 2012.

Baron-Cohen, Simon. 'The Extreme Male Brain Theory of Autism'. *Trends in Cognitive Science* 6 (2002): 248–54.

Baron-Cohen, Simon. *Mindblindness: An Essay on Autism and Theory of Mind*. Cambridge, Massachusetts: MIT Press, 1995.

Baron-Cohen, Simon. *Zero Degrees of Empathy*. London: Allen Lane, 2011.

Baron-Cohen, Simon, Auyeung, B., Nørgaard-Pedersen, B., Hougaard, D. M., Abdallah, M. W., Melgaard, L., Cohen, A. S., Chakrabarti, B., Ruta, L., and Lombardo, M. V. 'Elevated Fetal Steroidogenic Activity in Autism'. *Molecular Psychiatry* 20 (2015): 369–76.

Baron-Cohen, Simon, Bolton, P., Wheelwright, S., Short, L., Mead, G., Smith, A., and Scahill, V. 'Autism Occurs More Often in Families of Physicists, Engineers, and Mathematicians'. *Autism* 2 (1998): 296–301.

Baron-Cohen, Simon, Richler, J., Bisarya, D., Gurunathan, N., and Wheelwright, S. 'The Systemizing Quotient (SQ): An Investigation of Adults with Asperger Syndrome or High-Functioning Autism, and Normal Sex Differences'. *Philosophical Transactions of the Royal Society. Series B*. Special issue of 'Autism: Mind and Brain'. 358:1430 (2003): 361–74.

Baron-Cohen, Simon, Wheelwright, S., Skinner, R., Martin, J., and Clubley, E. 'The Autism-Spectrum Quotient (AQ): Evidence from Asperger Syndrome/High-Functioning Autism, Males and Females, Scientists and Mathematicians'. *Journal of Autism and Developmental Disorders* 31 (2001): 5–17. Accessed 4 July 2016. http://docs.autismresearchcentre.com/papers/2001_BCetal_AQ.pdf.

Baron-Cohen, Simon, Wheelwright, S., Stone, V., and Rutherford, M. 'A Mathematician, a Physicist, and a Computer Scientist with Asperger Syndrome: Performance on Folk Psychology and Folk Physics tests'. *Neurocase* 5 (1999): 475–83.

Baron-Cohen, Simon, Wheelwright, S., Stott, C., Nolton, P., and Goodyer, I. 'Engineering and Autism: Exploring the Link Further: Reply to Wolff, Braunsberg and Islam'. *Autism* 2 (1998): 98–104.

Baron-Cohen, Simon, Wheelwright, S., Stott, C., Nolton, P., and Goodyer, I. 'Is There a Link between Engineering and Autism?'. *Autism* 1 (1997): 101–9.

Barry, Alison. 'Autism: Lost in the Mirror?'. *Journal of Psychology and Clinical Psychiatry* 2:2 (2015). 1–5. Accessed 1 November 2016. http://medcraveonline.com/JPCPY/JPCPY-02-00063.pdf.

Bazian. 'People with Autism Are "Dying Younger", Warns Study'. nhs.uk. 19 March 2016. Accessed 20 December. http://www.nhs.uk/news/2016/03March/Pages/People-with-autism-are-dying-younger-warns-study.aspx.

Beauvoir, Simone de. *The Second Sex*. Translation by H. M. Parshley. London: Vintage, 1997. Originally published 1949.

Beckett, Samuel. 'Krapp's Last Tape'. In Beckett, Samuel. *The Complete Dramatic Works*. London: Faber, 1986: 187–97. Originally published 1958.

Belek, Ben. 2013. 'Bron/Broen (The Bridge)'. The Autism Anthropologist. Accessed 29 December 2016. https://theautismanthropologist.wordpress.com/2013/10/28/bron-broen-the-bridge/.

BestPracticeAutism.com. 'Best Practice Review: The Autism Diagnostic Observation Schedule'. 15 January 2012. Accessed 31 October 2016. http://bestpracticeautism.blogspot.co.uk/2012/01/best-practice-review-autism-diagnostic.html.

Bettelheim, Bruno. *The Empty Fortress: Infantile Autism and the Birth of the Self*. New York: The Free Press, 1972. Originally published 1967.

Biklen, Douglas. *Autism and the Myth of the Person Alone*. London: New York University Press, 2005. Kindle Edition.

Blake, William. 'London'. In Blake, William. *Songs of Innocence and Experience*. Oxford: Oxford University Press, 1970: 46. Originally published 1794.

Blake, William. *The Marriage of Heaven and Hell*. New York: Dover, 1994. Originally published 1793.

Blincoe, Nicholas. 'Feeling Frail'. *The Telegraph* (UK). 17 October 2004. Accessed 22 July 2016. http://www.telegraph.co.uk/culture/books/3625560/Feeling-frail.html.

Block, John, Dir. *Sounding the Alarm: Battling the Autism Academic*. New York: Blockburger, 2014.

Bloodaxe Books. 'Joanne Limburg: The Autistic Alice'. Accessed 5 October 2016. http://bloodaxebooks.com/ecs/product/the-autistic-alice-1138.

Bond, Henry. 'What Autism Can Teach Us about Psychoanalysis'. *The Guardian*. 12 April 2012. Accessed 2 November 2016. https://www.theguardian.com/commentisfree/2012/apr/16/autism-psychoanalysis-lacanian.

Bonnello, Chris. 'Taking Things Literally: When Having Autism's Actually Pretty Fun'. *Autistic Not Weird*. 27 April 2015. Accessed 27 October 2016. http://autisticnotweird.com/taking-things-literally-when-having-autisms-actually-pretty-funny/.

Boyle, Susan. 'Mad World'. In Boyle, Susan. *Someone to Watch over Me*. 2011. Columbia, CD.

Bradshaw, J. L. and Nettleton, N. C. 'The Nature of Hemispheric Specialization in Man'. *Behavioral and Brain Sciences* 4 (1981): 51–63.

The Bridge. Episode 1. Directed by Henrik Goergsson. Written by Camilla Ahlgren, Hans Rosenfeldt and Nikolaj Scherfig. BBC4, 21 April 2012.

The Bridge. Episode 2. Directed by Henrik Goergsson. Written by Camilla Ahlgren, Hans Rosenfeldt and Nikolaj Scherfig. BBC4, 21 April 2012.

The Bridge. Episode 19. Directed by Henrik Goergsson. Written by Camilla Ahlgren, Hans Rosenfeldt and Nikolaj Scherfig. BBC4, 1 February 2014.

Broderick, Alicia A. and Ne'eman, Ari. 'Autism as Metaphor: Narrative and Counter-narrative'. *International Journal of Inclusive Education* 12:5 (2008): 459–76.

Broomfield, Matt. '2 Charts That Show What Has Happened to Mental Health under the Conservatives'. *The Independent*. 9 January 2017. Accessed 10 January 2017. http://www.independent.co.uk/life-style/health-and-families/health-news/mental-health-figures-depression-anxiety-children-tory-government-theresa-may-pledge-end-stigma-a7517531.html.

Brown, Julie. *Writers on the Spectrum*. London: Jessica Kingsley, 2010.

Burks-Abbott, Gyasi. 'Mark Haddon's Popularity and Other Curious Incidents in My Life as an Autistic'. In Osteen, Mark, ed. *Autism and Representation*. Abingdon: Routledge. 289–296.

Bush, George W. 'President's Statement on Combating Autism Act of 2006'. White House Archives: President George W. Bush. Accessed 17 September 2016. http://georgewbush-whitehouse.archives.gov/news/releases/2006/12/20061219-3.html.

Butler, Judith. *Excitable Speech: A Politics of the Performative*. New York: Routledge, 1997.

Butler, Judith. *Gender Trouble: Feminism and the Subversion of Identity: Tenth Anniversary Edition*. Abingdon: Routledge, 1999. Kindle edition.

Cain, Sian. 'Emily Brontë May Have Had Asperger Syndrome, Says Biographer'. *The Guardian*. 29 August 2016. Accessed 8 January 2017. https://www.theguardian.com/books/2016/aug/29/emily-bronte-may-have-had-asperger-syndrome-says-biographer.

Cambridge Autism Research Centre. 'Fetal Steroid Hormones: A Longitudinal Study'. Accessed 14 December 2016. https://www.autismresearchcentre.com/project_15_foetaltst.

Cambridge University Autism Research Centre. Homepage. Accessed 18 October 2016. https://www.autismresearchcentre.com/.

Carroll, Lewis. *Through the Looking-Glass and What Alice Found There*. 1871. London: Macmillan. Kindle edition: location 182.

Centers for Disease Control and Prevention. 'Autism Spectrum Disorder'. Accessed 18 October 2016. http://www.cdc.gov/media/releases/2014/p0327-autism-spectrum-disorder.html.

Clayton Behavioural. 'Did Hans Asperger Have Asperger's Syndrome?' Accessed 12 August 2016. https://www.claytonbehavioral.com/did-hans-asperger-have-aspergers-syndrome.

Collins, Paul. 'Must-Geek TV'. *The Slate*. 2 February 2009. Accessed 23 October 2016. http://www.slate.com/articles/arts/television/2009/02/mustgeek_tv.html.

Coupland, Douglas. *JPod*. London: Bloomsbury, 2006.

Coupland, Douglas. *Marshall McLuhan: You Know Nothing of My Work!* New York: Atlas, 2011.

Coupland, Douglas. *Microserfs*. London: HarperCollins, 2004. Originally published 1995.

Crane, L. and Goddard, L. 'Episodic and Semantic Autobiographical Memory in Adults with Autism Spectrum Disorders'. *Journal of Autism and Developmental Discord* 38 (2008): 498–506. Reviewed by Dawei Li, Duke University, USA; Danilo Assis Pereira, Brazilian Institute of Neuropsychology and Cognitive Sciences, Brazil.

Davide-Rivera. 'Asperger's and Pregnancy'. Aspie Writer.com. 29 January 2013. Accessed 26 November 2016. http://aspiewriter.com/2013/01/aspergers-and-pregnancy-sensory-issues.html.

Davies, Helen. *Gender and Ventriloquism in Victorian and Neo-Victorian Fiction*. Basingstoke: Palgrave Macmillan, 2012.

Davies, Helen. *Neo-Victorian Freakery: The Cultural Afterlife of the Victorian Freak Show*. Basingstoke: Palgrave Macmillan, 2015.

Davis, Lennard J. *Enforcing Normalcy: Disability, Deafness and the Body*. New York: Verso, 1995.

Dawson, G., Webb, S. J., and McPartland, J. 'Understanding the Nature of Face Processing Impairment in Autism: Insights from Behavioral and Electrophysiological Studies'. *Developmental Neuropsychology* 27:3 (2005): 403–24.

Dawson, Michelle. 'Bettelheim's Worst Crime: Autism and the Epidemic of Irresponsibility'. 9 September 2003. Accessed 4 January 2017. http://www.sentex. net/~nexus23/md_01.html.

Deafblind UK. 'About Deafblindness'. Accessed 20 September 2016. http://deaf blind.org.uk/deafblindness/.

De la Cuesta, Gina Gomez and Mason, James. *Asperger's Syndrome for Dummies*. Chichester: John Wiley, 2011.

Deveney, C. 'Susan Boyle: My Relief at Discovering That I Have Asperger's'. *The Observer*. 8 December 2013. Accessed 30 December 2016. https://www.theguard ian.com/music/2013/dec/08/susan-boyle-autism.

'Diagnosing Bill Gates'. *Time*, 24 January 1994. Accessed 23 July 2016. http:// content.time.com/time/magazine/article/0,9171,979990,00.html.

Di Pellegrino G., Fadiga L., Fogassi L., Gallese V., and Rizzolatti G. 'Understanding Motor Events: A Neurophysiological Study'. *Experimental Brain Research* 91 (1992): 176–80.

Doc Martin. Episode 12. Directed by Ben Bolt. Written by Dominic Minghella and Edana Minghella. ITV. 15 December 2005.

Doc Martin. Episode 18. Directed by Ben Bolt. Written by Richard Stoneman. ITV. 8 October 2007.

Doc Martin. Episode 45. Directed by Nigel Cole. Written by Richard Stoneman. ITV. 14 October 2013.

Doc Martin. Episode 46. Directed by Nigel Cole. Written by Jack Lothian. ITV. 21 October 2013.

Donvan, John and Zucker, Caren. *In a Different Key: The Story of Autism*. London: Allen Lane, 2016.

Duffy, John and Dorner, Rebecca. 'The Pathos of "Mindblindness": Autism, Science, and Sadness in "Theory of Mind" Narratives'. *Journal of Literary & Cultural Disability Studies* 5 (2011): 201–16.

Dunne, Susan. *A Pony in the Bedroom*. London: Jessica Kingsley, 2015.

Eagleton, Terry. '*Zero Degrees of Empathy*: Review'. Review of *Zero Degrees of Empathy: A New Theory of Human Cruelty*, by Simon Baron-Cohen. *The Financial Times*. 1 April 2011. Accessed 3 August 2016. http://www.ft.com/cms/s/2/3fa57592-5be4-11e0-bb56-00144feab49a.html.

Einstein, Albert. *On Cosmic Religion and Other Opinions and Aphorisms*. New York: Dover, 1931.

European Commission for Social Rights. 'International Association of Autism-Europe v France, Complaint No.13/2002'. ESCR.net. Accessed 2 November 2016. https://www.escr-net.org/caselaw/2006/international-association-autism-europe-v-france-complaint-no-132002.

Fabri, M., Andrews, P.C.S. and Pukki, H. K. *A Guide to Best Practice in Supporting Higher Education Students on the Autism Spectrum*. Leeds: Leeds Beckett University, 2016.

Faherty, Catherine. 'Asperger's Syndrome in Women: A Different Set of Challenges?'. In Attwood, Tony and Grandin, Temple, eds. *Asperger's and Girls*. Arlington, Texas: Future Horizons, 2006. 9–14.

Fein, Elizabeth. 'Innocent Machines: Asperger's Syndrome and the Neurostructural Self'. *Sociological Reflections on the Neurosciences: Advances in Medical Sociology* 13 (2011): 27–49.

Feinstein, Adam. *A History of Autism: Conversations with the Pioneers*. Oxford: Wiley-Blackwell, 2010. Kindle edition.

Ferguson, Euan. 'Profile: Generation Next'. *The Observer* (UK). 28 May 2006. 28. Accessed 2 May 2016. www.lexisnexis.com.

Fernandes, Marriska. 'Director Gavin O'Connor Dishes on Ben Affleck Thriller *The Accountant*'. Tribute.ca. 13 October 2016. Accessed 22 October 2016. http://www.tribute.ca/news/index.php/director-gavin-oconnor-dishes-on-ben-affleck-thriller-the-accountant/2016/10/13/.

Feyerabend, Paul. *Against Method: Outline of an Anarchistic Theory of Knowledge*. London: NLB, 1975.

Fitzgerald, Michael. *Autism and Creativity: Is There a Link between Autism in Men and Exceptional Ability?* New York: Routledge, 2004.

Fitzgerald, Michael. *The Genesis of Artistic Creativity*. London: Jessica Kingsley, 2005.

Folmar, Kate. 'Channelling the Lives of Silicon Valley in Person'. *Globe and Mail*. 9 June 1995. Source: Nexis. Accessed 22 July 2016. www.lexisnexis.com.

Forster, E. M. *Aspects of the Novel*. London: Penguin, 2005. Originally published 1927.

Forster, E. M. *Howards End*. London: Penguin, 1989. Originally published 1910.

Forster, E. M. *Maurice*. London: Penguin, 1992. Originally published 1971.

Foucault, Michel. *Madness and Civilization: A History of Insanity in the Age of Reason*. Translated by Howard, Richard. London: Routledge, 2001. Originally published 1961.

Fox, Kate. *Portrait of the Autist as a Young Woman*. 2010. Accessed 2 December 2016. https://katefoxwriter.wordpress.com/2010/08/14/portrait-of-the-autist/.

Fowler, Christopher. 'Books: The Curious Incident of the Dog in the Night-Time by Mark Haddon'. *The Independent on Sunday*. 6 July 2003, 18. Accessed 17 October 2016. www.lexisnexis.com.

Frances, Allen. 'The Autism Generation'. *Project Syndicate*. 19 July 2011. Accessed 23 August 2016. https://www.project-syndicate.org/commentary/the-autism-generation.

Frances, Allen. *Saving Normal: An Insider's Revolt against Out-of-Control Psychiatric Diagnosis, DSM-5, Big Pharma, and the Medicalization of Ordinary Life*. New York: HarperCollins, 2013.

Frith, Uta, ed. *Autism and Asperger Syndrome*. Cambridge: Cambridge University Press, 1991.

Frith, Uta. *Autism: Explaining the Enigma*. Oxford: Blackwell, 2003.

Frith, Uta and Hill, Elisabeth, eds. *Autism: Mind and Brain*. Oxford: Oxford University Press, 2003.

Fryer, Jane. 'The Human Calculator'. *The Daily Mail*. 6 January. Source: Infotrac Newsstand. Accessed 28 July 2016. http://go.galegroup.com.

Gallagher, James. 2016. '"Super-parenting" Improves Children's Autism'. BBC News. Accessed 26 October 2016. http://www.bbc.co.uk/news/health-37729095.

Gardner, M., Suplee, P. D., Bloch, J., and Lecks, K. 2016. 'Exploratory Study of Childbearing Experiences of Women with Asperger Syndrome'. *Nursing for Women's Health* 20:1 (2016): 28–37.

Glendinning, Victoria. *Jonathan Swift*. London: Hutchinson, 1998.

Goodman, Andrew. 'Temple Grandin on Autism, Death, Celibacy and Cows'. *The New York Times Magazine*. 12 April 2013. Accessed 6 January 2017. http://www.nytimes.com/2013/04/14/magazine/temple-grandin-on-autism-death-celibacy-and-cows.html.

Gould, J. and Ashton-Smith, J. 2011. 'Missed Diagnosis or Misdiagnosis? Girls and Women on the Autism Spectrum'. *Good Autism Practice* 12:1 (2011): 34–42.

Grandin, Temple. 'How People with Autism Think'. In Schopler, E. and Mesibov, G. B., eds. *Learning and Cognition in Autism*. New York: Plenum Press, 1995.

Grandin, Temple and Scariano, Margaret M. 1986. *Emergence: Labeled Autistic*. Novato: Arena Press, 1989.

Gray, John. *Men Are from Mars, Women Are from Venus*. London: HarperCollins. 1992.

Greenberg, Gary. *The Book of Woe: The DSM and the Unmaking of Psychiatry*. London: Scribe, 2013.

Gross, Paul and Levitt, Norman. *Higher Superstition: The Academic Left and Its Quarrels with Science*. Baltimore: Johns Hopkins University Press, 1994.

Gunn, Simon and Bell, Rachel. *Middle Classes: Their Rise and Sprawl*. London: Orion, 2003.

Haagaard, Alexandra. 'How *The Accountant* Victimizes the Autistic Community'. *The Establishment*. 17 October 2016. Accessed 22 October 2016. http://www.theestablishment.co/2016/10/17/how-the-accountant-victimizes-the-autistic-community/.

Hacking, Ian. 'How We Have Been Learning to Talk about Autism: A Role for Stories'. *Metaphilosophy* 40:304 (2009): 419–516.

Hacking, Ian. 'Humans, Aliens and Autism'. *Daedalus* 138:3 (2009): 44–59.

Hacking, Ian. 'Making Up Autism', Inaugural C. L. Oakley Lecture in Medicine and the Arts, University of Leeds, 13 May 2013.

Hacking, Ian. *The Social Construction of What?* Cambridge, Massachusetts: Harvard University Press, 1999.

Haddon, Mark. *The Curious Incident of the Dog in the Night-Time*. London: Vintage, 2004. Originally published 2003.

Hall, Dinah. 'Innocents and Their Experiences'. *The Sunday Telegraph*. 20 April 2003, 13. Accessed 17 October 2016. www.lexisnexis.com.

Hamilton, C. R., ed. *Neuropsychologia: Paths in the Brain, Actions of the Mind: Special Issue in Honor of Roger W. Sperry* 36:10 (1998).

Happé, Francesca G. E. 1991. 'The Autobiographical Writings of Three Asperger Syndrome Adults: Problems of Interpretation and Implications for Theory'. In Frith, Uta, ed. *Autism and Asperger Syndrome*. Cambridge: Cambridge University Press, 1991. 207–42.

Hawkes, Nigel. 'Why a Dash of Autism May Be Key to Success'. *The Times* (London). 4 December 2001. Accessed 4 August 2016. www.lexisnexis.com.

Hirvikoski, T., Mittendorfer-Rutz, E., Boman, M., Larsson, H., Lichtenstein, P., and Bölte, S. 'Premature Mortality in Autism Spectrum Disorder'. *The British Journal of Psychiatry* 208 (2016): 232–38. Accessed 20 December 2017. http://bjp.rcpsych.org/content/bjprcpsych/208/3/232.full.pdf.

Hoban, Phoebe. 2014. *Lucian Freud: Eyes Wide Open*. Seattle: Amazon Publishing.

Hoggart, Richard. *The Uses of Literacy: Aspects of Working-Class Life with Special Reference to Publications and Entertainments*. London: Penguin, 1957.

Houston, Rab and Frith, Uta. *Autism in History: The Case of Hugh Blair of Borgue*. Oxford: Blackwell, 2000.

Huxley, Aldous. *Brave New World*. London: Vintage, 1932. Kindle edition.

Iacoboni, M. and Dapretto, M. 'The Mirror Neuron System and the Consequences of Its Dysfunction'. *Nature Reviews: Neuroscience* 7 (2006): 942–51.

IMDb. 'The Real Superhumans and the Quest for the Future Fantastic: The Human Calculator'. Canada, 2007. Accessed 28 July 2016. http://www.imdb.com/title/tt1621016/?ref_=nm_flmg_slf_2.

Jack, Jordynn. *Autism and Gender: From Refrigerator Mothers to Computer Geeks*. Urbana: University of Illinois Press, 2014.

Jacobson, Barbara. *Loving Mr Spock: Understanding an Aloof Lover – Could It Be Asperger's Syndrome?* London: Jessica Kingsley, 2006.

James, Ioan. *Asperger's Syndrome and High Achievement*. London: Jessica Kingsley, 2006.

James, Ioan. 'Singular Scientists'. *Journal of the Royal Society of Medicine* 96 (2003): 36–39. Accessed 30 June 2016. http://www.ncbi.nlm.nih.gov/pmc/articles/PMC539373/.

Jefferies, Stuart. 'The Bridge Recap: Season Two, Episodes Seven and Eight'. *The Guardian* TV and Radio blog. 25 January 2014. Accessed 5 May 2015. https://www.theguardian.com/tv-and-radio/tvandradioblog/2014/jan/25/the-bridge-recap-season-two-episodes-seven-eight.

Kanner, Leo. 'Autistic Disturbances of Affective Contact'. *Nervous Child* 2 (1943): 217–50.

Kanner, Leo. 'Irrelevant and Metaphorical Language in Early Infantile Autism'. *American Journal of Psychiatry* 103 (1946): 242–46.

Kanner, Leo and Eisenberg, Leon. 'Early Infantile Autism, 1943–1955'. In Read, Charles F., ed. *Psychopathology: A Source Book*. Cambridge: Harvard University Press. 3–14. Originally published in *The American Journal of Orthopsychiatry* 25 (1958): 556–66.

Kean, Danuta. 2008. 'Clare Morrall: The Author Explores Asperger's Syndrome in Her Latest Novel'. *The Independent*. 9 March 2008. Accessed 26 November 2014. http://www.independent.co.uk/arts-entertainment/books/features/claire-morrall-the-author-explores-aspergers-syndrome-in-her-latest-novel-792452.html.

Kiln, A., Jones, W., Schultz, R., and Volkmar, F. 2003. 'The Enactive Mind, or from Actions to Cognition: Lessons from Autism'. In Frith, Uta and Hill, Elisabeth, eds. *Autism: Mind and Brain*. Oxford: Oxford University Press. 127–59.

Kirkus Reviews. '*Tuesday* by David Wiesner'. 20 May 2010. Accessed 5 December 2016. https://www.kirkusreviews.com/book-reviews/david-wiesner/tuesday/.

Kroll, Jack. 'From the Who to the Whom'. *Newsweek*, 121:18, 3 May 1993, 67.

Krystal, A. 'It's Genre. Not That There's Anything Wrong with It!' *New Yorker*, 24 October 2012. Accessed 3 August 2016. http://www.newyorker.com/books/page-turner/its-genre-not-that-theres-anything-wrong-with-it.

Kuhn, Thomas S. *The Structure of Scientific Revolutions*. Chicago: University of Chicago Press, 1996. Originally published 1962.

Kurstilbud. 'Mad World. Gary Jules'. Accessed 19 December 2016. http://www.hjelptilhjelp.no/filmer/filmer-om-autisme-og-aspergers-syndrom/video/mad-world-gary-jules.

Lacan, Jacques. 'The Mirror Stage as Formative Function of the *I*', 1949. In Lacan, Jacques, ed. *Écrits: A Selection*. Abingdon: Routledge, 2001. 1–8.

Lainhart J. E., Bigler, E. D., Bocian, M., Coon, H., Dinh, E., Dawson, G., Deutsch, C. K., Dunn, M., Estes, A., Tager-Flusberg, H., Folstein, S., Hepburn, S., Hyman, S., McMahon, W., Minshew, N., Munson, J., Osann, K., Ozonoff, S., Rodier, P., Rogers, S., Sigman, M., Spence, M. A., Stodgell, C. J., and Volkmar, F. 'Head Circumference and Height in Autism: A Study by the Collaborative Program of Excellence in Autism'. *American Journal of Medical Genetics*, Part A, 140 (2006): 2257–74.

Lawson, Wenn. 'Gender Dysphoria and Autism'. *Network Autism*. 28 May 2015. Accessed 6 January 2017. http://network.autism.org.uk/sites/default/files/ckfinder/files/gender%20dysphoria%20article%20for%20pdf.docx.pdf.

Limburg, Joanne. 'Alice and the Red Queen'. *The Autistic Alice*. Hexham: Bloodaxe, 2017. 52–53.

Limburg, Joanne. 'Alice Between'. *The Autistic Alice*. Hexham: Bloodaxe, 2017. 39.

Limburg, Joanne. 'The Annotated Alice'. *The Autistic Alice*. Hexham: Bloodaxe, 2017. 56.

Limburg, Joanne. *The Autistic Alice*. Hexham: Bloodaxe, 2017.

Limburg, Joanne. 'Queen Alice'. *The Autistic Alice*. Hexham: Bloodaxe, 2017. 55.

Locke, David. *Science as Writing*. London: Yale University Press, 1992.

Locker, Ray. 'Pentagon 2008 Study: Russia's Putin Has Asperger's Syndrome'. *USA Today*. 5 February 2015. Source: Nexis. Accessed 10 February 2015. www.lexisnexis.com.

Loftis, Sonya, F. 'Dear Neurodiversity Movement: Put Your Shoes On'. Academia. edu. 2016. Accessed 26 November 2016. https://www.academia.edu/27111285/ Dear_Neurodiversity_Movement_Put_Your_Shoes_On.

Loftis, Sonya, F. *Imagining Autism: Fiction and Stereotypes on the Spectrum*. Indiana: Indiana University Press, 2015. Kindle edition.

Longmore, Paul. *Why I Burned My Book and Other Essays on Disability*. Philadelphia: Temple University Press, 2003.Originally published 1985.

Loomes, Gillian Quinn. 'It's Only Words: A Critical 'Insider' Perspective on the Power of Diagnosis in the Construction of Autistic Social Identity'. *Good Autism Practice*. 18:1 (2017): 5–10.

Lord, C., Rutter, M., Goode, S., Heemsbergen, J., Jordan, H., Mawhood, L., and Schopler, E. 'Autism Diagnostic Observation Schedule: A Standardized Observation of Communicative and Social Behaviour'. *Journal of Autism and Developmental Disorders* 19:2 (1989): 185–212.

Lutchmaya, Svetlana, Baron-Cohen, Simon, and Raggatt, Peter. 'Foetal Testosterone and Eye Contact in 12 Month Old Infants'. *Infant Behavior and Development* 25:3 (2002): 327–35.

Lutchmaya, Svetlana, Baron-Cohen, Simon, and Raggatt, Peter. 'Foetal Testosterone and Vocabulary Size in 18- and 24-Month Old Infants'. *Infant Behavior and Development* 24:4 (2002): 418–24.

Lyall, K., Constantino, J. N., Weisskopf, M. G., Roberts, A. L., Ascherio, A., and Santangelo, S. L. 'Parental Social Responsiveness and Risk of Autism Spectrum Disorder in Offspring'. *JAMA Psychiatry* 71:8 (2014): 936–42.

MacNeice, Louis. 'Snow'. In MacNeice, Louis. *Collected Poems*. London: Faber, 2002: 30.

Matthews, Morgan. *X+Y*, directed by Matthews, Morgan. Origin Pictures and Minnow Films, 2014.

McGrath, James. 'Ideas of Belonging in the Work of John Lennon and Paul McCartney'. Leeds Metropolitan University, 2010. Doctoral thesis.

McGrath, James. 'Reading Autism'. *Interdisciplinary Literary Studies* 8:2 (2007): 100–113.

McGrath, James. 'Ventriloquy Soliloquy'. In *Shadowtrain*, September 2012. https:// leedsbeckett.academia.edu/JamesMcGrath.

McGuire, Anne. *War on Autism: On the Cultural Logic of Normative Violence*. Ann Arbor: University of Michigan Press, 2016. Kindle Edition.

McIntosh, D. M., Reichmann-Decker, A., Winkielman, P., and Wilbarger, J. L. 'When the Social Mirror Breaks: Deficits in Automatic, but Not Voluntary, Mimicry of Emotional Facial Expressions in Autism'. *Developmental Science* 9:3 (2006): 295–302.

Meltzer, Donald. *Explorations in Autism*. London: Harris-Meltzer Trust, 1975. Kindle edition.

Milton, Damian E. M. '"Nature's Answer to Over-Conformity": Deconstructing Pathological Demand Avoidance'. *Autism Experts*. 2013. Accessed 10 December 2016. http://autismexperts.blogspot.co.uk/2013/03/natures-answer-to-over-conformity.html.

Milton, Damian E. M. 'On the Ontological Status of Autism: The "Double Empathy Problem"'. *Disability & Society* 27 (2012): 883–87.

Mitchell, David and Snyder, Sharon. *Narrative Prosthesis*. Ann Arbor: University of Michigan Press, 2000.

Mitchell, Kate. *History and Cultural Memory in Neo-Victorian Fiction*. Basingstoke: Palgrave Macmillan, 2010.

Moffat, Wendy. *E. M. Forster: A New Life*. London: Bloomsbury, 2010.

Morrall, Clare. 2008. *The Language of Others*. London: Sceptre.

Morrison, Sarah. 'David Freud: The Art of Forgiveness'. *The Independent*. 17 February 2013. Accessed 21 September 2016. http://www.independent.co.uk/news/people/profiles/david-freud-the-art-of-forgiveness-8498148.html.

Morton, Oliver. 'Think Different?'. *Wired*, 1 December 2001. Accessed 18 July 2016. http://www.wired.com/2001/12/baron-cohen/.

Muggleton, Joshua. *Raising Martians – From Crash-Landing to Leaving Home: How to Help a Child with Asperger Syndrome and High-Functioning Autism*. London: Jessica Kingsley, 2011.

Mukhopadhyay, Tito Rajarshi. *How Can I Talk If My Lips Don't Move?: Inside My Autistic Mind*. New York: Arcade Publishing, 2008. Kindle edition. Quote: Locations 140–52.

Murray, D. K. C. 1992. 'Attention Tunnelling and Autism'. In *Living with Autism: The Individual, the Family and the Professional*. Originally presented at the Durham Conference, UK. Proceedings available from Autism Research Unit, School of Health Sciences, University of Sunderland, Sunderland SR2 7EE, UK.

Murray, Dinah, Lesser, Mike, and Lawson, Wendy. 'Attention, Monotropism and the Diagnostic Criteria for Autism'. *Autism* 9:2 (2005): 139–56.

Murray, Les. *The Biplane Houses*. Manchester: Carcanet, 2006.

Murray, Les. 'It Allows a Portrait in Line Scan at Fifteen'. Australian Poetry Library. Accessed 12 June 2016. http://www.poetrylibrary.edu.au/poets/murray-les/it-allows-a-portrait-in-line-scan-at-fifteen-0617122.

Murray, Les. 'It Allows a Portrait in Line-Scan at Fifteen'. *Learning Human: New Selected Poems*. Manchester: Carcanet, 2001. 135–36.

Murray, Les. 'It Allows a Portrait in Line Scan at Fifteen'. *New Collected Poems*. Manchester: Carcanet, 2003. 412–14.

Murray, Les. 'It Allows a Portrait in Line-scan at Fifteen'. *PN Review* 100 (November–December 1994): 82.

Murray, Les. 'It Allows a Portrait in Line-scan at Fifteen'. *Quadrant* 38:6 (June 1994): 12–13.

Murray, Les. 'It Allows a Portrait in Line Scan at Fifteen'. *Subhuman Redneck Poems*. Manchester: Carcanet, 1996. 42–43.

Murray, Les. Poetry Reading, the Tai Chi Village Hall, Didsbury, Manchester, 13 October 2007.

Murray, Stuart. *Autism*. London: Routledge, 2012.

Murray, Stuart. *Representing Autism: Culture, Narrative, Fascination*. Liverpool: Liverpool University Press, 2008.

Nadesan, Majia H. *Constructing Autism: Unravelling the 'Truth' and Understanding the Social*. Abingdon: Routledge, 2005.

Narby, Caroline. 'Double Rainbow: Deconstructing "The Geek Syndrome"'. Bitch-Media. 10 February 2012. Accessed 24 September 2016. https://bitchmedia.org/post/double-rainbow-deconstructing-the-geek-syndrome-draft.

National Autistic Society, The. '11 Shocking Statistics about Autism and Employment'. *The Guardian* (website). 27 October 2016. Accessed 5 March 2017. https://www.theguardian.com/tmi/2016/oct/27/11-shocking-statistics-about-autism-and-employment.

National Autistic Society, The. *Ageing with Autism: A Handbook for Care and Support Professionals*. London: The National Autistic Society, 2013.

National Autistic Society, The. *Autism: A Brief Guide for Employers*. London: The National Autistic Society, 2011.

National Autistic Society, The. 'Autism Facts and History'. Accessed 18 October 2016. http://www.autism.org.uk/about/what-is/myths-facts-stats.aspx.

National Autistic Society, The. 'Autism Profiles and Diagnostic Criteria'. 27 June 2016. Accessed 6 January 2017. http://www.autism.org.uk/about/diagnosis/criteria-changes.aspx.

National Autistic Society, The. 'Gender and Autism'. Accessed 4 December 2016. http://www.autism.org.uk/about/what-is/gender.aspx.

National Autistic Society, The. 'Information for General Practitioners'. Accessed 1 August 2016. http://www.autism.org.uk/gp.

National Symposium on Neurodiversity at Syracuse University. 'What Is Neurodiversity?'. Accessed 5 June 2016. https://neurodiversitysymposium.wordpress.com/what-is-neurodiversity/.

Ne'eman, Ari. 'Screening Sperm Donors for Autism? As an Autistic Person, I Know That's the Road to Eugenics'. *The Guardian* (UK). 30 December 2015. Accessed 15 August 2016. https://www.theguardian.com/commentisfree/2015/dec/30/screening-sperm-donors-autism-autistic-eugenics.

Nielsen, J., Zielinski, B. A., Ferguson, M. A., Lainhart, J. E., and Anderson, J. S. 'An Evaluation of the Left-Brain vs. Right-Brain Hypothesis with Resting State Functional Connectivity Magnetic Resonance Imaging'. *PLOS One* 8:8 (2013): Accessed 14 January 2017. http://journals.plos.org/plosone/article?id=10.1371/journal.pone.0071275.

Nordicana 2014. 'The Bridge Q + A'. Nordicana Festival, London. 17 January 2014. Accessed 9 January 2017. https://www.youtube.com/watch?v=dPHN6ExsNhE.

Oakley, Ann. *The Sociology of Housework*. London: Martin Robertson, 1974.

Oberman, L. M. and Ramachandran, V. S. 'The Simulating Social Mind: The Role of the Mirror Neuron System and Simulation in the Social and Communicative Deficits of Autism Spectrum Disorders'. *Psychological Bulletin* 133:8 (2007): 310–27.

O'Dell, L., Rosqvist, H. B., Francisco, O., Brownlow, C., and Orsini, M. 'Critical Autism Studies: Exploring Epistemic Dialogues and Intersections, Challenging Dominant Understandings of Autism'. *Disability & Society* 31:2 (2016): 166–79.

O'Driscoll, Dennis. 'Interviews: Les Murray, The Art of Poetry No.89'. *The Paris Review* 173 (2005). Accessed 11 April 2014. http://www.theparisreview.org/interviews/5508/the-art-of-poetry-no-89-les-murray.

OED Online. 'Aspie, n. and adj.' Oxford: Oxford University Press, December 2016. Accessed 5 January 2017. http://www.oed.com/view/Entry/392643?redirected From=aspie.

OED Online. 'Dismember, v.' Oxford: Oxford University Press, June 2016. Accessed 14 August 2016. http://www.oed.com/view/Entry/54773?redirectedFrom=dismember.

OED Online. 'Neurotypical adj. and n.' Oxford: Oxford University Press, June 2016. Accessed 10 August 2016. http://www.oed.com/view/Entry/271429?redirected From=Neurotypical#eid.

OED Online. 'Super-, Prefix'. Oxford: Oxford University Press, September 2016. Accessed 26 October 2016. http://www.oed.com/view/Entry/194186?rskey= BAqSPF&result=20.

The Office. Episode 2. Directed by Ricky Gervais and Stephen Merchant. Written by Ricky Gervais and Stephen Merchant. BBC Two. 16 July 2001.

The Office. Episode 9. Directed by Ricky Gervais and Stephen Merchant. Written by Ricky Gervais and Stephen Merchant. BBC Two. 14 October 2002.

The Office. Episode 10. Directed by Ricky Gervais and Stephen Merchant. Written by Ricky Gervais and Stephen Merchant. BBC Two. 21 October 2002.

Orsini, Michael and Davidson, Joyce. ' "Introduction – Critical Autism Studies": Notes on an Emerging Field'. In Orsini, Michael and Davidson, Joyce, eds. *Worlds of Autism: Across the Spectrum of Neurological Difference*. Minneapolis: University of Minnesota Press, 2013. Kindle Edition, 74–346.

Orsini, Michael and Davidson, Joyce, eds. *Worlds of Autism: Across the Spectrum of Neurological Difference*. Minneapolis: University of Minnesota Press, 2013. Kindle edition.

Osteen, Mark, ed. *Autism and Representation*. Abingdon: Routledge, 2008.

Ouzounian, Richard. 'Pete Townshend Talks about The Who's *Tommy*'. *The Star*. 17 May 2013. Accessed 20 September 2016. http://www.thestar.com/entertainment/ stage/2013/05/17/pete_townshend_talks_about_the_whos_tommy.html.

Pacheco, Anthony. 'Mad World Deconstructed'. 2009. Accessed 5 January 2017. http://anthony-pacheco.com/2009/04/07/mad-world-deconstructed/

Pease, Allan and Pease, Barbara. *Why Men Don't Listen and Women Can't Read Maps*. London: Penguin.

Penguin Books. 'The Rosie Project' (summary). Accessed 8 January 2017. https:// www.penguin.co.uk/books/193470/the-rosie-project/9780718178550/.

Pickles, A., Le Couteur, A., Leadbitter, K., Salomone, E., Cole-Fletcher, R., Tobin, H., Gammer, I., Lowry, J., Vamvakas, G., Byford, S., Aldred, C., Slonims, V., McConachie, H., Howlin, P., Parr, J. R., Charman, T., and Green, J. 'Parent-mediated Social Communication Therapy for Young Children with Autism (PACT): Long-term Follow-up of a Randomised Controlled Trial'. *The Lancet*. 25 October 2016. Accessed 26 October 2016. http://www.thelancet.com/pdfs/journals/lancet/ PIIS0140-6736(16)31229-6.pdf.

Pinchevski, Amit. 'Bartleby's Autism: Wandering along Incommunicability'. *Cultural Critique* 78 (2011): 27–59.

Potts, Robert. 'Profile: Light in the Wilderness: Margaret Atwood'. *The Guardian*. 26 April 2003. Accessed 3 August 2014. http://www.theguardian.com/books/2003/ apr/26/fiction.margaretatwood.

Preston, John, Munévar, Gonzalo, and Lamb, David, eds. *The Worst Enemy of Science? Essays in Memory of Paul Feyerabend*. Oxford: Oxford University Press, 2000.

Quinn, Gillian. 'An Evaluation of the Use of Advocacy with an Adult Seeking a Diagnostic Assessment for Autism'. *Good Autism Practice*. 10:1 (2009): 50–52.

Ramachandran, Vilayanur S. and Oberman, Lindsay M. 'Broken Mirrors: A Theory of Autism'. *Scientific American*. November 2006, pp. 62–69. Accessed 3 November 2016. http://cbc.ucsd.edu/pdf/brokenmirrors_asd.pdf.

Reddy, Vasudevi, Williams, Emma, Costantini, Cristina, and Lang, Britta. 'Engaging with the Self: Mirror Behaviour in Autism, Down Syndrome and Typical Development'. *Autism* 14:5 (2010): 531–46.

Ribas, Denys. *Autism: Debates and Testimonies*. London: Free Association Books, 2006.

Rimland, Bernard. *Infantile Autism: The Syndrome and Its Implications for a Neural Theory of Behavior*. London: Jessica Kingsley, 2015. Kindle edition.

Rizzolatti, Giacomo and Fabbri-Destro, Maddalena. 'Mirror Neurons: From Discovery to Autism'. *Experimental Brain Research* 200 (2010): 223–37.

Robison, John Elder. *Look Me in the Eye*. New York: Three Rivers Press, 2008.

Ross, Andrew, ed. *The Science Wars*. Durham, NC: Duke University Press, 1996.

Ruzich, E., Allison, C., Chakrabarti, B., Smith, P., Musto, H., Ring, H., and Baron-Cohen, S. 'Sex and STEM Occupation Predict Autism-Spectrum Quotient (AQ) Scores in Half a Million People'. *PLOS ONE* 21 (2015). 1–15. Accessed 1 August 2016. http://journals.plos.org/plosone/article/asset?id=10.1371%2Fjournal.pone.0141229.PDF.

Sacks, Oliver. 'An Anthropologist on Mars'. *The New Yorker*. 27 December 1993, reprinted in Sacks, Oliver. *An Anthropologist on Mars: Seven Paradoxical Tales*. New York: Knopf, 1995.

Sacks, Oliver. *The Man Who Mistook His Wife for a Hat*. London: Picador, 2015.

Said, Edward W. *Orientalism*. London: Penguin, 2003. Originally published 1978.

Sainsbury, Clare. *Martian in the Playground: Understanding the Schoolchild with Asperger's Syndrome*. London: Sage, 2010.

Schunke, Odette, Schöttle, Daniel, Vettorazzi, Eik, Brandt, Valerie, Kahl, Ursula, Bäumer, Tobias, Ganos, Christos, David, Nicole, Peiker, Ina, Engel, Andreas K, Brass, Marcel, and Münchau, Alexander. 'Mirror Me: Imitative Responses in Adults with Autism'. *Autism* 20:2 (2016): 134–44.

Schwartz, Casey. 'Asperger's Overdiagnosed, Ill-Defined, May Not Be a Syndrome Much Longer'. *Daily Beast*. 7 February 2012. Accessed 4 July 2016. http://www.thedailybeast.com/articles/2012/02/07/asperger-s-over-diagnosed-ill-defined-may-not-be-a-syndrome-much-longer.html.

Scott, F. J., Baron-Cohen, S., and Brayne, C. 'The CAST (Childhood Asperger Syndrome Test): Preliminary Development of a UK Screen for Mainstream Primary-School-Age Children'. *Autism* 6:9 (2002): 231–37.

Scully, Jackie L. 'What Is a Disease?' *EMBO Rep* 5:7 (2004). 650–53. Accessed 21 October 2016. https://www.ncbi.nlm.nih.gov/pmc/articles/PMC1299105/.

Searle, Ruth. *Asperger Syndrome in Adults: A Guide to Realizing Your Potential*. London: Sheldon Press, 2010.

Severson, Katherine DeMaria, Aune, James Arnt, and Jodlowski, Denise. 'Bruno Bettelheim, Autism and the Rhetoric of Scientific Authority'. In Osteen, Mark, ed. *Autism and Representation*. Abingdon: Routledge, 2008. 65–77.

Shakespeare, Tom. *Disability Rights and Wrongs Revisited*. London: Routledge, 2014. Kindle edition.

Shakespeare, Tom and Watson, Nicholas. 2002. 'The Social Model of Disability: An Outdated Ideology?'. *Research in Social Science and Disability* 2 (2002): 9–28. Accessed 7 January 2017. http://disability-studies.leeds.ac.uk/files/library/Shakespeare-social-model-of-disability.pdf.

Shameful. 'About Shameful'. Accessed 2 November 2016. http://shamefuldocumentary.com/about.html.

Shaul, Joel. *Our Brains Are Like Computers!* London: Jessica Kingsley, 2016.

Shelley, Percy Bysshe. *A Defence of Poetry and Other Essays*. Public Domain Books. Kindle, 1840.

Silberman, Steve. 'The Geek Syndrome'. *Wired*. 1 December 2001. Accessed 3 July 2016. https://www.wired.com/2001/12/aspergers/.

Silberman, Steve. *Neurotribes*. London: Allen & Unwin, 2015.

Silberman, Steve. 'Was Dr. Asperger a Nazi? The Question Still Haunts Autism'. NPR. org. 20 January 2016. Accessed 19 August 2016. http://www.npr.org/sections/health-shots/2016/01/20/463603652/was-dr-asperger-a-nazi-the-question-still-haunts-autism

The Silent Wave, The. 'One Aspie's "Asperger Soundtrack Explained"'. 4 September 2016. Accessed 19 December 2016. https://thesilentwaveblog.wordpress.com/2016/09/04/one-aspies-asperger-soundtrack-explained/.

Simsion, Graeme. *The Rosie Effect*. London: Michael Joseph, 2014.

Simsion, Graeme. *The Rosie Project*. London: Penguin, 2013.

Sinclair, Jim. 'Don't Mourn for Us'. *Autonomy, the Critical Journal of Interdisciplinary Autism Studies* 1:1 (2012). Accessed 9 January 2017. http://www.larry-arnold.net/Autonomy/index.php/autonomy/article/view/AR1/pdf. Originally published 1993.

Smith, J. Mark. 'A Conversation with Les Murray'. *Image*. 64. Accessed 6 June 2016. https://www.imagejournal.org/article/conversation-les-murray/.

Snider, Mike. 'The X-Man: Douglas Coupland, from *Generation X* to Spiritual Regeneration'. *USA Today*. 7 March 1994. Source: Nexis. Accessed 22 July 2016. www.lexisnexis.com

Snow, C. P. *The Two Cultures*. Cambridge: Cambridge University Press, 2008. Originally published 1962.

Snyder, Sharon L. and Mitchell, David T. *Cultural Locations of Disability*. Chicago: University of Chicago Press, 2006.

Sokal, A. and Bricmont, J. '*Intellectual Impostures: Postmodern Philosophers Abuse of Science*'. London: Profile, 1999.

Sontag, Susan. *Illness as Metaphor & AIDS and Its Metaphors*. London: Penguin, 1991.

Southgate, Victoria and Hamilton, Antonia. 'Unbroken Mirrors: Challenging a Theory of Autism'. *Trends in Cognitive Neuroscience* XXX:X (2008): 1–5.

Sponheim, E. 'Changing Criteria of Autistic Disorders: A Comparison of the ICD-10 Research Criteria and DSM-IV with DSM-III-R, CARS, and ABC'. *Journal of Autism and Developmental Disorders* 26:5 (1996): 513–25.

Steinbeck, John. *Of Mice and Men*. London: Penguin Modern Classics, 2000. Originally published 1937.

Stronach, Roddy. *A Very Capitalist Condition: A History of Politics and Disability*. London: Bookmarks Publications, 2016. Kindle edition.

The Syndicate. Episode 1. Directed and written by Kay Mellor. BBC1. 2 June 2015.

The Syndicate. Episode 2. Directed and written by Kay Mellor. BBC1. 9 June 2015.

The Syndicate. Episode 3. Directed and written by Kay Mellor. BBC1. 16 June 2015.

Tammet, Daniel. *Born on a Blue Day*. London: Hodder & Stoughton, 2006.

Tantam, Digby. 'Asperger Syndrome in Adulthood'. In Frith, Uta, ed. *Autism and Asperger Syndrome*. Cambridge: Cambridge University Press, 1991. 147–83.

Tears for Fears. 'Mad World'. In Tears for Fears, *The Hurting*, Mercury, 1983.

Telegraph Men. 'Are You on the Autism Spectrum? Take the Test'. *The Telegraph – Men* (website). 4 November 2015. Accessed 5 March 2017. http://www.telegraph. co.uk/men/thinking-man/11974282/Are-you-on-the-autistic-spectrum-Take-the-test.html.

Tilton, Adelle, J. *The Everything Parent's Guide to Children with Autism*. Avon, Massachusetts: Adams Media, 2010.

Time. 'Medicine: The Child Is Father'. 25 July 1960. Accessed 25 October 2016. http://content.time.com/time/magazine/article/0,9171,826528,00.html.

Timimi, Sami; Gardner, Neil, and McCabe, Brian. *The Myth of Autism: Medicalising Men's and Boys' Social and Emotional Competence*. Basingstoke: Palgrave Macmillan, 2010.

Thinking Person's Guide to Autism. Accessed 3 August 2016. http://www.think ingautismguide.com/.

Titchener, Edward Bradford. *Lectures on the Experimental Psychology of the Thought Processes*. New York: Macmillan. 1909. Quoted in 'empathy, n.' *OED Online*, Oxford University Press. Accessed 8 August 2016.

Townshend, Pete. *Who I Am*. London: HarperCollins, 2012.

Trilling, Lionel. *E. M. Forster*. London: The Hogarth Press, 1969.

University of Cambridge. 'Research Links Testosterone Levels to Autistic Traits'. 13 January 2009. Research News. Accessed 13 December 2016. http://www.cam. ac.uk/research/news/research-links-testosterone-levels-to-autistic-traits.

Vitelli, Romeo. 'The Return of the Refrigerator Parent?'. *Huffington Post*. 5 January 2012. Accessed 7 June 2016. http://www.huffingtonpost.ca/romeo-vitelli/ sophie-robert-the-wall_b_1286360.html.

Walker, D. R., Thompson, A., Zwaigenbaum, L., Goldberg, J., Bryson, S. E., Mahoney, W. J., Strawbridge, C. P., and Szatmari, P. 'Specifying PDD-NOS: A Comparison of PDD-NOS, Asperger Syndrome and Autism'. *Journal of the American Academy of Child and Adolescent Psychiatry* 43:2 (2004): 172–80.

Waltz, Mitzi. *Autism: A Social and Medical History*. Basingstoke: Palgrave, 2013. Kindle edition.

Waltz, Robert B. 'Alice's Evidence: A New Look at Autism'. 2013. Accessed 5 October 2016. https://mnheritagesongbook.files.wordpress.com/2013/10/alicesevidence.pdf.

Watkins, Susan. 'Women's Post-Apocalyptic Fiction 1945-Present: Writing as Re-vision'. Professorial Inaugural Lecture. Leeds Beckett University, 26 October 2016.

Watson, Richard. 'In Silicon Valley, Young White Males Are Stealing the Future from Everyone Else'. *The Guardian*. 27 May 2016. Accessed 23 July 2016. https://www.theguardian.com/commentisfree/2016/may/27/in-silicon-valley-young-white-males-are-stealing-the-future-from-everyone-else.

Westfahl, Gary. '*Homo Aspergerus:* Evolution Stumbles Forward'. *Locus Online*, 6 March 2006. Accessed 2 August 2016. http://www.locusmag.com/2006/Features/Westfahl_HomoAspergerus.html.

Westfahl, Gary, ed. *Hugo Gernsback and the Century of Science Fiction*. Jefferson: McFarland, 2007.

Wheelwright, S., Baron-Cohen, S., Goldenfeld, N., Delaney, J., Fine, D., Smith, R., Weil, L., and Wakabayashi, A. 'Predicting Autism Spectrum Quotient (AQ) from the Systemizing Quotient-Revised (SQ-R) and Empathy Quotient (EQ)'. *Brain Research* 1079 (2006): 47–56. Accessed 10 December 2016. http://docs.autismresearchcentre.com/papers/2006_Wheelwright_etal_BrainResearch.pdf.

The Who. '1921', in *Tommy*, Polydor, 1996, CD.

The Who. 'Amazing Journey', in *Tommy*, Polydor, 1996, CD.

The Who. 'Christmas', in *Tommy*, Polydor, 1996, CD.

The Who. 'Go to the Mirror!', in *Tommy*, Polydor, 1996, CD.

The Who. 'Pinball Wizard', in *Tommy*, Polydor, 1996, CD.

The Who. *Tommy: Super Deluxe Edition*. London Polydor, 2013. Liner notes.

Wiesner, David. *Tuesday*. Boston: Houghton Mifflin Harcourt, 1991.

Wilde, Oscar. *The Importance of Being Earnest*. In Wilde, Oscar. *The Complete Works of Oscar Wilde*. Glasgow: HarperCollins, 1994. Originally published 1895.

Willey, Liane Holliday. *Pretending to Be Normal: Living with Asperger's Syndrome*. London: Jessica Kingsley, 1999.

Williams, Donna. *Nobody Nowhere*. London: Jessica Kingsley, 1992.

Williams, J. H. 'Imitation, Mirror Neurons and Autism'. *Neuroscience and Biobehavioural Reviews* 25:7 (2001): 287–95.

Wing, Lorna. 'Asperger's Syndrome: A Clinical Account'. *Psychological Medicine* 11 (1981): 115–29.

Wing, Lorna. *Autistic Children: A Guide for Parents and Professionals*. Levittown: Brunner/Mazel, 1985.

Wing, Lorna. 'The Definition and Prevalence of Autism: A Review'. *European Child and Adolescent Psychiatry* 2:2 (1993): 61–74.

Wing, Lorna. 'Reflections on Opening Pandora's Box'. *Journal of Autism and Developmental Disorders* 35:2 (2005): 197–203.

Wing, Lorna and Gould, Judith. 'Severe Impairments of Social Interaction and Associated Abnormalities in Children: Epidemiology and Classification'. *Journal of Autism and Childhood Schizophrenia* 9 (1979): 11–29.

Wired Staff. 'Take The AQ Test'. *Wired.* 1 December 2001. Accessed 15 July 2016. http://www.wired.com/2001/12/aqtest/.

Wolff, Sula. 'Letters to the Editors'. *Autism* 2 (1998): 96–97.

Wolitzer, Meg. *The Interestings.* London: Vintage, 2014. Originally published 2013.

Woodbury-Smith, M. R., Robinson, J., Wheelwright, S., and Baron-Cohen, S. 'Screening Adults for Asperger Syndrome Using the AQ: Preliminary Study of Its Diagnostic Validity in Clinical Practice'. *Journal of Autism and Developmental Disorders* 35 (2005): 331–35.

Wordsworth, William. 'My Heart Leaps Up When I Behold'. In Wordsworth, William. *Selected Poems.* London: Penguin Classics, 2004. 134–35.

WPSPublish.com. 'Autism Diagnostic Observation Schedule, Second Edition (ADOS®-2)'. Accessed 31 October 2016. http://www.wpspublish.com/store/p/2648/autism-diagnostic-observation-schedule-second-edition-ados-2.

Wrong Planet.net. 'Asperger Syndrome and Popular Music'. 22 April 2009. Accessed 19 December 2016. http://wrongplanet.net/forums/viewtopic.php?f=3&t=97201&sid=53c26d432a7a5f7b2d372fb815123b84.

Wrong Planet.net. 'Homepage'. Accessed 27 January 2017. http://wrongplanet.net/.

Wrong Planet. 'Oryx and Crake'. Accessed 28 March 2016. http://wrongplanet.net/forums/viewtopic.php?t=877&sid=573c714cb97893b827cda5e50dfedbdf.

Wrong Planet. 'Oryx and Crake (No Spoilers)'. Accessed 28 March 2016.http://wrongplanet.net/forums/viewtopic.php?t=91895&sid=9d37d7a33235a9962592a0284b7854b9.

Yaull-Smith, Dale. 'Girls on the Spectrum'. *Communications* (Spring 2007): 30–31.

Zamoscik, Vera, Mier, Daniela, Schmidt, Stephanie N. L., and Kirsch, Peter. 'Early Memories of Autistic Individuals Assessed Using Online Self-Reports'. *Frontiers in Psychiatry* 7:79 (2016): 1–10. Accessed 2 November 2016. https://www.ncbi.nlm.nih.gov/pmc/articles/PMC4852178/.Department of Clinical Psychology, Central Institute of Mental Health, Mannheim and Medical Faculty Mannheim, Heidelberg University, Mannheim, GermanyEdited by: Qinghua He, Southwest University, China.

Index

Aberg, C. A., 133–34
ability, autistic: academic, 18–19,
  58–62; Asperger on, 13, 48;
  creativity and, 37–38, 39, 49,
  131; intellectual, 48–49, 58–62;
  numeracy and, 27–28, 152, 154;
  reading comprehension, 21, 50; social
  circumstances and, 18–19, 158–60,
  169; STEM and, 38–39, 51–52.
  See also expectations; UCARC
ableism, 14, 91, 110, 112, 114, 116–17,
  142, 169; autism otherized by,
  72–73, 87, 90; gaze of, 79–80;
  internalization of, 109, 161, 164
academics, autistic, 18–19, 23, 34, 49,
  61–62, 69, 110–11, 119n2
academic skills, autism and, 18–19
Accountant, The (film by O'Connor),
  82–83, 199
achievement, 128, 170; neurotypical
  expectations of autistic, 127, 159,
  198; privilege and, 158–60, 169, 170
acting. *See* passing
adjective, casual use of 'autistic' as, 77, 81
adolescence, 54–55, 70, 107, 112.
  See also 'It Allows a Portrait in Line
  Scan at Fifteen' (Les Murray)
Adorno, Theodor W., 9, 128, 144, 146,
  174, 209, 212

adult autism: agency and, 73, 116–17,
  151, 163, 175, 186, 196, 197;
  assessment for, 12, 73–75; cultural
  marginalization of, 69, 72, 174–77;
  cultural trivialization of, 2, 33, 78, 94;
  development and, 109, 112; diagnosis
  of, 176–77, 185; exploitation and,
  82; infantilization of, 7, 73–75;
  otherizing of, 70, 78, 81; parenting
  and, 74; science fiction and, 54–56;
  socialising, 112; streamlining, risk of,
  60–62, 165; uncertainties around the
  meaning of, 2, 6, 7, 47, 75; weight
  and, 114. *See also* expectations;
  gender; identity; parenting; women
Adult Autism-Spectrum Quotient (AQ)
  Test (questionnaire by Baron-Cohen
  et al.), 6, 39, 142, 215n43; aims of,
  6, 40–46; bias and, 40; as clinical
  screening tool, 5–6, 40, 42–43,
  44, 45, 61, 135; datedness of, 43;
  'everyone's a little bit autistic notion
  and', 162; fiction and, 6, 43, 135;
  imagination and, 25, 43; Internet
  novelty of, 42; journal publication
  of, 6, 42; and mathematicians, 6, 43,
  59; as mirror index of normalcy, 71;
  piloting of, 40, 42; ramifications of
  scoring, 61, 136; scientific validity

237

About the Author

Dr James McGrath is Senior Lecturer in Literature and Cultural Studies at Leeds Beckett University. His doctoral thesis explored ideas of belonging in the work of John Lennon and Paul McCartney. He has published widely on the topics of music, literature and cultural history. His poems have appeared in publications including *DreamCatcher, International Times, Guardian Higher, PN Review, Junkyard Procession, Smiths Knoll, Shadowtrain and The Interpreter's House.*

Lightning Source UK Ltd.
Milton Keynes UK
UKOW04n2229310817
308344UK00001B/45/P